Phenomenology of Black Spirit

We dedicate this book to the innumerable Black lives we failed to name.

Phenomenology of Black Spirit

Biko Mandela Gray and Ryan J. Johnson

EDINBURGH
University Press

Edinburgh University Press is one of the leading university presses in the UK. We publish academic books and journals in our selected subject areas across the humanities and social sciences, combining cutting-edge scholarship with high editorial and production values to produce academic works of lasting importance. For more information visit our website: edinburghuniversitypress.com

© Biko Mandela Gray and Ryan J. Johnson, 2023

Edinburgh University Press Ltd
The Tun – Holyrood Road
12(2f) Jackson's Entry
Edinburgh EH8 8PJ

First published in hardback by Edinburgh University Press 2023

Typeset in Bembo
by R. J. Footring Ltd, Derby, UK, and
printed and bound by CPI Group (UK) Ltd, Croydon, CR0 4YY

A CIP record for this book is available from the British Library

ISBN 978 1 3995 1097 4 (hardback)
ISBN 978 1 3995 1098 1 (paperback)
ISBN 978 1 3995 1099 8 (webready PDF)
ISBN 978 1 3995 1100 1 (epub)

The right of Biko Mandela Gray and Ryan J. Johnson to be identified as the authors of this work has been asserted in accordance with the Copyright, Designs and Patents Act 1988, and the Copyright and Related Rights Regulations 2003 (SI No. 2498).

Contents

Acknowledgements vii
List of Abbreviations viii

Introduction. Black and White, Gray in Gray 1

I. Fighting, Uplifting, and Thinking
1 Master-Slave Dialectic 27
  Frederick Douglass and Harriet Jacobs
2 Stoicism 73
  Booker T. Washington and Ida B. Wells
3 Scepticism 101
  W.E.B. Du Bois and Anna Julia Cooper

II. (Un)Happy (Black) Consciousness
4 Devotion 143
  Marcus Garvey and Zora Neale Hurston
5 Sacramental Work and Desire 177
  Dr Martin Luther King, Jr and Ella Baker
6 Self-mortification 219
  Malcolm X and Angela Davis

Conclusion. Idealism and Black Power 261

Bibliography 275
Index 285

Acknowledgements

We would like to acknowledge, first of all, Dustin Atlas, for being our brilliant, weird, hilarious friend who brought us together. Nate Jones for copy-editing and feedback. Kwesi Thomas for reading the whole book and offering incredibly helpful copy-editing and content advice.

There are so many people at Elon University who we must gratefully acknowledge. The students in the Fall 2018 Senior Seminar in Philosophy (Victoria Iglesias, John Layher, Halaj Mack, Lyn Nelson, and Nathan Ravenal). The Provost's office for its support, and especially Tim Peoples. The amazing Buffie Longmire-Avital and the African and African-American Studies department. The support of every member of the Philosophy department – Stephen Bloch-Schulman, Ann Cahil, Nim Batchelor, Anthony Weston, Yoram Lubling, Martin Fowler, Lauren Guilmette, and Rob Leib – was essential.

We give great gratitude to our teachers and mentors, both official and unofficial. We would not have been able to write this book without those who cared for and came before us – George Yancy, Charles Mills, Niki Kasumi Clements, Jennifer Bates, Rebecca Comay, Jim Vernon, James Cone, Rocío Zambrana, Christina Sharpe, Rinaldo Walcott, and so many others.

We are grateful to Carol Macdonald and all the wonderful people at Edinburgh University Press for trusting us with this project, and to the anonymous reviewers who offered very helpful feedback. We hope that we have repaid your trust and fulfilled your expectations.

Most of all, thank you to our partners, Erin and Andrea, who put up with us and our irrepressible fascinations with philosophical questions that are far more existential than theoretical. Thank you for your love, patience, and partnership.

Abbreviations

BF   Frederick Douglass, *My Bondage and My Freedom* (The Library of America, 1994)

MX   Malcolm X, *The Autobiography of Malcolm X: As Told to Alex Haley* (Ballantine Books, 1992)

NL   Frederick Douglass, *Narrative of the Life of Frederick Douglass, an American Slave*, in *Autobiographies* (The Library of America, 1994)

PO   Marcus Garvey, *Philosophy and Opinions of Marcus Garvey*, ed. Amy Jacques-Garvey, *The Journal of Pan African Studies* (ebook, 2009)

PS   G.W.F. Hegel, *The Phenomenology of Spirit*, trans. A.V. Miller (Oxford University Press, 1977)

SBF   W.E.B. Du Bois, *The Souls of Black Folk* (Penguin Books, 2018)

UP   Booker T. Washington, *Up From Slavery* (Dover, 1995)

WW   Martin Luther King, Jr., *Why We Can't Wait* (Signet, 2000)

Introduction

Black and White, Gray in Gray

Despite what the title may suggest, this is not a book about Hegel. Or, put slightly differently, this is not a book *about* Hegel. It is about a text he wrote, his 1807 *Phenomenology of Spirit*. To the extent that the *Phenomenology* gives us insight into what he, as well as many other white men, were thinking in early nineteenth-century Germany, Hegel shows up in this text as merely one of many characters. He might be *a* main character, but he is not the only one. This book, then, is a conversation – between the *Phenomenology* and Black thinkers, between a dominant and canonical philosophical text and a chorus of thinkers, writers, and activists who either illuminate or trouble the *Phenomenology's* assertions and conclusions.[1] Perhaps it is more a conversion than a conversation.

For some, this kind of approach will feel lopsided, since it is very specific. At first glance, this text will reveal that it does not engage with the *Phenomenology* in its totality, but only its fourth chapter: 'Self-Consciousness'. We begin at the master-slave dialectic, and end with the third movement of what Hegel calls the 'unhappy consciousness'. In the *Gesammelte Werke* edition, we only cover about forty pages. There are times where we acknowledge the deep resonances between the *Phenomenology's* phases and some of the thinkers we chronicle in this volume. An equally brief glance at this text might lend itself to the conclusion that we are reading Black thinkers *through* Hegel, but while this is partly true, it is not the whole story. Cursory glances, after all, never suffice; what appears at first can be deceptive; immediacy is pretence. So, from the outset, we ask that you, dear reader, take your time. The prose

---

1 Following W.E.B. Du Bois' case for capitalising 'Negro', we capitalise 'Black' (but not 'blackface') even when a quoted author does not originally do so.

will not be difficult, but even simple prose can be deceptively complicated. And so we repeat, from the outset, please take your time.

We do not ask this of you lightly. We ask you to take your time because writing this book took some time – a lot more than we anticipated. The pandemic, antiblackness, and global neoliberalism got in the way. The book was drafted during the period when Breonna Taylor, George Floyd, Tony McDade, and Ahmaud Arbery were killed. It was written as western governments – particularly but not only the United States – chose profits over people, opting to neglect lives in the name of keeping oppressive and dispossessive economies going. Both of us have, in different ways, suffered from the effects of Covid: we have lost family members; we have gotten sick ourselves. Exhaustion set in, depression took hold. We share personal details here not to garner sympathy, but to highlight the structural impediments to making sense of a pressing problem. We also share these details to explain why this book took time.

These are not the only reasons, though. The book also took time because, before it became a reality, we did not know each other. This book is a conversation, but it is also the result of *conversations*. It is the result of two philosophers – a Black philosopher of religion and a white philosopher interested in continental and ancient philosophy – thinking and struggling to make sense of anti/blackness together. We have different vantage points. We come from different places. While we would not claim that this book is a model for something like 'racial reconciliation' (that term is problematic in a host of ways), it is the result of us *tarrying* together, as George Yancy might say.

What you hold in your hands, then, is the result of many long conversations about Hegel, Black life, and antiblackness. This book is the product of a relationship, cultivated over time, between two philosophers who are deeply troubled by the state of affairs in this world. To this end, it might be helpful to briefly tell the story of the book's emergence. This will help to situate its contours, its movements, its limitations, and what is at stake for us both personally and philosophically.

INTRODUCTION

Writing Together in Black and White

It began on a plane. Well, sort of. We were both headed to the same conference, but we did not know each other; it just so happened that our connecting flights converged. We both got off the plane, went to baggage claim and, in introducing ourselves to one another, realised that we had been on the same flight. After a bit of nervous laughter, we headed to our hotel.

At the conference, Ryan presented a paper on theophagy, asking a student to eat pancakes cooked with a cross at the centre; Biko presented a paper on Toni Morrison, Martin Heidegger, and wonder. By the time the first day of the conference was finished, we were drinking, eating, and laughing together.

And then, the question. Ryan asked it sheepishly, though straightforwardly: *I'm thinking about this book on Hegel and Black thinkers. Would you be interested? You don't have to answer now.* Biko said yes, and the rest, as they say, is history.

Except that it isn't. There were more layers beneath that simple proposition made to a stranger to work on a text together. Ryan had been trying to make sense of his own complicity in antiblackness as a white man, and Biko was struggling both with the reality of antiblackness as well as imposter syndrome. There weren't – there aren't – that many Black philosophers in the academy, let alone Black philosophers of religion. Fresh out of graduate school, Biko was concerned that he could not live up to the label. This book, therefore, would afford Biko the opportunity to make sense of a canonical figure in western philosophy, and conversely, it would afford Ryan the opportunity to critically engage with this philosopher on matters of antiblackness and white supremacy.

By the time we started working together, things became clearer – and therefore more complicated. Biko had read enough about Hegel to recognise the antiblackness at the heart of his thinking, while Ryan had read so much Hegel that he recognised a disturbance at the heart of Hegel's *Phenomenology*: Blackness. Without attention to the chattel slavery running rampant at the time of the *Phenomenology*'s publication, it seemed that the

3

dialectic would not work. Seeking to make sense of this, Ryan turned to various Black thinkers, and Biko provided commentary and insight. In short, we taught each other: one taught Hegel; the other taught Blackness and Black studies – until the two began to intertwine into something unexpected, something material.

There were rubs and disagreements along the way, but by the time we really got going, it was clear: as Susan Buck-Morss points out, Hegel's *Phenomenology* cannot be read without attention to anti/blackness.[2] With this as our starting point, we mapped out chapters and read thinkers together; we started writing – and continued tarrying – together. The *Phenomenology of Black Spirit* is therefore the result of long conversations, personal struggles, and constant tarrying in the space of anti/blackness and the logics that both inform and fuel its continued presence as a structure of engagement in this world. It is the result of profound moments of dis/agreement – which is to say, it is the result of two people *philosophising*. The *Phenomenology of Black Spirit* is not merely a commentary on Hegel, and neither is it merely a commentary on Black thinkers. It is certainly not white verification. It is, rather, an expression of a philosophical conversation, a real relationship, one that traverses time and space to make sense of one deceptively simple question: *What if the protagonist of Hegel's* Phenomenology *was Black?*[3]

What If the Protagonist of Hegel's Phenomenology was Black?

We did not ask this question haphazardly. By the time we had worked through the *Phenomenology*, and had mapped out who would go where, we realised that, at least from the master-slave dialectic forward, *the protagonist in Hegel's* Phenomenology of

---

2 Susan Buck-Morss, *Hegel, Haiti, and Universal History* (Pittsburgh: University of Pittsburgh Press, 2009).
3 This is partly our answer to Frank M. Kirkland's 'How Would Hegel's *Phenomenology of Spirit* Be Relevant Today?', *Logos: The Journal of Modern Society and Culture* 7:1 (Winter 2008).

INTRODUCTION

Spirit *begins as the slave*.[4] As we say in the first chapter, there is a Blackness at the heart of Hegel's *Phenomenology* – one that he cannot abide but also cannot explicitly account for. Most people read the slave (*Knecht*, in German, which A.V. Miller translates the 'bondsman' and Terry Pinkard as 'servant') as a deracialised figure – which is to say, most people read it as white and male. But such a reading seems inconsistent with, and certainly not self-aware of, the time in which the *Phenomenology* was written. Even if Hegel also had ancient mytho-historical slavery or feudalism in mind, chattel slavery was very much a thing – aside from colonialism and indigenous genocide, it was *the* thing – and to miss or overlook this is to un/willingly delude oneself. Reading the *Phenomenology* without attention to Blackness is bad philosophical magic; it is a smoke and mirror show that is no longer understood as mere smoke and mirrors. And it is dishonest (and implicated).

But it is time to clear the air, we think. If negation is the engine that powers the dialectic, then the slave (a figure that cannot help but be Black in modernity) is the embodiment of this negation and its development. The slave develops; Blackness develops. Recognising this, we set out to lay bare that Blackness *is* Hegel's negation; Blackness is what develops in, as, and through the negation – and therefore the nothingness – that it is. As we claim in the final chapter, Blackness has been deemed nothing, mortified, and it would seem that the activity of this Black nothingness – which is to say, negation – is precisely the fuel for the development of Hegelian spirit.

But as we also point out in the last chapter, nothingness cannot, and should not, be easily dismissed. As Hegel's repeats from Spinoza, negation is itself a determination; nothingness might not have direct positive content (though this too might be disputed),

---

4   Our point is to read Hegel's slave as Black, not to treat 'Black' and 'slave' as synonymous, so that people on the continent of Africa may want to unbind, or slow, the equivocation between Blackness and slavery. In other words, we admit a US-centric construal of Blackness, even as we seek to open up toward the many experiences of Blackness throughout the diaspora.

but it does have content. Nothing(ness) lives. *Blackness* lives. And it lives beyond the attempts to ignore, eliminate, obscure, or erase it. In this regard, this book also sets out to do one other thing – namely, challenge the field of contemporary philosophy to engage with Black thinkers.

But don't misread us here – this text is not a philosophical enactment of 'Diversity, Equity, and Inclusion' strategies. Focusing on the Blackness internal to Hegel's dialectical thinking does not simply expose *Hegel*; it announces the centrality of Blackness to the development of philosophical thought from modernity moving forward. To think with the chorus of Black lives we chronicle here is to recognise how Black life *shapes* modernity, how it informs and influences the movements and changes of the world – even if this shaping, informing, and influencing occurs through violence. The stories we tell here are not always pleasant. In fact, they are often tragic.

But that is also, sadly, the point. The lives we engage with in this text might exemplify, critique, or wholly detract from the *Phenomenology*'s logic, but in doing and being so, these lives make up part of the content of negation, of nothingness. They name and claim nothingness as resistance and subterfuge (Chapter 1); they underscore how nothingness can be both naively foolish and soberingly realist in its stoic commitments (Chapter 2); they announce the double- and triple-divisions with (in and through) which nothingness must wrestle (Chapter 3).

So split, Black spirit struggles with unhappiness – perhaps unhappy because it has been deemed nothingness, a divided nothingness at that – and this struggle shows up in three phases: first, it devotes itself to externally transcendent or immanent ideals (Chapter 4); finding little solace there, it puts in the sacramental work of desiring to change its conditions – even as it constantly gets in its own way (Chapter 5); and eventually, recognising that it does get in its own way, the phenomenology of Black spirit engages in the work of self-mortification, either living into the nothingness that it is, or channelling that nothingness into larger transformative projects of collective revolution (Chapter 6). Throughout this text, we try to tell a story of nothingness and its activity. We lay claim to nothingness and negation as determinations of *plenitude*, not loss; fullness, not sheer absence.

Blackness and Nothingness

Such thinking is not easy; neither is it simple. This book conceptually runs counter to the longstanding philosophical collapsing of nothingness, meaninglessness, and Blackness. If we consider, for example, Calvin Warren's *Ontological Terror*, we are met with a fierce thinker whose ruminations on the nothingness of Blackness compellingly underscore the totalising nature and aims of antiblackness. *Ontological Terror* clearly delineates that the world militates against Blackness in an attempt to secure meaning. In this view, Blackness becomes the (Heideggerian) equipment through which the meaning of the being of the world is worked out. No different from a hammer, Warren argues, Blackness – and therefore Black people – are relegated to the ontological realm of non-being, where hope is a ruse, metaphysics is a trap, and the very question of something like Black subjectivity is nonsensical. Given the ways Blackness figures as nothingness in law, science, and visual images, Blackness and therefore Black people do not have a say in the movement of the world – or, put differently, what they say is quickly interdicted by the violence of antiblackness.[5] According to Warren, Blackness is nothing; denying this is to willingly engage in an ontological illusion.

We cannot deny this. The way Warren figures both nothingness and Blackness – which, again, are synonymous in Warren's thinking – is logically, epistemologically, and conceptually sound. Yet there is a curious line in *Ontological Terror*, one that comes toward the end of the text: 'The nothing Black being must incarnate is the metaphysical entity an antiblack world obsessively attempts to purge, but fails in this enterprise, *since the world cannot eradicate nothing*.'[6] Warren goes on to claim that this fact – the

---

5   Calvin Warren, *Ontological Terror: Blackness, Nihilism, and Emancipation* (Durham, NC: Duke University Press, 2018).
6   Ibid., 143.

fact that the world cannot eradicate nothing – actually keeps the process of antiblackness going: 'failure does not preclude the enterprise; rather, it serves as its pernicious fuel'. 'The metaphysical holocaust, the obsessive attempt to eradicate the Black nothing', Warren claims, 'requires an extensive arsenal of destruction'.[7] In this regard, even if nothing cannot be eradicated, there is no way out for Blackness; it is relegated to the realm of the dismissed, the killed, the perpetually terrible, terrifying, and terror-inducing position of lawlessness and loss.

Listen. That line still sticks out: *the world cannot eradicate nothing*. If nothing cannot be eradicated, then nothing is *excessive*. It exceeds the violence of this world, even as it is called upon to call and recall the world into being again and again. Nothing is called to a task, and though this self-negating labour is neither life-giving nor life-sustaining in a world hellbent on its destruction, such labour names that nothing has activity, that it *does* something.[8]

Hegel calls it negation. Perhaps, in agreement with Warren, we might claim that it is this very negation, the very activity of (those who have been determined) nothing – which is so excessive that it cannot be eradicated, so plentiful that it cannot be fully erased, so overwhelming in its haunting and haunted presence that it cannot be fully done away with – that makes philosophy, particularly Hegelian phenomenology, possible. In so doing, it does more than serve as a mere condition of possibility for others. Nothingness and its activity – negation – announces something *other* and other*wise* than the limited range of possibilities this world presents; perhaps it is the expansion of freedom. Sometimes, as is the case with thinkers like Booker T. Washington (Chapter 2), such possibilities are obscured and denied by a desire to be a part of the world; but in other cases – as with thinkers like Harriet Jacobs (Chapter 1), Ida B. Wells (Chapter 2), Zora Neale Hurston (Chapter 4), Ella Baker (Chapter 5), and Angela Davis (Chapter 6) – the devastating and brutal life of nothingness nevertheless

---

7 Ibid.
8 One might consider this not self-negating but a form of negation that does not work on the determinate 'something', that is, 'whiteness'.

announces other possibilities, other ways of engaging, that cannot always be captured by the reductive and annihilating logics of an antiblack world. If Blackness is nothing – and, according to Warren, it is – then such nothingness contains and produces multitudes.

In a way, then, our *Phenomenology of Black Spirit* both draws from and critiques nihilistic accounts of Blackness, offering another vision of nothingness as active – even if such activity is interdicted, interrupted, denied, and violated by the antiblack world within which we find ourselves (and which we find within ourselves). In fact, Warren himself opens the door for such an engagement when he claims:

> The important task for Black thinking ... is to imagine Black existence without Being, humanism, or the human. Such thinking would lead us into an abyss. But we must face this abyss – its terror and its majesty. I would suggest that this thinking leads us into the spirit, something exceeding and preceding the metaphysical world.[9]

To this, we respond with a resounding *yes*. To imagine Black existence without Being; to imagine Blackness, Black life, Black *lives* as the activity of negation; to think Black life in a way that preserves the 'terror and majesty' at the heart of its development; this – *this* – is what this text seeks to do. To what extent this text fulfils or satisfies a Black nihilistic vision, or to what extent we develop this phenomenology of Black spirit well, is for the reader to decide.

But we can try.

And that is what we have done.

'We are still on the path to developing a phenomenology of Black spirit', Warren writes.[10]

Maybe this text might aid us along that path.

---

9 Warren, *Ontological Terror*, 171.
10 Ibid.

Black Studies and Hegel Studies

This book will not satisfy everyone, we well know. We invoked Warren here because he is, to our knowledge, the most prominent philosophical thinker on Black nihilism and the development of Black spirit. But we also invoked him to signal what will not always be present throughout the text – namely, that this book is situated between two worlds that rarely touch: Black studies and Hegel studies. In this regard, our *Phenomenology of Black Spirit* does not try to satisfy Hegel scholars, nor does it offer a full account of or engagement with Black studies. In drawing from both fields, it runs the risk of satisfying neither and irritating both.

But this is a risk we are willing to take – not simply because we find it useful, but because we are convinced that philosophy must become more robust, more expansive, and more engaged if it is to have any kind of purchase in this world. For too long, philosophy has largely sequestered itself from the larger world, often contenting itself with producing more commentaries on thinkers, texts, and movements that have already gotten a significant amount of attention.

This dynamic has rendered the professional practice of philosophy unjustifiably myopic in its scope, and irrelevant – if not pernicious – in its effects. With the exception of what we might call 'prepositional philosophers' – philosophers *of* race, gender, sexuality, religion, and the like – or what we might call the 'adjectival philosophers' – political philosophers, poststructural philosophers, postmodern philosophers, and so on – much of the field has been steeped in thinking with and about the same figures, turning a blind eye to the exigent issues and problematics that face us collectively. We do not consider Ella Baker an ethicist; we do not underscore the social- and political-philosophical insights of Zora Neale Hurston.[11] And perhaps that is all to the good.

---

11 Although there is a beautiful text by Lindsay Stewart, entitled *The Politics of Black Joy: Zora Neale Hurston and Neo-Abolitionism* (Evanston: Northwestern University Press, 2021), that engages with Hurston as a political philosopher. We cannot overstate the philosophical complexity and contributions of this text.

INTRODUCTION

Apart from Anna Julia Cooper, Angela Davis, and perhaps W.E.B. Du Bois, it is doubtful that many of the thinkers we engage in this text would have envisioned themselves as doing philosophy. Our goal here, then, is not to fashion these Black thinkers as philosophers so much as it is an attempt to push the field to further engage with Black life as constitutive for its very possibility and continued emergence. If Heidegger could engage with poetry; if Kant read travelogues; and if Hegel could engage with Antigone, it is certainly not beyond the pale to recognise the profound (as in, essential and constitutive) influence Black life has had in the development of western thought.

In this regard, this text *is* an engagement with Black studies. Many Black studies scholars have long articulated the centrality of Blackness to the development of modern thought. The slave trade was not some addendum to an already-formed epistemological, political, and social structure; it was central to it – slavery formed its foundation, gave the modern project its coherence.

To this extent, underscoring the Blackness in Hegel's *Phenomenology* is an attempt to further the critical project of Black studies. If, as Fred Moten writes, Blackness claims everyone,[12] then this text announces what we already know – or at least what we already should know: that Blackness claimed Hegel, disturbed his thinking, left him bothered, even if he himself could not figure out why.[13] He could not and did not acknowledge it explicitly. But he could write around it, trace it as the contour of constitutive nothingness. Though she is speaking of and from different regional and disciplinary contexts, Toni Morrison's discussion of

---

12 Fred Moten, "Black Op", in *Stolen Life* (Durham, NC: Duke University Press, 2018), 155–60.
13 Pinkard points out how, when the *Phenomenology* was published in 1807, Hegel was 'virtually unknown, barely employed ... [It was] written hurriedly while Hegel was in extreme dire circumstances ... during its composition he had no tenable job, no real prospects, and an illegitimate child on the way ... He had been supporting himself in a condition rapidly approximating to a state of penury'; in sum, 'The *Phenomenology* was a book born out of despair.' Terry Pinkard, 'Introduction' to G.W.F. Hegel, *The Phenomenology of Spirit*, trans. and ed. Terry Pinkard (Cambridge: Cambridge University Press, 2018), ix.

'evasion' names the dynamic that seems to be central to Hegel's phenomenological ruminations and the standard commentaries upon them. As Morrison writes:

> In matters of race, silence and evasion have historically ruled ... Evasion has fostered another substitute language in which the issues are encoded and made unavailable for open debate. The situation is aggravated by the anxiety that breaks into discourse on race. It is further complicated by the fact that ignoring race is understood to be a graceful, liberal, even generous habit.[14]

While Morrison is most certainly speaking of 'American' literary authors and their preoccupations with notions of rugged individualism, transformation, and the like, we think her discussion can be applied to Hegel's context as well. Though Hegel probably did not evade notions of race and Blackness in the *Phenomenology* (though he certainly took them on in other places – and in racially chauvinistic ways), the text nevertheless reads like an act of constant evasion, of darting and moving, trying to remain situated within the universalist frame of an idealist epistemology.[15] There is no way Hegel was completely ignorant about the realities of slavery, and yet, in the name of the development of (what has been assumed to be – even perhaps by Hegel himself) spirit, the *Phenomenology* courts, to use Morrison's words, 'another substitute

---

14 Toni Morrison, *The Source of Self Regard* (New York: Vintage Books, 2019), 142. For a take on Hegel, habits, and race, see Andreja Novakovic, 'Hegel's Real Habits', *European Journal of Philosophy* 27:4 (2019): 882–97; and Novakovic, *Hegel on Second Nature in Ethical Life* (Cambridge: Cambridge University Press, 2017).
15 On Hegel's racial chauvinism, see, for example: Frank M. Kirkland, 'Hegel on Race and Development', in *The Routledge Companion to Philosophy of Race*, ed. Paul C. Taylor, Linda Martín Alcoff, and Luvell Anderson (New York: Routledge, 2018), 42–60; Robert Bernasconi, 'With What Must the Philosophy of World History Begin? On the Racial Bias of Hegel's Eurocentrism', *Nineteenth-Century Contexts* 22 (2000): 171–201; Michael Hoffheimer, 'Race and Law in Hegel's Philosophy of Religion', in *Race and Racism in Modern Philosophy*, ed. Andrew Valls (Ithaca: Cornell University Press, 2005), 194–216, and Hoffheimer, 'Hegel, Race, Genocide', *Southern Journal of Philosophy* 39 (2001): 35–62; Patricia Purtschert, 'On the Limit of Spirit: Hegel's Racism Revisited', *Philosophy & Social Criticism* 36:9 (2010): 1039–51.

language in which the issues are encoded and made unavailable for open debate'.

The 'substitute language' is not *that* disguised, though. Even if translators often use the terms 'lord and bondsman' to describe the master-slave dialectic, we think it is clear what Hegel is talking about. But for too long, many readers have read this phase as not having anything to do with Blackness and chattel slavery. As we said above, thinkers like Stefan Bird-Pollan, Michael Monahan, Sybol S.C. Anderson, Rocío Zambrana, Kimberly Ann Harris, Elvira Basevich, and others are starting to change this terrain.[16] For now, however, too many philosophers are more than happy to recast the dialectic as not having anything to do with the millions of Black people subjected to the brutal arithmetic of slavery and its accounting.

Maybe they do this out of a 'graceful, liberal, even generous habit'.[17] Perhaps philosophers stray away from problems of antiblack violence because a liberal colour-blindness filters their philosophical lenses. We cannot comment here on such possibilities, and neither are we interested in denigrating specific philosophers or philosophical schools. We – like Charles Mills, Leonard Harris, Cornell West, George Yancy, Lewis Gordon, Adrian Piper, Jacqueline Scott, and too many others to name – simply want the field to reckon and struggle with its own complicity in antiblackness and white supremacy, and one way to do that is to underscore the centrality of Blackness to philosophical thought, especially modern philosophical thought.

---

16 Stefan Bird-Pollan, *Hegel, Freud and Fanon: The Dialectic of Emancipation* (London: Rowman & Littlefield, 2015); Michael Monahan (ed.), *Creolizing Hegel* (London: Rowman & Littlefield, 2017); Sybol S.C. Anderson, *Hegel's Theory of Recognition: From Oppression to Ethical Liberal Modernity* (London: Continuum, 2009); Rocío Zambrana, 'Hegelian History Interrupted', *Crisis & Critique* 8:2 (2021): 410–31; Kimberly Ann Harris, 'Hegel's Dialectic and African Philosophy: Du Bois, Fanon, and James', PhD diss., Penn State University, 2018; Elvira Basevich, 'Reform or Revolution? On the Political Use of Violence in the Historical Constitution of Objective Spirit in Du Bois and Hegel', special issue of *Hegel Bulletin* (forthcoming).
17 On habits and Hegel, see Rocío Zambrana, 'Bad Habits: Habit, Idleness, and Race in Hegel', *Hegel Bulletin* 42:1 (2021): 1–18.

In *this* regard, this text is also an enactment of Hegel studies. Though we ask what might be understood as an unorthodox question – what if the protagonist of the *Phenomenology* was Black? – and though we provide a different reading of Hegel that attends to Blackness and Black people, we are neither flippant about nor dismissive of Hegel. Both of us were taught that the best forms of critique are those that take the object of critique seriously – which is to say, both of us were trained in the practice of critical philosophical engagement. Merely dismissing or simply denigrating the *Phenomenology* offers little. Hegel wrote the text, and the field has canonised it.[18] With this in mind, our move is not to ignore or minimise the *Phenomenology* and its contributions and limitations, but instead to situate it, to tease out what it and its commentators seem to miss.

This text, then, is engaged in both Hegel studies and Black studies.[19] It might even be an enactment of Hegel studies *as* Black studies – by which we mean that any engagement with Hegel is already an engagement with the problematics of slavery and its afterlives. Neither Hegel nor his thought can be disentangled from the antiblack violence of modernity; to dismiss this or suggest otherwise is to misread the past.

The Structure of the Text

We have to start somewhere.

As we said, we see this text as a conversation and a conversion, but also as continuing a conversation started by others.[20] Thinkers

---

18 Hegel, of course, had a major role in the formation of the canon as very white, male, Eurocentric story. See Peter K.J. Park, *Africa, Asia, and the History of Philosophy: Racism in the Formation of the Philosophical Canon, 1780–1830* (Albany: SUNY Press, 2013).
19 Here we evoke one of the earliest African American Hegels, William H. Ferris. Ferris's Hegelianism can be found throughout *The Philosophical Treatise of William H. Ferris: Selected Readings from* The African Abroad or, his Evolution in Western Civilization, ed. Tommy J. Curry (London: Rowman & Littlefield, 2016).
20 We build upon works such as Robert Bernasconi and Sybol Cook (eds), *Race & Racism in Continental Philosophy* (Bloomington: Indiana University Press,

like Frederick Douglass, W.E.B. Du Bois, C.L.R. James, Frantz Fanon, Aimé Césaire, Édouard Glissant, and others have already begun the conversation on dialectical thinking in relation to Blackness.[21] While we do not claim to have the acumen of these thinkers, we do see the *Phenomenology of Black Spirit* as furthering the dialogue on dialectics and Blackness.[22] Douglass appropriated dialectical thinking in his work, Du Bois stalled it, Fanon criticised it, C.L.R. James politicised it, Rocío Zambrana refined it.[23] We are inspired by all of these thinkers, but here take a different approach.

We call it *dialectical parallelism*.[24]

2003); and Naomi Zack (ed.), *The Oxford Handbook of Philosophy and Race* (New York: Oxford University Press, 2017).

21 See especially C.L.R. James, *Notes on Dialectics: Hegel, Marx, Lenin* (Westport, CN: Lawrence Hill & Co, 1980); as well as John H. McClendon III, *C.L.R. James's Notes on Dialectics: Left Hegelianism or Marxism-Leninism* (Lanham, MD: Lexington Books, 2005). See also Lou Turner, 'On the Difference between the Hegelian and Fanonian Dialectic of Lordship and Bondage', in *Fanon: A Critical Reader*, ed. Lewis R. Gordon, T. Denean Sharpley-Whiting, and Renee T. White (Oxford: Blackwell, 1996).

22 For a similar project, see Ulrike Kistner and Philippe Van Haute (eds), *Violence, Slavery and Freedom between Hegel and Fanon* (Johannesburg: Wits University Press, 2020).

23 See Rocío Zambrana's approach to Hegel's racism in 'Hegel, History, and Race', in *The Oxford University Handbook*, ed. Naomi Zack (Oxford: Oxford University Press, 2017), 251–60. Apologists excuse Hegel's bigotry through his historical context, while critics discard all of Hegelianism due to his undeniable racial bigotry and chauvinism. Zambrana, however, offers a 'critically interruptive' reading that confronts Hegel's contradictions forthrightly, yet examines them for the insights that they still provide. Like Zambrana, we want to critique and never excuse Hegel, but also believe there is great value in his core dialectical thinking.

24 We see resonances with Fred Moten's sense of 'appositional encounter', that which 'demands an investigation, which is to say a remixing, of prior tracks and the laying down of some new ones; some movement, down and across ruptured, restricted avenues, nowhere, no place, but not there; some eccentric avenue given and made in being broken in and into and down, uptown, Los Angeles, Arkansas. Movement like this *isn't parallel* but off and out; tangent as much as crossing; *asymptotic, appositional encounter*. As soon as we call this line we're on derailment we'll begin to study how all this out root goes.' Fred Moten, *Black and Blur* (Durham: Duke University Press, 2017), 22, 296n.30. Others have staged such appositional encounters, such

By reading the *Phenomenology* through and alongside Black thinkers – and by reading those thinkers against the *Phenomenology* – we attempt a mode of thinking that illuminates both. This shows up in two different ways.

First, there is a conversation between the *Phenomenology* and Black thinkers. For the most part, this should feel straightforward. The book is broken into two parts. In each, we pair Hegel with Black thinkers, showing how the latter embody, augment, critique, and depart from the *Phenomenology*.

In Part I, we engage the first half of Hegel's chapter on self-consciousness: the master-slave dialectic, the stoic, and the sceptic. Frederick Douglass and Harriet Jacobs/Linda Brent are tended to in relation to the master-slave dialectic (Chapter 1); Ida B. Wells and Booker T. Washington critique and embody the *Phenomenology's* stoic (Chapter 2); W.E.B. Du Bois and Anna Julia Cooper inaugurate and articulate a tradition of critical Black scepticism (Chapter 3).

In Part II, we engage the second half of Hegel's chapter on self-consciousness: 'the unhappy consciousness [*das unglückliche Bewußtein*]'. Part II is also broken up into three chapters and structured along pairs. In Chapter 4, we sit with how Marcus Garvey and Zora Neale Hurston were fierce devotees of Blackness – albeit in different ways; Chapter 5 names Martin Luther King, Jr and Ella Baker as agents of sacramental work and desire (again, in different ways); and Chapter 6 chronicles the lives of Malcolm X and Angela Davis as differential enactments of what we see as 'self-mortification [*Selbstkasteiung*]'. In each of the chapters, the *Phenomenology* is paired with two Black thinkers to show the insights, resonances, and limitations of Hegel's text, especially its unsaid and repressed white core.[25]

---

as David Kazanjian in his' review of Buck-Morss, 'Hegel, Liberia', *Diacritics* 40:1 (2012): 6–39; or, more fully, Jim Vernon, *Hegel, Hip Hop, and the Art of Emancipation* (Basingstoke: Palgrave Macmillan, 2018).

25 For clarification, we want to admit the simultaneously hegemonic yet precarious and unsettled nature of how we are using the term 'white', especially given its variable and changing uses through time and place, such as in Hegel's Germany versus the contemporary United States (from which

But this is only one dimension of our dialectical parallelism. Reading Hegel's *Phenomenology* alongside Black Thought and life is dialectical, but it does not speak to a parallel. In this regard, there is a second, more constructive dimension in this text: *the Black thinkers we engage form a dialectic unto themselves.* More often than not, the Black men in this text resonate more with the *Phenomenology*'s movements, while the Black women often disrupt the standard phenomenological logic – and in doing so, call attention to how Black women remain the ones who are often called upon to move Black life, forward, elsewhere, now here.

The sexism and misogynoir of both the *Phenomenology* and many of the Black male thinkers in this text, however, is not the whole story. It cannot be. The Black women we engage with here allow us to see the limitations of their male counterparts, but they also demonstrate profound creativity, commitment, and vision. In this regard, each of the Black women discussed announce a movement within and beyond the frame of the normative; they call us, and they call us out. Harriet Jacobs/Linda Brent could not fight her way out of slavery – subversion was her strategy of self-recognition and self-assertion. Ida B. Wells was stoically committed to Black life, but she had no truck with Washington's minstrel antics nor his limited and warped agenda for Black uplift. Anna Julia Cooper detected another split beyond Du Bois' sceptical double-consciousness, inaugurating the concept of 'intersectionality' through what some Black feminist thinkers have called 'triple-consciousness'. In Part I, we see three women thinkers who were less interested in the oppositional and pugnacious logics undergirding the *Phenomenology* and their male counterparts than they were with finding new and alternative

---

we write). There are many arguments for this that we assume here, but the essential argumentative core concerns Hegel's central and definitive role in the formation of the Eurocentric canon of philosophy, knowledge, and civilisation, as well as the racialised categories through which our contemporary perspective looks back to Hegel's Germany, especially insofar as he has been part of a formulation of (at least) American whiteness. We thank Kwesi Thomas for help on this. For one take, see Nell Irvin Painter, *History of White People* (New York: W. W. Norton, 2011), especially chapters 4 to 6.

ways of cultivating, protecting, and critiquing Black life in service of its betterment.

Part II runs a bit differently, like Hegel's text. Zora Neale Hurston, Ella Baker, and Angela Davis also develop alternative modes of living and thinking, but they also *do not fit easily into the dialectical categories*. Hurston was devoted, but her devotion was to Black life in its immanent plenitude; she was uninterested in appealing to a transcendent 'Africanness', as Garvey was, so her life and works move beyond an investment in the 'Unchangeable' as an external and transcendent force or ideal. In so doing, she straddles the line between the devotee and the agent of sacramental work and desire – the content of the next chapter, Chapter 5. Hurston is neither a devotee nor an agent of sacramental work and desire because she is *both*. This is also the case for Baker, who, instead of falling prey to the unintended self-aggrandising dynamics of sacramental work, asserted her selfhood within and in relation to those she taught and worked with. As we say in Chapter 6, most people do not remember Baker – not because she did not know who she was or because she lived a life of submissive subservience, but because her legacy lives on in the lives of those with whom she worked. But that is the point: Baker did *not* fall prey to the trap of self-aggrandisement like King did, and in this way she is read as a woman doing the work of self-mortification – a work that characterised X's life.

In Chapter 6 we argue that Malcolm X only began to have a rigorous sense of self through becoming El-Hajj Malik El-Shabazz. Before that, he had lost himself – or was robbed of a self – by others, several times. But Angela Davis – who ends, and perhaps culminates, the text – channelled that practice of self-mortification into something generative. In losing herself, in pursuing herself to the point that it became much more than she can could control, she *gained* a sense of self-in-and-through-community – so much so that she could not think of herself outside of the work she did with others and was forced to grapple with what that meant for her own self-conception.

The chapters, of course, go into more detail regarding these dynamics. What is important here, though, is to say that the dialectical parallelism we unfold is not merely an attempt to read Black Thought through Hegel's *Phenomenology*. This text is not yet another reading *of* philosophy; it is an attempt to *philosophise*. We want to think constructively about the possibilities and pitfalls – the possibilities within the pitfalls – of Blackness and Black life. Our *Phenomenology of Black Spirit* shies away from neither the violence nor the generativity of Blackness, but instead tries to hold both in creative philosophical tension. To the extent we are successful at this endeavour, only the reader can decide.

Limitations of the Text; or, Invitation for Future Study

More than anything else, *Phenomenology of Black Spirit* is about trying to change things. At its core, it is an attempt to lay bare and criticise the violence of antiblackness – as well as articulate other possibilities within that violence, within and beyond Hegel.

But that is the thing with normative texts: though they seek to transform, they rarely, if ever, do everything they set out to do and they always do more. This text is no different, it has its limitations, and we could never deny that.

Part of this is due to both of our subject-positions. We are both cisgendered males, and while neither of us are particularly interested in liberal identity politics – or the epistemic frailty that comes with that politics – we realise that such a position necessarily entails violent blind spots, realities with which we have not yet engaged, or engaged sufficiently.[26]

One area in which this shows most clearly is the way women are figured in the text. While we have tried our best to express the tragic and generative complexity and power that the women figures embody in this text, we recognise that our engagements with them are not as full as they need to be. Our goal here was to expose the anti/blackness central to the *Phenomenology*, and

---

26 For an Hegelian take on identity politics, see Victoria Burke, 'Essence Today: Hegel and the Economics of Identity Politics', *Philosophy Today* 51:1 (2007): 79–90.

yet, as Zakiyyah Jackson tells us, there is no way for one to think Blackness without recognising the way antiblackness is an already-violent structure of gendering.[27] There is no way to think Blackness without recognising how it has been refracted through what we have come to call 'gender', and yet this very notion articulates gendering as a violent affair, an onto-epistemic structure of mutilation and violation. The world mourns George Floyd, but it pities Breonna Taylor, capitalising off that pity and rendering her death somehow less significant.

To certain readers, the text will read as if the women are less significant. While this is not the case for us personally, we recognise that there is more work to be done on this front, that the phenomenology of *Black* spirit must begin and end with the reality that Black flesh is ungendered, and that those who are not figured as 'men' are the preeminent enfleshments of this ungendering. To this extent, we are also acutely aware of the implicit heteronormativity and gender binary present in the unfolding of this work. To this we simply say: we can and will do better, and we hope that others will join us in destabilising the normative structures inherent to western philosophical thinking.

The other limitation of the text is that, despite our conclusions, this book still runs the risk of being understood as a reading of Black thinkers through a single philosophical text published by a white German man who had no desire to think with Blackness – save from denigrating it.[28] We only deal with a small portion of one of Hegel's giant books, just forty pages of the *Phenomenology*, which means that the structure of the text may make it feel like his philosophy can encompass quite a bit of what Black life is about. A certain reading of this text, then, might lead people to think we are reinforcing, not deconstructing, the universalist aims of the

---

27 See Zakiyyah Iman Jackson, *Becoming Human: Matter and Meaning in an Antiblack World* (New York: New York University Press, 2020).
28 According to the Oxford English Dictionary, 'denigration' means 'to sully or stain', as in a sullied reputation or character. It comes from the Latin *denigrare*, meaning 'to blacken, to defame', which combines *de-* ('completely') + *niger* ('black'), the basis for 'Negro' and the N-word. Denigration is, in a sense, a degradation of the form of life deemed Black.

Phenomenology, but such a reading – while not unimaginable – is nevertheless not what this book aims to do.

Instead, our positioning of multiple Black thinkers in relation to the one text is a structural attempt to overwhelm Hegel's *Phenomenology* with the Blackness that already constitutes it, but that it cannot acknowledge. Again, the thinkers we engage do more than fulfil or embody the movements of Hegel's *Phenomenology*. They augment, critique, and detract from it in their lives, their work, and, when available, their writings, and they do so obliquely, immanently, and unexpectedly.[29] This is both far more Hegelian and anti-Hegelian than Hegel ever could have, but always should have, been. As Hegel says of the emergence of new truths or new forms of consciousness, this work 'takes place for us, as it were, *behind the back* of consciousness' (PS 87;[30] emphasis added). The work of calling philosophy to account for its violence is a work that must deal with what philosophy has designated itself to be. This work must, therefore, deal with and deconstruct those thinkers and texts that have been central to its development and maintenance through what is immanently unsaid and unseen, that is, from the innermost outside. If it is to mean anything to the future of philosophy, Hegel's *Phenomenology* has to be dealt with; it has to be subjected to rigorous ethical and philosophical scrutiny *because* it has become so canonical.

The trick, then, is to engage with the canon in ways that situate it and its violence. The work to be done is to *relativise* the prevalence of these canonical thinkers and texts by announcing their limitations, their violence, their constraints. Hegel was just a man; the *Phenomenology* is just a text. It is a smart one. But in the end, it is the ruminations of one man who, armed with a certain set of violent assumptions and an uncharacteristically keen epistemological eye, developed a philosophical approach and

---

29 For more on *oblique* approaches to Hegel, albeit in a text that is not directly about Blackness, see Angelica Nuzzo, *Approaching Hegel Obliquely: Melville, Molière, Beckett* (Albany: SUNY Press, 2018).
30 PS numbers refer to section numbers in the A.V. Miller translation, not to pagination.

method to contend with the problems of his day. *We* make him important, which means that *our* readings of his work must wrestle with the quotidian reality that he was no more special than the enslaved Black people who, through various strategies and tactics, survived and/or revolted against the overwhelming epistemological, political, religious, and social violence visited upon them.

Such an account does not minimise Hegel or his contributions (and even if it does, we can live with that). But it does *situate* the man and his work, giving us a different lens through which to understand his work and its implications. As we said at the outset, this book is *not* about Hegel. It is not *about* Hegel.

Or, put most precisely, it is not about *Hegel*.

And for us, shifting that attention is precisely what opens the possibility of doing responsible philosophy.

What We Yearn For ...

Our *Phenomenology of Black Spirit* might not be for everyone. Technical in its prose, circular in its unfolding, unorthodox in its method and conclusions, this text is an attempt to open a door (probably a back door, the one marked for servants, slaves, and segregated subjectivities) to a conversation that started long before we arrived and that, we hope, will continue long after we die.

Actually, no: we *don't* hope that. To hope that would be to hope for antiblackness's continued presence – which is to say, to hope for that would be to hope for the continuation of this world as it stands. We do not hope that this world will continue as such. In fact, we're not sure 'hope' is the right term for what we desire, for hope speaks to a telos, which, in the end, would reduce the work we've done here (and the work others have done) to an instrumentalising project of 'progress'. Perhaps Yancy is onto something with his notion of post-hope.

What we yearn for, then, is the destruction of a world which has antiblackness as its foundation. We yearn for a world in which Blackness is so disruptive that the very notion of world needs to be reconfigured. We chronicle some of that in this text, though often implicitly. In this regard, this introduction has sought to make explicit what will not always be easily detectable in the pages that follow. That is often what introductions do, at least.

But now it is time to get to the work.

Let's see what a phenomenology of Black spirit is about.

I. Fighting, Uplifting, and Thinking

1

Master-Slave Dialectic

Frederick Douglass and Harriet Jacobs

> Everything must be absolute here.
> – Frederick Douglass (BF 200)

Wanting to Live: Hegel, Haiti, and the Master-Slave Dialectic

Let us begin with lines from the best-known passage in all of Hegel:

> Since to begin with they are unequal and opposed, and their reflection into a unity has not yet been achieved, they exist as two opposed shapes [*Gestalten*] of consciousness; one is the independent [*selbtständige*] consciousness who essential nature is to be for itself, the other is the dependent [*unselbtständige*] consciousness whose essential nature is simply to live or to be for another. The former is lord [*Herr*], the other is bondsman [*Knecht*]. (PS 189)

It is possible, though perhaps difficult, to miss the profundity of these lines. One could forget that with the violence inherent in the two 'shapes [*Gestalten*]' Hegel was, of course, working out a logic. After all, this moment is merely one among many in a larger moment amongst others. As 'shapes', the lord and the bondsman are figures, forms advancing a dialectic. This moment keeps thought – Hegel's, (white) philosophy's, ours – moving along its course.

But let's read closer – or, perhaps, let's go back a section. 'The Master, *Herr*' and 'the slave, *Knecht*' are forms – 'shapes' – but they are not mere imaginary figments.[1] Something *real* is bothering

---

1 We admit that 'master' and 'slave' are unsettled translations of *Herr* and

Hegel, something that has life-and-death implications. The 'dependent [*unselbtständige*]' shape of the bondsman's consciousness didn't begin as such. In fact, just a paragraph earlier, there wasn't dependence. There were only two desires for *in*dependence – desires that were deadly.

> Death certainly shows that each staked his life and held it of no account, both in himself and in the other; but that is not for those who survived this struggle. They put an end to their consciousness in its alien setting of natural existence, that is to say, they put an end to themselves, and are done away with as *extremes wanting to be for themselves*, or to have an existence of their own. But with this there vanishes from their interplay the essential moment of splitting into extremes with opposite characteristics; and the middle term collapses into a lifeless unity which is split into lifeless, merely immediate, unopposed extremes; and the two do not reciprocally give and receive one another back from each other consciously, but leave each other free *only indifferently*, like things. (PS 188)

Here Hegel announces an internal disturbance of the desire for independence and its lethal implications. Before the bondsman and the lord appear as shapes, there was a fight to the death. The desire for absolute independence is a death wish (*Todeswunsch*). If the fight continues, the death will be total. Extreme opposition leads to mutually assured destruction. At least this is how Hegel configured it. Something *was* bothering him.

Some say it was the Haitian revolution. After all, that revolution was brutal, and it had everything to do with masters and bondspeople. Susan Buck-Morss comes to this conclusion: the life and death battle between the lord and the bondsman must have been inspired by the revolution in what would become Haiti.[2]

Knecht, likely traceable to the post-Kojève/Hyppolite French translations, *maître* and *esclave*, and thus guilty of what Van Haute calls the 'anthropological reading'. Philippe Van Haute, 'Through Alexandre Kojève's Lens: Violence and the Dialectic of Lordship and Bondage in Frantz Fanon's *Black Skin, White Masks*', in *Violence, Slavery and Freedom between Hegel and Fanon*, ed. Kistner and Van Haute, 39.

2 Buck-Morss, *Hegel, Haiti, and Universal History*, 49. To the contrary, Andrew

That revolution was a brutal and supernatural fight; conjurers, priests, and priestesses – and perhaps 'root' workers (this will become important later) – turned to the gods, the ancestors, and nature who, in turn, encouraged them to fight back. Out of that 'natural setting', Haiti was born.[3] But the death toll was high – on both sides. According to Buck-Morss, Hegel was well aware of this fight to the death, and it *bothered* him.[4] Haiti and France became 'unopposed extremes', who had left 'each other free only indifferently, like things'. This indifferent freedom, it seems, offered no possibility of mutual recognition, mutual exchange.[5] The reciprocal relations founding recognition had stalled. There was nowhere to go and no way forward. The fight resulted in a metaphysical standstill.

But this was not the case everywhere. Slavery was still thriving in the United States. Perhaps Hegel was aware of those other places, too. One can imagine, then, that Hegel's next move, in paragraph 189, was his way of overcoming the standstill that had resulted in both his logic and in the revolution. Hegel wanted a logic that *lives*. 'Their act [that of the opposed extremes-turned-indifferent-things] is an abstract negation, not the negation coming from consciousness, which supersedes in such a way as to preserve and maintain what is superseded, and consequently *survives* [*überlebt*] its own supersession' (PS 188; emphasis added).

Cole argues that this famous scene depicts eighteenth-century German feudalism, rather than ancient or modern chattel slavery. Andrew Cole, *Birth of Theory* (Chicago: University of Chicago Press, 2014), 65–85.

3 Ciccariello-Maher argues that C.L.R. James and Frantz Fanon, rather than Buck-Morss's resuscitation of Hegel's universal history, are 'more generative for the task of decolonizing dialectical thought'. George Ciccariello-Maher, '"So Much Worse for the White": Dialectics of the Haitian Revolution', *Journal of French and Francophone Philosophy/Revue de la philosophie française et de langue française* 22:1 (2014): 19–39.

4 Of the many criticisms of Buck-Morss, see Celucien L. Joseph, 'On Intellectual Reparations: Hegel, Franklin Tavarès, Susan Buck-Morss, Revolutionary Haiti, and Caribbean Philosophical Association', *Africology: The Journal of Pan-African Studies* 9:7 (2016).

5 For a take on mutual recognition in Hegel and Fanon, see Charles Villet, 'Hegel and Fanon on the Question of Mutual Recognition: A Comparative Analysis', *The Journal of Pan African Studies* 4:7 (2011): 39–51.

Hegel wanted a living logic, and may have assumed that everyone else had the same understanding of life.

This is all speculative, of course, but Hegel himself was speculative.[6] More to the point, we are not speculating out the blue. Consider the first line of paragraph 189: 'In this experience, self-consciousness *learns that life is as essential to it as pure self-consciousness.*' Life is essential, but to have it, division is necessary. The opposed extremes are not suitable for life because of the threat of death. Thus, something must give – logically and existentially. But only for one side, since the splitting isn't equal. One side must be dependent on the other; 'the master' and 'the slave' are born – or, at least, they show themselves for the first time.

Who Is This Lord? Who Is This Slave?

This chapter is about Hegel's master-slave dialectic, but it is also about the Black life, the Black *lives*, that expose (if not constitute) the limitations of his thought. In his *Phenomenology*, 'the master' and 'the slave' are logical positions, 'shapes [*Gestalten*]' of consciousness. While this allows the power of Hegel's thought to shine, it also misses much – and, in turn, raises critical questions: Does the fight to the death always engender the emergence of the lord and the bondsman, or could the fight be between these two logical positions? What about 'dependence'? Does it always and actually show up as (close to) absolute – where the desires of the enslaved are subsumed under those of the masters? Does gender make a difference? After all, males weren't the only people who were enslaved. What if 'the slave' was not a bonds*man*, but a bonds*woman*? What might a female perspective do to Hegel's dialectic? We ask these questions, and we sit with them here.

---

6 We admit we are risking equivocation here. For Hegel, 'the *speculative* or *positively rational* apprehends the unity of the determinations in their opposition, the *affirmative* that is contained in their dissolution and in their transition'. Stephen Houlgate, *Hegel on Being* (London: Bloomsbury Academic, 2021), 11. See G.W.F. Hegel, *Science of Logic*, trans. George D. Giovanni (Cambridge: Cambridge University Press, 2010), 41.

To respond to them, we go to the United States. Buck-Morss's account is so tempting, if not totally convincing, that we are intrigued by what would happen if we shifted our focus in reading Hegel's master-slave dialectic from Haiti to life and death conflicts between masters and slaves in American chattel slavery.[7] Acknowledging the admittedly unfounded desire to believe Hegel was truly concerned with Haiti, our strategy resonates with Buck-Morss's, as she writes: Hegel 'inaugurate[s], as the central metaphor of work, not slavery versus some mythical state of nature (as those from Hobbes to Rousseau had done earlier), but slaves versus masters, thus bringing into his text the present, historical realities that surrounded it like invisible ink'.[8] It is possible, then, that the bondsman-lord dialectic is not merely a logical unfolding of spirit, but also – and perhaps primarily – a reflection on the existential-phenomenological dialectic between the enslaved and the slaveholding class.[9] To stay with historical texts and actors who do the thinking themselves – perhaps this approach might offer different insights.

But let us be specific. Perhaps, during the period of legal and formal enslavement, there are thinkers who wrote and thought dialectically from the perspective of the enslaved. We could,

---

7   In another resonance with Buck-Morss's argument, Douglass was the United States Minister Resident and General Consul to the Republic of Haiti from 1889 to 1891. We also recognise the many risks in such a temptation. For these, see Frank Kirkland, 'Hegel and the Saint Domingue Revolution – Perfect Together?: A Review of Susan Buck-Morss' *Hegel, Haiti, and Universal History*', *Logos: The Journal of Modern Society and Culture* 11:2–3 (2012).
8   Buck-Morss, *Hegel, Haiti, and Universal History*, 52.
9   In *Roll Jordan Roll*, Eugene Genovese offers a dialectical history of the relationship between the enslaved and the slaveholding class in the United States. Genovese structures this history through the concept of paternalism, whereby the slaveholding class envisioned themselves as benevolent caretakers of the enslaved. A dialectic unfolds: the paternalistic slaveholders need enslaved Black people to ensure their role as benefactors, and, in turn, the enslaved begin to recognise the fallacy of such a claim. The logic fails as soon as the work, the whips, the chains, the 'punishments', and the sexual assaults unfold. See Eugene Genovese, *Roll Jordan Roll: The World the Slaves Made* (New York: Vintage, 1976).

then, trace the bloody path across the Atlantic, through the Middle Passage, and to the major slave ports running up along the Eastern United States. And there, we might stop in South Carolina, where a young girl named Harriet Jacobs was born.[10] Or, we could stop in Talbot County, Maryland, where a Black boy of African, Native American, and European heritage, 'named' Frederick Augustus Washington Bailey, was born into slavery in (possibly) February 1818. We will stop in both places. In a way, Hegel's work demands it.

We turn to both places because they announce unseen openings in Hegel's thought. In addition to its unabashed and virulent antiblack racism, Hegel's work also turns on a vicious normative masculinity, pugnacious in its presentation and categorical in its thinking. This masculinity does not show itself simply in the male pronouns or the fighting. It also shows itself through a kind of logical cleanness, a sterility that is allergic to opacity. 'The lord' and 'the bondsman', then, are logical (dis)positions, figures who are both more and less than the historical people who were enslaved and who were exercising domination. 'The slave' had names. 'The master' did, too. And these names make a difference. They make differences.

One difference is clear: the difference between a logical position and an ontological *disposition*. The *slave* is defined by its dialectical and logical relation to the master; the *en*slaved are also defined by this relation, but this relation takes different, and often more complex, forms than 'the slave's' relation. The figure and the names connect, but they are not connected by identification.

Who is the slave, then? As we will show, Hegel's '*Knecht*' is a logical position of absolute dependence, it is 'for another'. The slave derives his — and it is a 'he' — existence, his recognition, from the master's gaze. His position, is, therefore, a logical one; he is a kind of necessary negation. That is, necessary for Hegel's logic. Hegel needs him for his logic to work. But in order for Hegel's logic to work, the slave must also work — in a very

---

10 Harriett Jacobs/Linda Brent, *Incidents in the Life of a Slave Girl* (New York: Harvest Books, 1973).

specific way (we'll say more about this later). The slave's work *does work* – for Hegel's logic, for the slave himself. But enslaved people didn't always share Hegel's meaning of work. Some, like Frederick Douglass, move the dialectic forward through fighting; others, like Harriet Jacobs, move the dialectic forward through practice. As this chapter unfolds, we will see the implications of these different meanings.

Conversely, Hegel's master is the one who is being 'for himself' (and 'he' is a *he*, too, for reasons that will soon become clear). He, too, does logical work. But again: the master and the historical masters are not the same. Harriet's master Dr Flint did not fight with Jacobs (though he did hit her); the slaver breaker Edward Covey was not *actually* Douglass's master. There are slippages. And these slippages matter. They make us think differently. They give us pause. They offer different perspectives. And they push us to change our language. For this reason, unless we're quoting someone else, we reserve the term 'the slave' for the logical position in Hegel's thought. When we discuss historical examples, we use the term 'enslaved'. 'Enslaved [*Versklavt*]' announces an ontological disposition that, even in its constraint, announces plasticity. Enslavement can and will look different, but 'the slave' is locked in his logical relation.[11]

There are other changes to language, too. After all, Harriet was an enslaved female (we follow Hortense Spillers in using the 'female' designation).[12] 'The slave' is figured as male; he fights, and he works. But Harriet's life disrupts the masculinity implicit in Hegel's (and Douglass's) dialectical line(s) of thinking. This isn't merely tokenism. We do not 'tack' Harriet on to the end to 'include' women in our analysis. As we will show, she is perhaps

---

11 We should not understand the term 'locked' to imply a stasis, though. Hegel's slave doesn't simply stand still; he is the logical engine of the dialectic. Make no mistake: the slave changes; he finds self-recognition. He grows over time. The slave is not stuck; he moves. But the meaning of his movement is already overdetermined. We'll hear more about this as the chapter unfolds.
12 Hortense Spillers, 'Mama's Baby, Papa's Maybe: An American Grammar Book', *Diacritics* 17:2 (1987): 64–81.

the strongest expression and critique of the dialectic through her own narrative of self-recognition. She works, but not like Hegel's slave. She finds herself, but not like Douglass does. Her process is a slow, tedious unfolding that comes through small moments of clarity. Her process is a practice.

If this is the case for the enslaved and 'the slave', though, then what about 'the master'? If there is a slippage, an unacknowledged difference, between Hegel's slave and the enslaved, between the slave and his names, then is there a slippage between the master and *his* names? The answer is yes and no.

On the one hand, there is a slippage. As we noted above, Flint and Covey do things differently than Hegel's master. Covey is broken through his fight with Douglass; Harriet continuously thwarts Flint's sexual desires. So, yes: there is a slippage. But they, each of them, eventually fall back into place in Hegel's logic. The masters find themselves in their bondspeople; they find their recognition through the gaze of the other – even if this other isn't nearly as subservient or dependent as Hegel's bondsman initially is. Covey's self-image changes when he loses; Flint becomes recalcitrant in his desire to never sell Harriet when he learns she is pregnant.

Some might claim that there is a gendered slippage here. After all, there were mistresses as well as masters. Harriet's struggles are as much against Mrs Flint as they are against Dr Flint. This gendered difference should matter; and perhaps it did. But consider what Spillers says about mistresses – referring to Harriet's narrative as evidence. Spillers references Mrs Flint's constant whispering in Harriet's ear; she whispered things that Dr Flint might say. This whispering was meant to catch Harriet off-guard, to see if Harriet was, indeed, telling the truth about declining and avoiding Dr Flint's sexual advances. Spillers lays out the effects of Mrs Flint's actions:

> The mistress in the case of Brent's [Harriet's] narrative becomes a metaphor for *his* madness that arises in the ecstasy of unchecked power. Mrs. Flint enacts a male alibi and prosthetic motion that is mobilized *at night*, at the material place of the dream work. In

both male and female instances, the subject attempts to *inculcate* his or her will into a vulnerable, supine body.[13]

The mistress, it turns out, ends up becoming a proxy for the master; even her normative gender is subsumed under his manhood. 'In the ecstasy of unchecked power', the mistress takes on the role of the master, and in so doing, reaffirms the logical and historical position of 'the master' in the dialectic. Like Dr Flint, Mrs Flint needs Harriet's (denied) recognition in order to understand herself. Like Dr Flint, Mrs Flint fails to change.

For this reason, we retain the masculine pronoun 'he' for 'the master' – in both logical and historical terms. Though there are slippages, they are not slippery enough to dislodge the work 'the master' does in Hegel's thought. 'The master' and the historical masters were not the same, but the difference between them may not make enough of a difference to warrant the introduction of a distinction here.

The other slippages do, though. And in such a profound way that we are compelled to attend to them. In Douglass and in Harriet, we find different pathways to self-recognition: Douglass fights his way out; Harriet hides and evades her way out. These differences matter. They open up different lenses through which to understand and critique the *Phenomenology*. And, perhaps more importantly than understanding and critique, they open up a different dialectic – one that runs parallel to Hegel's. Douglass critiques Hegel's dialectic; Harriet critiques both Hegel and Douglass. In so doing, Douglass and Harriet offer alternatives; they open up a different master-slave dialectic in the phenomenology of Black spirit.

Fighting Your Way Forward: Frederick Douglass

We begin in Talbot County, Maryland, with Frederick. When he grew into a man and, through toils and troubles, became a free man, taking on the surname 'Douglass', he became the most

---

13 Ibid., 77.

famous enslaved Black American in history and the most photographed American of the nineteenth-century. Frederick Douglass, then, needs little or no introduction. He wrote so much, and so much has been written about him. He wrote three narratives. He was a powerful orator and abolitionist, a diplomat, a writer, a publisher, and above all a thinker.

A *thinker*: it boggles the mind that, save for those texts and classes on 'philosophy of race', Frederick Douglass doesn't make it into 'canonical' discourses on philosophical thinking. Or maybe it is not so mind-boggling. Maybe that is precisely the way a certain kind of philosophical thinking unfolds: through the erasure of an entire tradition.

But the erasure is never total. Something remains, a remnant. Some kind of residue is left in the wake of 'erasure'. Douglass would not – could not – be erased. And neither would Jacobs. And both – *both* – have something to say about dialectics. Which is to say, both have something to say about Hegel. In this way, our strategy also draws from Paul Gilroy, who writes:

> I want to propose that we read a section of Douglass' narrative as an alternative to Hegel: a supplement if not exactly a trans-coding of his account of the struggle between lord and bondsman. In a rich account of the bitter trial of strength between Edward Covey, the slave breaker to whom he has been sent, Douglass can be read as if he is systematically reworking the encounter between master and slave in a striking manner which inverts Hegel's own allegorical scheme.[14]

Hegel's Lordship and Bondage

We now turn to Hegel's account of the structure of human subjectivity, beginning in the 'Lordship and Bondage' section, to see what it can offer to an understanding of Douglass and this first moment in a dialectic of Black Thought.[15]

---

14 Paul Gilroy, *The Black Atlantic: Modernity and Double Consciousness* (Cambridge, MA: Harvard University Press, 1993), 60.
15 David Blight claims that 'Douglass seemed intuitively aware of Georg Hegel's

For Hegel, subjectivity begins in self-consciousness. Subjectivity requires another subject to recognise it *as* a subject, and the same requirement goes in both directions. One subject needs another subject just as much as that other subject needs the first subject. It is through another's recognition that one can be a subject because one subject only encounters itself as a subject insofar the other gives its self back. Let us now pull apart this twisted logic of recognition.

The structure of subjectivity is a 'unity-in-its-duplication [*Einheit in seiner Verdopplung*]' (PS 178). In the process of recognition, two subjects are pulled out of their respective interiorities. Each loses its hold in itself because it is no longer able to fully determine what it is. We are pulled out of our heads when we feel we are being watched. Seeing that another beholds us in their sights, we find ourselves in an *other* being. We encounter ourselves only insofar as another holds us.

To be held. Or, conversely, *to hold*. Hegel's structure of subjectivity is one of holding, of *the* hold. The dialectical structure of subjectivity requires a beholding, and the hold is not always symmetrical or reciprocal. To be 'held' isn't always reciprocal – even if the one who holds finds its subjectivity in the hold of the one already held.

This is not mere wordplay. Hegel's 'unity-in-its-duplication' is a structure of subjectivity that opens to the question of holding, to the question of *the hold* – leading back to the hold of the ship. Jacobs and Douglass do not exist without a prior holding that calls them into existence. The bondsperson is thrust into this dialectic

---

famous insight about the mutual dependence of the master and the slave, of their inherent need for recognition from each other for the system to work. From experience, Douglass had his own ways of showing how the more perfect the slave, the more enslaved the master. And he showed how slavery, no matter how brutal its forms and conditions, was the meeting of two kinds of consciousness in a test of wills, and that total domination or absolute authority by the master was only rarely possible. He understood just how much the master's own identity as an independent, powerful person depended on the slave's recognition through his willing labor of that master's authority.' David W. Blight, *Frederick Douglass: Prophet of Freedom* (New York: Simon & Schuster, 2018), 40–1.

as one already in holding and from whom life is *withheld*, as the victim of what Hortense Spillers calls a '*theft of the body* – a willful and violent ... severing of the captive body from its motive will, its active desire'.[16]

The embodied bondsperson, the bondsperson that is nothing more than a body, returns a look, but the look isn't reciprocal. Just as we are pulled out of ourselves in order to confront how others see us, we simultaneously overcome the other's hold on us insofar as the other becomes merely a means for our encounter with ourselves, almost like a lifeless mirror that merely reflects us back our own, albeit distorted, image. As the other is overcome, their hold on us is thus reduced to nothing. *The other is placed (back) in the hold.*

But the other also and nevertheless undoes the subject in the process. The hold isn't totalising – or, put differently, the hold isn't a total abnegation. While this overcoming and reduction is needed for the subject to be certain of itself, it also, and simultaneously, overcomes and reduces itself because it is reliant on another subject to recognise it *as* a subject. As Hyppolite puts it, 'the negation of the other ... becomes self-negation as well'.[17] Hegel considers this double-sensed or bi-directional structure 'ambiguity [*Doppelsinnes*]' – a double-sensed, double-movement (PS 179–81).

This double-movement proceeds along three moments. First, the subject, beginning in itself, is pulled out of itself as it senses that another recognises it. Second, the first *recognised* subject locates itself in the *recognising* other. Third, the first subject then returns to itself, reclaiming the sense of self that was given to it by the second subject as its own. The first and third moments are the extremes; the second moment is the middle term. In Hegel's words:

> Each [subject] is for the other the middle term through which each mediates itself with itself and unites with itself; and each is for itself, and for the other, an immediate being on its own account,

---

16 Spillers, 'Mama's Baby', 67.
17 Jean Hyppolite, *Structure and Genesis*, trans. Jean Heckman (Evanston: Northwestern University Press, 1979), 168.

which at the same time is such only through this mediation. They *recognize* themselves as *mutually recognizing* each other [*gegenseitig sich anerkennend*]. (PS 184)

Battle for Recognition

Recognition, for Hegel, cannot be merely an internal or external relation. It cannot be merely an external relation because then the other would be inessential, not necessary for subjective development. Thus, the relation to the other must, it seems, be internalised. But it cannot be merely internal because then neither subject would be independent of, separate and different from, the other. Put differently, the two subjects could never be free of each other if it was mere internal relation. Recognition is thus a synthesis of external and internal relations, a union of separateness or independence and connectedness or dependence.

As stated earlier, this process of recognition of subjectivities is not symmetrical or equal. Hegelian recognition is not a mirroring relationship because that relation does not capture the inverted directedness that we see in this account of recognition. Two struggling beings are brought into conflict because they are each trying to demonstrate that they are all of reality, that the world is how the subject determines it to be. Subjects want the world to be the way they think about it, just as they want to have the right understanding of the world. My goal is to eliminate the other so that they cannot get in the way of my determining the world in the way in which I determine it. Hegel considers this a 'life-and-death' battle in which both seek to 'raise their certainty of being *for themselves to truth*', both for themselves and for the other (PS 187). They both seek to prove that each is more than a mere living *thing*; they both seek to force the other to recognise that they are self-consciousnesses above and beyond what Agamben calls 'bare life', *zoe* (ζωή).[18] This fight for recognition, Hippolyte writes, is a seeking 'to prove to others as well as to oneself that one is an

---

18 Giorgio Agamben, *Homo Sacer: Sovereign Power and Bare Life*, trans. Daniel Heller-Roazen (Stanford: Stanford University Press, 1998), 8.

autonomous self-consciousness. But one can prove that to oneself only by proving it to others and by obtaining that proof from them.'[19] This will become clear when we turn to Douglass in a more sustained fashion.

Recognition involves an 'inequality of the two' subjects that 'are opposed to one another, one being *recognized [Anerkanntes]*, the other only *recognizing [Anerkannendes]*' (PS 185). Since 'they have not yet exposed themselves to each other ... as self-consciousness ... [e]ach is indeed [only] certain of its own self, but not of the other' (PS 186). As Hyppolite puts it, '[i]ts certainty remains subjective'.[20] However, since each lacks the certainty of the subjectivity of the other, both of their 'own self-certain[ties] still ha[ve] no truth' (PS 186). There must be two self-certain subjects for the possibility of any self-certainty at all. The *contents of their intentions are the same but the direction is opposed*. Each subject must simultaneously sustain two opposed points of view.

There is, then, a simultaneous recognition of two inverted points of view. One point of view is centred on my particular desire in which the other counts as the object of that desire – the desire to kill – and the other point of view escapes the centring on myself, thus de-centring me, and which is reflected through the other's point of view in which I am the object of their desire, their desire to kill me.

What leads to this battle is the shared but inverted desire of each subject to be the only source of determination of all of reality. The problem is that if the other is killed, there is no other to recognise the winner *as* the winner; the winner cannot be the master if there is no slave to recognise the master *as* master. The master can only win if both subjects survive the battle, simply because to be self-conscious requires being alive. The dialectical structure of slavery, then, is necessarily a structure that aims to *keep the enslaved alive*, even though it often failed in that endeavour. If the enslaved just dies, leaving only the master (who would then not be the master), this would be an act of what Hegel calls

---

19 Hyppolite, *Structure and Genesis*, 169.
20 Ibid.

'abstract negation', negation without determination (PS 188). For Hegel, the (eventual) master recognises that the risk of life for the purpose of being recognised as the determining force of all things is a necessary condition for self-consciousness. The master must keep the enslaved alive; to lose the enslaved would be to lose a sense of oneself.

This sense of keeping the enslaved alive traces back to slave ships. The Middle Passage was unfathomably wretched, but the goal was not to allow enslaved people to die. Theologian Anthony Pinn notes that keeping the enslaved in the hold was a way of keeping them from revolting. But even the most recalcitrant captives needed to be kept alive and healthy. Pinn puts it this way:

> In the darkness of the hold, ventilation was limited and sanitation difficult to maintain. But to keep [the enslaved] in somewhat good health, captains would bring the slaves on deck to allow the hold to be cleaned and disinfected as well as to provide space for feeding. On many ships, slaves were fed an array of beans, yams, plantain, and other cheap goods. In addition, exercise was considered important in order to maintain the slaves' health and muscle tone and to bring a good price once in the colonies. As one might imagine, Africans taken from the familiarity of their families and homes were not in the mood for a good workout. Hence, slave traders forced them to dance under the threat of punishment.[21]

Moreover, in keeping the captives alive, slave traders had to endure the brutal conditions of the Atlantic as well. The Middle Passage was brutal for everyone involved, but it has to be emphasised: the goal was to keep the enslaved alive, albeit for economic (rather than, as is the case with Hegel's master, for psychological) reasons. The hold is a hold, indeed.

For Hegel, the slave of the dialectic is the one who *endures*, while for historical slavery some slaves must survive.[22] They

---

21 Anthony Pinn, *Terror and Triumph: The Nature of Black Religion* (Minneapolis: Fortress Press, 2003), 31.
22 It is important to note that many enslaved Africans and their descendants chose death instead of life. But as a philosophical identity, the slave is the

survive to fight or labour another day. The slave compromises their claim to be an independent self-consciousness; they do not strive to be all of reality. Freedom is the spoil at stake, as Hegel writes: 'it is only through staking one's life that freedom is won' (PS 187). To be completely free to self-determine, one subject must make the other completely submit to its will, must make the other a slave.[23]

Consciousness in Bondage

The being of the slave first appears outside of their consciousness because the slave is owned, in body and soul, by the master. The slave is chained to mere life, though it might be better to say that they are *animated*. They respire. They circulate blood. They move (or rather *are* moved). But this animation is not for themselves. As Spillers writes, 'the captive [i.e. the enslaved] body reduces to a thing, becoming *being for* the captor'.[24] The enslaved's being is only for-another, for the master, and not in-itself, not their own. The slave must thus regard the master as the source of their meaning and motion. The freedom that the slave sees in the master becomes the slave's ideal, his model for being a subject. As Hegel puts it, 'servitude has the master for its essential reality' (PS 194). The master appears as the truth of the slave, an external truth, because the meaning of their existence as a slave is completely determined by the position of the master.

---

one who endures and, in the process, abnegates their claim to independent self-consciousness.
23 We should note that Orlando Patterson finds fault with 'Hegel's failure to take account of the free nonslaveholding members of the master's society', which leads to 'an extremely important, if paradoxical, conclusion about the nature of slave-based timocratic cultures: namely, that they are possible only where slavery does not totally dominate society'. Thus, he concludes: 'A truly vibrant slave culture, if it is to avoid the crisis of honor and recognition, must have a substantial free population. Conversely, a society with only masters and slaves cannot sustain a slave culture.' Orlando Patterson, *Slavery and Social Death: A Comparative Study* (Cambridge, MA: Harvard University Press, 2018), 100.
24 Spillers, 'Mama's Baby', 67.

The master therefore consciously treats the slave as a mere means, as an instrument intended simply to satisfy his masterly desires. He puts them on hold, in holding, but there is a slippage: unconsciously, the master recognises the slave as an intentional human being because he speaks to them. He gives orders. He commands. This is not a monologue, for the slave recognises and understands the meaning of these orders, these commands. So, there is some recognition and some lack of recognition, just as there is some conscious and some unconscious recognition. Grégoire Chamayou sees this logic in the obscene pleasure that is part of the long history of manhunts: 'The supreme excitement and at the same time the absolute demonstration of social superiority is, in fact, to hunt beings one knows to be men [sic] and not animals.'[25] In the history of hunting people that Chamayou examines, the 'peculiar challenge' of trying to erase the distance between humans and animals is precisely what makes manhunts so delectable and widespread: 'Recognizing the humanity of the prey and at the same time challenging it in practice are thus the two contradictory attitudes constitutive of the manhunt.'[26]

When he uses the slave as an instrument for his own ends, the master consumes the product of the slave's labour. The master does not fret about food, water, pleasure, shelter, but simply enjoys them. The master is identified with the object consumed, overlooking the process of its production. The master's position is thus static. Without a reason to act, the master just stays the same, a mere identity wherein I = I; he wants to keep that identity, to stay the master who consumes and enjoys. *The master stays the same.*[27]

---

25 Grégoire Chamayou, *Manhunts: A Philosophical History*, trans. Steven Rendall (Princeton: Princeton University Press, 2012), 2.
26 Ibid.
27 It is possible to hear in this 'sameness' the 'Same' of Emmanuel Levinas. The same consumes. It digests. The 'ipseity' of its 'I' needs to consume external realities. But the other serves to disrupt this. See Emmanuel Levinas, *Totality and Infinity*, trans. Alphonso Lingis (Pittsburgh: Duquesne University Press, 1969).

Chamayou calls this sameness an 'absolute nonsubject' that derives from the positing of a radical inferiority.[28] The master begins as an absolute nonsubject and becomes a nonabsolute subject. The subjectivity of the slave 'consists solely in the negation of their own autonomy'.[29] The minimal power of action – recognition – is denied when they are seen as the master's accomplice – the master's slave. The slave is thus not allowed to be an agent, even of their own slavery; they are the purely passive instrument of another's will.[30] This reflects, on the side of the master, the inversion of the slave: rather than 'absolute nonsubject', the master is the 'nonabsolute subject', which involves what Jean Hyppolite calls the 'inherent contradiction in the state of domination'.[31] The master is master only because he is recognised by the slave as a master. As the master becomes increasingly dependent on the slave to fulfil his desires, his independence diminishes. But the slave *works*. And for this reason, the slave grows. They change. They do not remain the same.

The master is totally dependent on the other, the slave, whom he does not recognise as worthy of recognition. Even more, the master disdains the very being that gives him his masterly status. The master's dependence on the slave seeds resentment. Such an asymmetrical form of recognition fails because it is too one-sided and unequal, and this cannot abide. The master must have what he wants: if he wants the slave to be happy, the slave must oblige. They must 'be' happy – which is to say, they must perform happiness. Saidiya Hartman puts it this way:

> the brutal command to merrymaking suggest[s] that the theatricality of the Negro emerges only in the aftermath of the body's brutal dramatic displacement – in short, after the body has been made subject to the will of the master ... what else could jigs danced in command performances be but the gentle indices of

---

28 Chamayou, *Manhunts*, 51.
29 Ibid., 50.
30 For an examination of slavery and agency, see Walter Johnson, 'On Agency', *Journal of Social History* 37:1 (2003): 113–24.
31 Hyppolite, *Structure and Genesis*, 173.

domination[?] … Such performances cast the slave as a contented bondsman and elide the difference between volition and violation.[32]

There is, of course, a difference between being forced to perform happiness and actually *being* happy; this difference – the difference between violation and volition – is elided in the slave's position in the dialectic. The slave's actions are thus not really their own, but actions compelled by another. The master, writes Hegel, 'is the pure essential action in this relationship, while the action of the slave is impure and unessential' (PS 191).

This elision between volition and violation has serious implications. The slave must make the master's desires appear to be their own. For some, the appearance eventually takes too much of a hold: the master's desire becomes the slave's desire. Malcolm X might call this type of slave a 'house negro'. 'Whenever the master says "we", he says "we". That's how you can tell a house negro.' The master says, 'I want cotton', the slave says, '*we* want cotton', though this desire does not originate within the slave. 'He identifies himself with his master more than the master identifies with himself.'[33] The slave is subsumed: they cannot even think for themselves, or their thought of themselves is blocked by the omnipresence of the master. The slave, then, is merely what Hegel calls a person, a house negro, because 'he [*sic*] has not attained to the truth of this recognition as an independent self-consciousness' (PS 187). This move, the deliberation of the slave's desires, is not a self-relation but a relation to the master.

Optimistically, Hegel thinks that this leads to a twist in the order of independence and dependence between master and slave insofar as their roles mutually depend on each other. The 'one-sided and unequal' nature of this relation reveals the inherent contradiction of mastery, as Hyppolite puts it; 'the truth of the

---

32 Saidiya Hartman, *Scenes of Subjection: Terror, Slavery, and Self-Making in Nineteenth-Century America* (New York: Oxford University Press, 1997), 43.
33 Malcolm X, 'The House Negro and the Field Negro', <https://www.youtube.com/watch?v=7kf7fujM4ag>

master reveals that he is the slave of the slave'.[34] Or, as Douglass notes: 'There is more truth in the saying, that slavery is a greater evil to the master than to the slave, than many who utter it, suppose' (BF 189).[35]

Fear of Death

To keep animated: this is the project of slavery. Masters need to keep slaves alive, but in a way that ensures the enslaved do not develop *lives*. To maintain that life without living, masters developed a psychic technology in the other's self: the fear of death. The master had to make it appear as if he was the sole source of life or death. The development of this technology traces from the American South back to the first plunder of Africa, when white Europeans hunted down and captured Black bodies. 'The experience of hunting', Chamayou writes, 'establishes for the prey [who became slaves] a relationship to the world that is structured by a radical anxiety. Each perception, including that of its own body, becomes a foreboding of danger.'[36]

The hunt, however, is not simply existential; it is also sexual. When it comes to the violence of slavery, this hunt – and the danger it poses – is figured *through* the female. The threat of death is bodily, and it finds its source in a 'powerlessness' that, as Spillers shows, has its source in the 'irresistible, destructive sensuality' radiating from the captive female body. In other words, the hunt is brutally and – perhaps lethally – seductive; the hunted are powerless, and this powerlessness allures the hunter, making the hunt all the more riveting. Spillers puts it this way: 'As a category of "otherness," the captive body ... embodies sheer physical powerlessness that slides into a more general "powerlessness," resonating through various

---

34 Hyppolite, *Structure and Genesis*, 172.
35 'The slaveholder, as well as the slave, is the victim of the slave system ... there is no relation more unfavorable to the development of honorable character, than that sustained by the slaveholder to the slave. Reason is imprisoned here, and passions run wild' (BF 171).
36 Chamayou, *Manhunts*, 59.

centers of human and social meaning.'[37] The 'manhunt', it turns out, hinges upon hunting those who are *not* 'men'.

Consider, drawing from Spillers, how enslaved female bodies were 'accounted for' and put to work to reproduce. An enslaved person begins their life in what Orlando Patterson calls 'natal alienation', and often dies in the darkness of anonymity and ignorance.[38]

While some might not see natal alienation as the threat of death, consider this: if slavery is about keeping the enslaved animated, then the threat is not merely physical death. It is, instead, to draw from Jared Sexton (who is drawing from Patterson), a social death. Sexton puts it this way:

> A living death is as much a death as it is a living ... Black life is not social life in the universe formed by the codes of state and civil society, of citizen and subject, of nation and culture, of people and place, of history and heritage, of all the things that colonial society has in common with the colonized, of all that capital has in common with labor – the modern world system ... Black life is *lived* in social *death*.[39]

To be kept 'alive' in order to remain socially dead; to be animated in order to be threatened by the selling of one's beloveds (which is to say, to *not* have children *or* a beloved, and conversely, to have a maternal relation be fragmented and one's love stunted); to be threatened with the inevitable eventuality that one will not have *had* a life but will only have had this life *taken away*; to know that escape could and would entail one's own demise: this is the life of the slave. From the early days of the African slave hunting and trading to the final days of American slavery, the fear of physical *and* social death – and of the master who embodied the power to

---

37 Spillers, 'Mama's Baby', 67.
38 Patterson, *Slavery and Social Death*, 99. Patterson makes a number of important and convincing critiques of Hegel's account of the master-slave dynamic, particularly in terms of the connections between slavery and labour (98–101).
39 Jared Sexton, 'The Social Life of Social Death', *Intensions* 5 (Fall/Winter 2011).

enact both and exercised it willingly – structured (and still structures) consciousness in bondage.[40]

Slave owners had complicated and expansive ways of instilling fear. We've mentioned one strategy above: natal alienation – and, in turn, the fragmentation of the maternal – but there are others. Most strategies were rooted in pseudo-scientific classifications that organised anthropological races according to tendencies supposedly essential to each. Black people, since they were (and are) not-quite-human, were alleged to be inherently susceptible to passions and violent urges. As not-quite-human, they were understood to be lacking the rational capacity to control their desires.

Another strategy was to convince slaves of this inability to control themselves by creating conditions in which they became drunk, irrational, and as out of control as wild animals. Douglass gives as an example of this the masters' manipulation of the days between Christmas Day and New Year, which were supposed to be given to the slaves as holidays.[41]

During these days, slaves were not supposed to work. Even if a slave might want to work, the masters thought such a slave 'undeserving of the holidays' because they were seen as having 'rejected the favor of the master' (MF 289). Instead, the slaves were supposed to be continuously drunk. To remain sober was, according to the masters, 'disgraceful', for 'he was esteemed a lazy and improvident man who could not afford to drink whiskey during Christmas' (BF 289).[42] Though the holidays were supposed to be a time of freedom and gaiety, Douglass saw this strategy

---

40 Too many have discussed Saidiya Hartman's claim that we live the 'afterlives of slavery'. We only mention it here to note that this dynamic still remains.
41 See also Hartman's discussion: 'as Douglass himself recognized, on rare occasions the pleasures available within the confines of slavery indeed possessed glimmerings of insurgency and transformation'. Hartman, *Scenes of Subjection*, 48.
42 This custom had long-lasting effects, even after the end of slavery. Booker T. Washington describes what he saw during his first winter at the Tuskegee Institute: 'We found that for a whole week the colored people in and around Tuskegee dropped work the day before Christmas, and that it was difficult to get any one to perform any service from the time they stopped work until the New Year. Persons who at other times did not use strong drink thought

for the cruel cunning that it was. 'I believe', he writes, 'these holidays to be among the most effective means, in the hands of the slaveholders, of keeping down the spirit of insurrection among the slaves' (BF 290). Though the holidays were supposed to show the benevolence and compassion of the masters, Douglass knew they were 'a fraud, instituted by human selfishness, the better to secure the ends of injustice and oppression' (BF 291). Slavery was not simply a matter of chaining arms and legs, whipping backs, or raping women; it was also, perhaps more so, a matter of constraining and constituting the soul. Slavery consumed the entire being of the slave, and the holiday 'trick' was a means to keep thoughts of freedom and autonomy far from their minds.

'These holidays', Douglass continued, 'serve the purpose of keeping the minds of the slaves occupied with the prospective pleasure, within the limits of slavery' (BF 290). Here is the cunning of the masters' understanding of human desires. If enslaved people were continuously and always kept under chain and whip, they would burst. The anger, drives, and desires would build and build until they exploded. The holidays, then, acted as 'conductors or safety valves to carry off the explosive elements inseparable from the human mind, when reduced to the condition of slavery' (BF 291). The goal of the holidays is not the 'slave's happiness ... but, rather, the master's safety', and the 'safety of the slave system' (BF 291). To ensure this, the masters kept the slaves drunk for days, encouraging if not compelling them to keep 'plunging ... into exhausting depths of drunkenness and dissipation' (BF 291). The intended effect was 'to disgust the slaves with their temporary freedom, and to make them as glad to return to work, as they were to leave it' (BF 291). Some slave masters played 'cunning tricks' on the drunken slaves, such as betting on some to drink more than the others, 'and so to induce a rivalry among them' (BF 291, 292). After days of induced debauchery, the slaves found themselves, upon waking, 'stretched out in brutal drunkenness, at once helpless and disgusting' (BF 292). This strategy (a sort of

---

it quite the proper thing to indulge in it rather freely during the Christmas week' (UP 65).

proto-cognitive behaviour training) of overindulging the slaves in anything that they might desire was common in slavery. Douglass gives the example of a slave who stole molasses. The master would then 'go away to town, and buy a large quantity of the *poorest* quality, and set it before his slave, and, with whip in hand, compel him to eat it, until the poor fellow is made to sicken at the very thought of molasses' (BF 292).

Another example is given by Douglass drawn from his time working for the slave breaker Edward Covey. Since Covey was convinced that the 'fear of punishment is the sole motive for any sort of industry', he constantly used 'a series of adroitly managed surprises' so that it was 'scarcely necessary for [him] to be really present in the field, to have his work go industriously' (BF 266, 265). Covey would sometimes get on his horse and make it seem like he was headed back to the house, when, in actuality, Douglass 'would find his horse tied in the woods, and the snake-like Covey lying flat in the ditch with his head lifted above its edge, or in a fence-corner, watching every movement of the slaves' (BF 265).[43] Slaves were kept in a constant sense of being watched, ever-seized with dread by the pervasive gaze of the slave-master, without a moment's relief for reflection and self-possession. Douglass was well aware that many strategies practised by 'the art of negro breaking, consisted ... in this species of cunning' (BF 265).

Such strategies were part of the larger cunning of the institution of slavery designed to inculcate in the slave a constant 'fear of death [*Furcht des Todes*]' (PS 194). Fear is a mechanism of detachment from the given. The mere introduction of the fear of death is the ultimate form of destabilisation. Yet the slave is not fearful of 'this or that particular thing or just at odd moments', writes Hegel, 'but its whole being has been seized with dread' (PS 194). In this, Hegel continues, the slave 'has trembled in every fiber of

---

43 Cf. Olaudah Equiano's description of his attempts to escape into the woods when European slavers hunted him in Africa: 'I began to consider that, if possible I could escape all other animals, I could not those of the human kind; and that, not knowing the way, I must perish in the woods. – Thus was I like the hunted deer.' Olaudah Equiano, *The Interesting Narrative and Other Writings* (New York: Penguin Books, 1995), 50.

its being, and everything solid and stable has been shaken to its foundations' (PS 194). His body flogged and shattered, his mind shocked and awed, his soul crushed and twisted, the life of the slave was completely consumed by this mortal fear.[44]

To understand how, we can assign an ambiguity to what Hegel sees as the means through which the 'master relates himself mediately to the slave' (PS 190). Hegel is here referencing 'a being [a thing] that is independent' in that it 'holds the slave in bondage' (PS 190). While it is possible to interpret this 'independent thing' as some object on which the slave works, it can also be interpreted, when read in light of Douglass's autobiographies, as the institution of chattel slavery. Hegel's words then acquire a new, compelling meaning. 'The master', in his terms, 'is the power over' the institution of slavery, and just as slavery 'is the power over the slave, it follows that he [the master] holds the other in subjection'. Hegel continues: 'the master relates himself mediately to [the institution of slavery] through the slave' (PS 190). This means that the master and the slave are related through this third thing – chattel slavery – though in opposed and radically unequal ways. The master relates to slavery *mediately*, that is, through the slave insofar as the slave is the one who labours, who is enslaved. The slave, by contrast, relates to slavery *immediately*, that is, the slave is the one caught in the vicious institution of slavery.

As we said, to keep the slave inescapably caught in slavery, the master attempts to infuse every part of the slave's life with the constant fear of death. 'A perpetual institution', Mbembe writes, 'the plantation lived under a perpetual regime of fear'.[45] Yet this fear is not just a fear of any ordinary danger in life, but becomes synonymous with the master himself. The fear of death *is* thus 'the fear of the lord [*Furcht des Herrn*]' (PS 195). The master is a ubiquitous *memento mori* because he is the way in which the

---

44 Hartman, however, emphasises not only the presence of resistance in innocent amusements, but also the evasion of complete domination and constitution of slave subjectivity. Hartman, *Scenes of Subjection*, chapter 1.
45 Achille Mbembe, *Critique of Black Reason* (Durham, NC: Duke University Press, 2013), 19.

fear of death gains stability, physical presence. Lacan calls this the 'law of the father' (*nom du père*). Its presence is clear in Douglass's account of learning about the 'queer old master', Col. Edward Lloyd, who, shrouded in the threat of death, became a 'fearful and inexorable *demi-god*, whose huge image on so many occasions haunted my childhood's imagination' (BF 146, 147).[46]

Work Will Not Set You Free

So far, Douglass has provided the concrete, embodied context for thinking through Hegel's master-slave dialectic. Yet it is essential that we see how Douglass also shows us the shortcomings of Hegel's account. One way to see this is to compare Hegel's description of the slave's emancipation with Douglass's actual path toward freedom. Where for Hegel it is work that sets the slave free, for Douglass it is fighting. We start with Hegel's account.

Both Hegel and Douglass recognise that freedom is the result of a complex set of relations. Gaining freedom is not about gaining absolute independence. Rather, it is a relation of the right kind of dependence. This is the core Hegelian thought: *freedom is finding the formation of my relation to the other that is not self-defeating but emancipating*. The master-slave relationship must become a dynamic process that allows for a continual overcoming of nature within and without, inside and outside, the slave. Although the master was the master of the slave, which emptied the slave of all sense of subjectivity in that the master's desires became the slave's desires, there is a Hegelian twist: *work sets the slave free*.

The master desires a plantation house, orders the slave to build it, and the slave takes up this desire as their own. To do so, however, the slave must voice their opinion. They must confront and engage with the material that will constitute the plantation house. So, for example, they tell the master that the house might be

---

46 Another example is the experience of slaves who tended the horses in Col. Lloyd's stables and carriage house: 'They never knew when they were safe from punishment. They were frequently whipped when least deserving, and escaped whipping when most deserving' (NL 26).

better if it had columns. The master, having little idea as to how to actually build columns, agrees with the slave's judgment and takes this new desire as *his* desire. The slave has not yet overcome the nature within, because they merely take on the desires imposed on them, but they are able to overcome the nature without (the natural world) by working on it, by forming matter into a house. Through their work, Hegel contends, the slave overcomes the power of nature by working on it.[47]

Hegel defines work as the repression of desire and the taking up of an order. As Hegel writes, 'Work … is desire held in check [gehemmte *Begierde*]' (PS 195). The object on which the slave is working is somewhat recalcitrant. They cannot just point at the object and make it do what they want it to do. They have to 'deal with it', to work on it, to form and shape it. Work forms and shapes things, including the working subject. 'Working on it' means working on both themselves and on the thing. Hence Hegel calls working a 'formative activity [*Das Formieren/das Bilden*]', wherein the slave forms a robust sense of self by forming the external world and seeing himself in his work, such as a finished Greek Revival plantation house (PS 196). Work involves the transformation of random activity into goal-directed action. As the product of the work is formed and gains permanence, the worker gains solidity, too. The slave gains a sense of permanence because they see themselves in their concrete labour product, which also has a sense of permanence. Since the worker sees themselves in the object, they become an object to be known. The slave thus becomes an object for themselves; they come to know themselves as an object *and* a subject. The object is, however, not external but is *themselves in* the object: the slave recognises themselves in the object, and thus they become a self-consciousness. Thus, for Hegel, there are two key moments in the slave's development: 1) fear of death (in the

---

47 This is not, however, work as a sort of *Bildung* or formative education, but work as *Arbeit*, which does not necessarily entail the sense of development and edification. See Anke Wischmann, 'The Absence of "Race" in German Discourses on *Bildung*: Rethinking *Bildung* with Critical Race Theory', *Race, Ethnicity and Education* 21:4 (2018): 471–85.

form of the master), and 2) formative activity (by working on the object).

With American chattel slavery, however, work was not the way out of slavery but the brutal institution's very engine. The more a slave worked, the stronger was the institution. The more the slaves produced, the more those leading and upholding the economy based on slavery grew in power. In this sense, Hegel got it backwards. The fight does not lead to enslaved labour; labour leads to the fight. Africans did not become slaves because they lost a battle between equals. They were enslaved as the result of a vast, international legal, social, technological, and political process – undergirded by racist anthropological classification systems – which unfolded and crystallised over centuries. A fight was the result not the cause. Frantz Fanon put it this way:

> here the master differs basically from the master described by Hegel. For Hegel there is reciprocity; here the master laughs at the consciousness of the slave. What he wants from the slave is *not recognition but work*. In the same way, the slave here is in no way identifiable with the slave who loses himself in the object and finds in his work the source of his liberation. The Negro wants to be like the master. Therefore he is less independent than the Hegelian slave. In Hegel the slave turns away from the master and turns toward the object. Here the *slave turns toward the master and abandons the object*.[48]

In chattel slavery, work will never set you free. Work reinforces the chains and sharpens the sting of the whip. Douglass worked hard and long, and saw himself in the fields, landscapes, ships and other objects into which he put his transforming labour. Yet freedom never came to him from work. The only way for him to set out on the path out of slavery and into freedom was to turn away from the object on which he worked and face the master in order to fight. Hence, Douglass's fight with Covey.

---

48 Frantz Fanon, *Black Skin, White Masks*, trans. Richard Philcox (New York: Grove Press, 2008), 220n8; emphases added. See also Brandon Hogan, 'Frantz Fanon's Engagement with Hegel's Master-Slave Dialectic', *Africology: The Journal of Pan African Studies* 11:8 (2018): 16–32.

Southern Honour Culture

Before digging into Douglass's fight, however, we should take a brief look at the nature of a 'fight' in the American South at the time. One influential interpretation of the social structure of the South describes it as a 'culture of honor'.[49] As Orlando Patterson explains: 'part of the [slaveholder's] ideology referred to the master's own conception of himself, and it is generally agreed that its pivotal value is the notion of honour, with the attendant virtues of manliness and chivalry', as well as pride, militarism, and regional identity.[50] The culture included a simultaneous idealisation and yet exclusion of southern white women (the purity of whom it was the duty of 'honourable' white men to protect) from socially significant roles. As John Hope Franklin already noted: 'The honor of the Southerner causes him to defend with his life the slightest suggestion of irregularity in his honesty or integrity; and he was fiercely sensitive to any imputation that might cast a shadow on the character of the women in his family. To him nothing was more important than honor.'[51] This in no way means that true honour – in the sense of a universal moral value – was the law of the land, as this was the land of slavery. In fact, it shows something intrinsic to the dialectic of slaveholding: 'Those who most dishonor and constrain others', writes Patterson, 'are in the best position to appreciate what joy it is to possess what they deny.'[52] An honour culture thus means that it was, for example, a

---

49 Richard E. Nisbett and Dov Cohen, *Culture of Honor: Violence in the South* (New York: Westview Press, 1996). Rollin G. Osterweis is another scholar who has noted the connection between slavery and timocracy in the American South. He claims that the civilisation of the Old South rested on a tripod: 'cotton and the plantation system form one leg, Negro slavery a second', and the 'Southern cult of chivalry' the third. Rollin G. Osterweis, *Romanticism and Nationalism in the Old South* (New Haven: Yale University Press, 1949), vii, 49. Osterweis draws a direct lineage from the ideal of European romanticism to the timocratical tendencies of the American South (ibid., 247).
50 Patterson, *Slavery and Social Death*, 95.
51 John Hope Franklin, *The Militant South 1800–1861* (Boston: Beacon Press, 1956).
52 Patterson, *Slavery and Social Death*, 95.

'necessity for men to appear strong and unwilling to tolerate an insult'.[53] Cultures of honour are typically cultures of extensive and persistent violence. Given that the South was a relatively lawless, herding society, reputation was valued above all else, and violence was the proper response to threats or challenges to one's honour. Thus, as Nesbitt and Cohen write, the 'culture of honor differs from other cultures in that violence will be used to attain and protect this kind of honor'.[54]

At the heart of this whole Southern culture of honour is the notion of respect among equals. One can only be dishonoured if one is deserving of equal respect and honour. If one white man insults or offends another white man, the insulted man is dishonoured, treated as less equal. The proper response to this is to fight, in a duel or some other form of ritualised violence. Most importantly, a true fight must occur between equals. Otherwise, it is not really a fight: if two people are not of equal social standing, such as a white man and a white woman or a white master and an enslaved Black person, then a proper fight between them is not possible.[55] When a master is violent to a slave, it is not a fight; it is just violence. Hence, when Covey tries to beat Douglass, he is not expecting a fight at all, for Douglass, as the slave, is not capable of standing equal to Covey, as the (proxy for) the master. Indeed, to a southern slaveholder like Covey, Douglass was the embodiment of dishonour and degradation, and the slave who had the gall to stand up for himself was the force of dishonour. However, such a surprise fight resulted, at the very least, in the first steps toward equality. As Patterson notes, in the 'antebellum South, the exaggerated sense of honor and quixotic chivalry of the ruling class proved to be the major cause of its undoing'.[56]

---

53 Nisbett and Cohen, *Culture of Honor*, xvi.
54 Ibid., 4.
55 Ibid., 50.
56 Patterson, *Slavery and Social Death*, 97. Despite its undoing, Nancy K. MacLean demonstrates the role of Southern honour culture in a later revival of this culture in the formation of the Klu Klux Klan in the 1920s. See her *Behind the Mask: The Making of the Second Klu Klux Klan* (Oxford: Oxford University Press, 1994).

The Fight with Covey

Douglass had no other means to be recognised as a person by Covey, his owner Captain Auld, or any other white person than to fight back against any physical attack upon his body. Let us recount the context of the fight to make it clear.

Douglass turned away from his work, to eventually face Covey, at a very specific time. He had been working during the hottest days in August 1834, alongside four other slaves, on a task that 'required strength and activity, rather than any skill or intelligence' (BF 271). At around 'three o'clock, while the sun was pouring down its burning rays, and not a breeze was stirring, I broke down', Douglass writes, 'I was seized with a violent aching of the head, attended with extreme dizziness, and trembling in every limb' (BF 271). Since the work required all four slaves, the whole process stopped – which Covey, who had been near the house, about a hundred yards away, immediately noticed. By the time Covey came over, Douglass had crawled to a fence. When Douglass, barely able to speak, failed to respond adequately to Covey's interrogation, Covey kicked him in the side, demanding that he get up and back to work. Douglass tried to rise, but fell back down, and received another swift kick to the ribs. Unable to make Douglass start working again, 'the merciless negro breaker took up the hickory slab' that the slaves had been using to do the work and beat Douglass with it. Douglass was unable to move, and resigned himself to death, in fact desiring its mortal relief. Incapable of willing Douglass back to work, Covey left him in a pool of blood. Though he could not have expected his real owner to sympathise with his pain, Douglass 'resolved to go straight to Capt. Auld, thinking that, if not animated by the motives of humanity, he might be induced to interfere on my behalf from selfish considerations' (BF 273). While his master initially 'seemed somewhat affected by the story of my wrongs', Douglass continues, 'he soon repressed his feeling and became cold as iron' (BF 275). Since, as far as Auld was concerned, Douglass was a slave and thus automatically deserving of Covey's wrath – and Covey was always already innocent in his actions – Douglass received nothing more from his master than 'a huge dose of *epsom salts*', and was ordered to 'return to the den of horrors' first thing next morning (BF 276).

After a sleepless night away from Covey, Douglass was forced to face the slave breaker, come what may. When he reached the farm, 'Covey, true to his snakish habits, darted out at me', Douglass writes, 'from a fence corner, in which he had secreted himself, for the purpose of securing me. He was amply provided with a cowskin and a rope; and he evidently intended to *tie me up*, and to wreak his vengeance on me to the fullest extent' (BF 277). Though Douglass was weak from the beatings and from not eating for some time, he was able to escape into the woods using the high corn fields as cover. This only made Covey even more angry, which he exclaimed when he returned to the house without his desired object of violence. Douglass remained safely hidden until well after sunset. During the night, he noticed a man walking through the dark woods. Finally having some degree of luck, the man was another slave, a friendly face from a nearby farm, Sandy Jenkins. Douglass showed himself, hoping for, though not expecting, shelter and safety. Though they risked a brutal beating, Sandy and his wife took in Douglass, fed him and tended to his wounds as best they could.

Following supper, Douglass and Sandy considered what Douglass could to do next. '[M]ust I go back to Covey', Douglass asked, 'or must I now attempt to run away?' (BF 280). Since escape was impossible, partially due to geographical constraints, they concluded that Douglass must return to Covey. Fortunately, Sandy had a trick in his bag. He was a conjurer, so Douglass turned to his magic for help in overcoming the threat of death. '[W]ith great solemnity', Sandy offered Douglass 'a certain *root*', promising that, if he carried 'it *always on my right side*, [it] would render it impossible for Mr. Covey, or any other white man, to whip me' (NL 63). Sandy himself 'said he had carried it for years, and that … he had never received a blow from a slaveholder since he carried it' (BF 280–1). At first, Douglass thought this talk of the magic root 'very absurd and ridiculous, if not positively sinful' (BF 281).[57] And yet, as Sandy pointed out, all of Douglass's book learning 'had not kept Covey off' (BF 281). Partially out of deference to the kindness Sandy had shown him, and being caught between the fear of death and the last hope for survival, Douglass accepted the root, which made him feel that 'a slight *gleam or shadow* of his [Sandy's] superstition had fallen upon me' (BF 586; emphasis added). But in resolving to return to Covey, he accepted either result: the gleaming light of recognition or the shadow of brute death. Between gleam and shadow, he started back to Covey's in order to face his master.

To Douglass's astonishment, when he returned to the farm that Sunday morning, Covey and his wife were 'smiling as angels', all clean and dressed for church (BF 282). 'There was something really benign in his countenance', Douglass reports, which made Douglass think that the magic root was more powerful than Sandy had promised (BF 282). Still, Douglass suspected that it was the Sabbath that had brought on a temporary kindness in the ruthless Covey, who, Douglass knew, 'had more respect for the *day*, than for the *man*' (BF 282). He was correct, as the viciousness of the slave breaker returned on Monday morning. While, on Covey's orders, Douglass was preparing the horses for the fields, Covey seized on him by surprise, aiming to 'get a slip knot on my legs'. Though Covey 'seemed to think he had me very securely in his power', he did not know of Douglass's new resolve (BF 283). Whether from his two days' rest or from the magical root, Douglass had left behind the fear that the master used to embody. In its place was a determination to fight back: '*I had resolved to fight*', Douglass writes, and 'the fighting madness had come upon me' (BF 283). To Covey's utter astonishment, this madness pulsed through Douglass's body as he clamped down on Covey's throat. 'Every blow of [Covey's] was parried', Douglass continues, 'though I dealt no blows in return'. All the while he remained 'strictly on the *defensive*' (BF 283). Every time Covey came at

---

57 *My Bondage and My Freedom* recounts the root story differently than the *Narrative* does. In the *Narrative*, Douglass is much less ambivalent about the root than he is later on; he's quite thankful for it.

him, Douglass flung him to the ground or choked him until he momentarily relented.

While the fight was, at least initially, between two *equals*, Covey could not stand to see himself as equal to a slave, and thus called out for help in quashing the fight in Douglass. Covey's cousin Hughes joined in, which forced Douglass to change strategy slightly: 'I was still *defensive* toward Covey', reports Douglass, 'but *aggressive* toward Hughes' (BF 284). When Hughes tried to 'catch and tie my right hand, I gave him the kick which sent him staggering away in pain, at the same time that I held Covey with a firm hand'. Seeing that even two white masters could not subdue Douglass, Covey asked if he would continue to resist; Douglass responded that he '*did mean to resist, come what might*' (BF 284). While Covey had tried to annihilate Douglass's humanity and reduce him to a beast, Douglass would 'stand it *no longer*' (BF 284). After several hours, the hired hand, Bill, returned, and Covey asked him to join his side in the fight. 'My master hired me here, to work, and *not* to help you whip Frederick', Bill responded (BF 285). Douglass warned Bill off and Bill reaffirmed that he had no order to fight, instead heading back to the fields to start working as he had been hired to do. The same refusal to join the fight came from Caroline, Covey's own slave woman, thus leaving Covey to stand defeated before a man who had proven to be at least his equal.

Though Covey had lost the fight, he could not admit it. After hours of bleeding, huffing, and puffing, he finally relented, ordering Douglass to start working, but adding this lie: 'I would not have whipped you half as so much as I have had you not resisted.' Yet the 'fact was, *he had not whipped me at all*', Douglass reports (BF 285). Covey had not even drawn Douglass's blood, even though Douglass left Covey covered in his own blood. Even months later, when he became angry at Douglass, Covey repeated the false report of the fight; Douglass corrected him: 'you need not wish to get hold of me again, for you will be likely to come off worse in a second fight than you did in the first' (BF 286).

The fight with Covey, Douglass wrote, was 'the turning point in my "*life as a slave.*" It rekindled in my breast the smoldering embers of liberty' (BF 286). Notice the ontological claims

Douglass makes: 'I was a *changed being* after that fight. I was *nothing before*; I WAS A MAN NOW. It recalled to life my crushed self-respect and my self-confidence, and inspired me with a renewed determination to be A FREEMAN' (BF 286). The fight with Covey transformed his *being*; he became a different type of being – a freeman not a slave. He continues:

> After resisting, I felt as I had never felt before. It was a resurrection from the dark and pestiferous tomb of slavery, to the heaven of comparative freedom. I was no longer a servile coward, trembling under the frown of a brother worm of the dust, but, my long-cowed spirit was roused to an attitude of manly independence. I had reached the point, at which I was *not afraid to die*. This spirit made me a freeman in *fact*, while I remained a slave in *form*. (BF 286)

Though he remained enslaved by Thomas Auld and temporarily in the possession of Covey, Douglass's ontological transformation – from a slave into a man – expresses the overcoming of Hegel's two moments of the slave: 1) fear of death (in the form of the master), and 2) formative activity (in this case, fighting with the master). Though Gilroy thinks that Douglass inverts Hegel's logic, writing that 'the slave actively prefers the possibility of death to the continuing condition of inhumanity', Douglass actually fulfils this logic.[58] To say that Douglass prefers the possibility of death is precisely to say that the slave overcomes the fear of death at the hands of the master. To win recognition, Fanon notes, it is not enough that 'the White Master, *without conflict*, recognized the Negro slave'; rather, 'the former slave wants to *make himself recognized*'.[59] Though he would never admit it, Covey was compelled to recognise that Douglass was more than a slave – that he was a man, just like himself.[60]

---

58 Gilroy, *Black Atlantic*, 63.
59 Fanon, *Black Skin, White Masks*, 217.
60 Given the importance of recognition in Hegel, we should at least mention the role of photography in recognition in the lives of enslaved people, especially given the centrality in Douglass's life and thought. Matthew Amato-Fox's *Exposing Slavery: Photography, Human Bondage, and the Birth of Modern Visual*

The fact that Covey did not try to beat Douglass again was surprising, given that the punishment for a slave resisting a beating from the master was to be 'publicly whipped, as an example to other slaves, and as a means of deterring' them (BF 287). Yet this never happened, Douglass was never punished publicly in this way, which surprised him a great deal. The only reason for this lack of subsequent punishment, Douglass surmised, was Covey's pride. 'Mr. Covey enjoyed the unbounded and very valuable reputation, of being a first rate overseer and *negro breaker*' (BF 287). Even when, in his remaining months with Covey, Douglass tried to provoke Covey into attacking him, he 'could never bully him into another battle' (BF 287). Covey ignored every provocation in silence, because he could not risk others finding out that he was a second- or third-rate slave breaker, unable to tame them all. After all, '[o]ne bad sheep', Douglass noted, 'will spoil a whole flock. Among the slaves, I was a bad sheep' (BF 288).

A Different Type of Fight

Placing Douglass's experience in a dialectical parallel with Hegel's master-slave dialectic reveals three significant differences, which might derive from the unacknowledged whiteness in Hegel's thought.

Politics in America (Oxford: Oxford University Press, 2019) is excellent on the diverse and contradictory roles of photography during American slavery. Amongst the many fascinating features of the text, Amato-Fox shows how photography allowed enslaved people to see themselves like never before, which is a condition for recognition of one's face and place in the world. It was Douglass, though, who engaged the technology of photography to shape how both he and slavery were recognised. Not only was Douglass the most photographed American in the nineteenth-century, he also lectured and wrote plenty about photography. On this see also John Stauffer, Zoe Trodd, and Celeste-Marie Bernier, *Picturing Frederick Douglass: An Illustrated Biography of the Nineteenth Century's Most Photographed American* (New York: W.W. Norton, 2015).

Starting Points

The first difference is the respective starting points of each conflict. The Hegelian fight is between equals, while the conflict between the enslaved and the master is due to the already well-entrenched system of slavery. As Chamayou puts it, here the 'initial situation is in fact not a face-off between two undifferentiated [and thus interchangeable] consciousnesses that, through a free confrontation, will establish a relationship of domination, but instead a situation in which domination already exists'.[61] Slave resistance occurs in the context of domination, not in open and equal relationships. Even before American slavery, when the Portuguese began hunting and stealing Africans, there was no fight on an equal footing.[62] Instead, there was a hunt for humans. The Africans who became slaves began as prey, while the white masters began as predators. This is why the relationship of master and slave was always asymmetrical.[63] In terms of the originary equality of its combatants, Douglass's fight with Covey, like any kind of slave resistance or rebellion, differs significantly from the fight as Hegel depicted it.

Order of the Fight

The second difference, which aligns with the first, is the order of the conflict: Douglass's fight is the inversion of Hegel's. As Chamayou writes, 'Douglass puts at the end what in Hegel comes at the beginning: The moment of the battle to the death appears as what dissolves the relationship of domination and not what constitutes it.'[64] For Douglass, the battle destructs, rather than constructs, the master-slave relationship.

---

61 Chamayou, *Manhunts*, 56.
62 See Ibram X. Kendi, *Stamped from the Beginning* (New York: Nation Books, 2016), chapter 2.
63 In terms of manhunting, which was essential to the slave system, 'even before [slave] operations begin, the hunter is already in a position to be the master', while the 'prey, taken by surprise, is not in a position to confront a group of hunters'. Chamayou, *Manhunts*, 58.
64 Ibid., 62.

Escape

The third difference is the presence of a third option, other than working or fighting: escape. Even though Douglass's fight made him conscious of himself as a man, equal to Covey or any white man, he remained in chains for years after. To realise his freedom, Douglass had to escape. So-called fugitive slaves produce a crisis in the order of domination, one that requires the fear of the master to be expanded beyond the plantation, beyond even the South, into the entire country. This included the passing of laws like the Fugitive Slave Act of 1850.[65]

Though Hegel does not engage the possibility of the slave escaping the master, we still see here the emergence of new kinds of knowledge in runaway slaves, perhaps analogous to the formative work in Hegel's story. Successfully escaping from slavery required a special kind of knowledge and awareness. Harriet Tubman's incredible work on the Underground Railroad is a famous example of this kind of sagacity. So-called 'fugitive' slaves, especially those chased through the woods, had to be aware of how the slave catchers would hunt them down. They had to see themselves, on the run, as those chasing them would see them. As Chamayou puts it: the 'hunted man has to learn to interpret his own actions from the point of view of his predator'.[66] In what might be a seed of what Du Bois calls 'double consciousness', the escaping slave became conscious of himself as both the master and the slave catcher might view him.[67] Previously, this was a type of paralysing fear of the master. But now, on the run, this

---

65 See Steven Lubet, *Fugitive Justice: Runaways, Rescuers, and Slavery on Trial* (Cambridge, MA: Harvard University Press, 2010); John Hope Franklin and Loren Schweninger, *Runaway Slaves: Rebels on the Plantation* (Oxford: Oxford University Press, 2000); or Sally Hadden, *Slave Patrols: Law and Violence in Virginia and the Carolinas* (Cambridge, MA: Harvard University Press, 2001).
66 Chamayou, *Manhunts*, 70.
67 See Nasar Meer, 'W.E.B. Du Bois, Double Consciousness and the "Spirit" of Recognition', *The Sociological Review* 67:1 (2019): 47–62; see also Shamoon Zamir, '"Double-Consciousness": Locating the Self', in *Dark Voices: W.E.B. Du Bois and American Thought, 1888–1903*, (Chicago: University of Chicago Press, 1995), 113–69.

fear had transformed into a kind of reasoning, or what Descartes calls *sagacitas*: 'discernment in the methodical deduction of one thing from another'.[68] Sagacity is a hunting trope, connoting the ability to track down or follow a desired object just as a hunter carefully and methodologically tracks down prey. Slave catchers were sagacious if they tracked down the fugitive slave by following the traces they left in their path. But if the slave can transform the fear of the master into sagacity, if the 'fugitive can foresee the sagacity of his pursuers and cover his tracks', then the slave can successfully escape to freedom.[69]

When Fighting Is Not an Option: Harriet Jacobs

Douglass could fight his way out. His battle with Covey indeed involved an ontological transformation: in the context of his life, this moment punctuates his transition from 'brute' to human. But this was not the case for many enslaved females.[70]

The reason, writes bell hooks, is that 'the two forces, sexism and racism, intensified and magnified the sufferings and oppressions of Black women' beyond the experience of enslaved men.[71] 'Slavery is terrible for men', writes Harriet Jacobs, 'but it is far more terrible for women. Superadded to the burden common to all, *they* have wrongs, and sufferings, and mortifications peculiarly their own.'[72] As Jacobs explains, in addition to the pervasive and constant terror that Douglass or any enslaved male experienced, enslaved females also experienced the pervasive and constant terror of sexual assault, violence, torture, and rape. For

---

68 René Descartes, *The Philosophical Writings of Descartes, Volume I*, trans. John Cottingham, Robert Stoothoff, and Dugald Murdoch (Cambridge: Cambridge University Press, 1985), CSM I, 33/AT X, 400.
69 Chamayou, *Manhunts*, 70.
70 For more on a feminist reading that directly engages Hegel and Douglass, see Cynthia Willet's *Maternal Ethics and Other Slave Moralities* (New York: Routledge, 1995), 95–156.
71 bell hooks, *Ain't I a Woman: Black Women and Feminism* (New York: Routledge, 2014), 22.
72 Jacobs, *Incidents*, 86.

an enslaved woman, as Angela Davis poignantly puts it, '[r]ape was the rule'.[73]

Rape was the rule. Perhaps this phrase offers an opening to a different understanding of the threat of death in Hegel's dialectic. It could be interpreted to mean that not simply the actuality, but, along the lines of social death, *the threat* of rape was included in its reign. As we leave Maryland and travel down to North Carolina, Harriet Jacobs provides a different dialectical approach – one that does not sharply demarcate the transition from slave to human as Douglass's life does. Jacobs's relation to her master Dr Flint was not one of forceful challenge, but of sagacious subterfuge.

By now, Hegel's formulation of the master-slave relationship should be clear. The master and the slave need one another; the master receives his subjectivity from the fragmented and constrained recognition of the slave. The slave, in turn, recognises the master's ideas, thoughts, and desires as their own; the slave works to fulfil those desires; but, in working, the slave finds a sense of self *in* the work.[74] In the end, it is the slave, not the master, who develops in Hegel's dialectic. Douglass inverts that dialectic, 'ending' with the 'beginning', making the fight the dissolution of the relationship. But, as we've shown, Douglass's fight discloses dimensions of Hegel's dialectic, too. With Jacobs, however, we do not find the same similarities.

There are resonances, of course. In Jacobs's narrative, her second cousin Benjamin and her brother William both find themselves operating in a similar dialectical relation to their masters as Douglass did. William fights with one of his masters and, like Douglass, comes out on top: 'William fought bravely, and the young master, finding he was getting the better of him, undertook to tie his hands behind him. He failed in that likewise. By dint of

---

[73] Angela Davis, *Angela Y. Davis Reader*, ed. Joy James (Oxford: Blackwell, 1998), 154.
[74] For the problematic logic of recognition in or through slavery, see Frank Kirkland, 'Enslavement, Moral Suasion, & Struggles for Recognition: Frederick Douglass' Answer to the Question – "What is Enlightenment?"', in *Frederick Douglass: A Critical Reader*, ed. B.E. Lawson and F.M. Kirkland (Oxford: Blackwell, 1999), 242–310.

kicking and fisting, William came out of the skirmish none the worse for a few scratches.'[75] Like Douglass, William secured his selfhood through battle; he 'did not mind the smart of the whip, but he did not like the *idea* of being whipped'.[76] William was not (and never was) a mere body; he had begun to understand the conceptual terrain through which slavery's technologies of social death operated.

Benjamin didn't fight, but he did run away. He was captured and returned to the South, where he was placed in jail. Here, we find yet another dynamic and critique of Hegel's dialectic: sometimes, the threat of bondage can take so tight a hold over the slave that they no longer want to live. Benjamin says to Harriett and his mother (Harriett's grandmother) during one of their visits: 'Here I will stay till I die, or till he sells me.'[77] Benjamin had a desire to *die*, and it wasn't until he ran away again and *remained free* that 'life was worth something'.[78] Benjamin didn't abnegate his self-consciousness; his ideas were not subsumed or totalised by the master. He was either going to die, or he was going to be free.

William's and Benjamin's stories, along with Jacobs's narrative, provide a different perspective on Hegel's dialectic. In fact, they call into question the certainty Hegel has about the *process* of self-recognition and development. William and Benjamin are, indeed, enslaved, and for this reason they do provide a mirror for the master: William remains enslaved; Benjamin is put back in his place by being thrown into jail. Their masters needed them, and, as Spillers reminds us, if they were not there, they would have had to have been invented.[79]

But, from the position of the slave, things are not so clean cut as Hegel makes them out to be. As noted above, Hegel sees work as the way toward a kind of self-recognition. Despite the brutality of it, for him work is a virtue (we will return to this in subsequent

---

75 Jacobs, *Incidents*, 16.
76 Ibid., 17.
77 Ibid., 21.
78 Ibid., 24.
79 Spillers, 'Mama's Baby', 65.

chapters). But neither Douglass, William, nor Benjamin find (or free) themselves in labour. Instead, they find themselves in their resistance to work, in their recognition that the work itself was contestable – and in the punishments that come with *not* working. They find themselves in and through other means: for Douglass it was through a root and a fight; for William it was through the dignity of his father, who refused to acquiesce to the demands of others; while for Benjamin it was through running away. They find themselves somewhere beyond, or perhaps in contradistinction to, the purview of the work that fulfils the master's desires. They were not, in Malcolm X's sense, house negroes. Or, if they were, they were not so for long.

Neither was Harriet. Although she worked in the house – for reasons that will become clear later – she, too, did not make the master's desires her own. In fact, it was precisely the difference between her desires and the master's that prompted her subversive behaviour, which eventually led to her freedom. Those familiar with Harriett's narrative will know that she stayed in a cramped space for seven years, hiding away from her master – and keeping watch over her children – before she made her escape. That is perhaps the most defining feature of her story: *while Douglass fought his way out, Harriett hid her way out.*

The context for this hiding, this subversive act of freedom, betrays yet another unthought dimension of Hegel's dialectic. Harriett develops her self-recognition – and eventually overcomes Dr Flint – through *subversion* rather than conflict. Dr Flint rarely resorted to physical violence, but when he did, it had everything to do with the rule of rape.

> 'So you want to be married, do you? said he, 'and to a free nigger.'
> 'Yes, sir.'
> 'Well, I'll soon convince you whether I am your master, or the nigger fellow you honor so highly. If you *must* have a husband, you may take up with one of my slaves.'
> ... I replied, 'Don't you suppose, sir, that a slave can have some preference about marrying? Do you suppose that all men are alike to her?'
> 'Do you love this nigger?' said he, abruptly.

'Yes, sir.'
'How dare you tell me so!' he exclaimed, in great wrath. After a slight pause, he added, 'I supposed you thought more of yourself; that you felt above the insults of such puppies.'
I replied, 'If he is a puppy I am a puppy, for we are both of the negro race. It is right and honorable for us to love each other. The man you call a puppy never insulted me, sir; and he would not love me if he did not believe me to be a virtuous woman.'
He sprang on me like a tiger, and gave me a stunning blow.[80]

Harriett doesn't 'fight back' here. Her honesty is resistance, but she did not throw blows. Moreover, Dr Flint is not upset that Harriett wants to marry, but instead upset that she is in love. This love was more important to her than marriage itself – but more than this, it indicated that Flint's power over her would never fully take hold. The master's subjectivity waned as the slave's self-recognition strengthened. But not through work. Jacobs worked, but, perhaps in a proto-Marxian twist, she knew that the labour was not hers.

Harriet's *body* was not hers. Flint was not simply mad that she loved, but that he could not get full access to her body. He was frustrated by her constant evasion of his attempts to try to have sex with her. And, in fact, it was precisely through this continued denial – through fugitive movements, through the movement of her body that was not hers – that Jacobs exercised agency and announced her own self-recognition. Where Hegel and Douglass find conflict to be the primary site of dialectical development, Harriet *evades* her way to self-determination.

Flint wanted Harriet's body; he'd already fathered multiple enslaved children by enslaved women. But, as she tells us, 'I shuddered to think of children that should be owned by my old tyrant.'[81] Harriett knew – and *knew* is key here – that she couldn't evade Flint's attempts forever, unless she 'favored another'. Having met and befriended an unmarried white man, she deliberated:

> I had seen several women sold, with his [Flint's] babies at the breast. He never allowed his offspring by slaves to remain long in

---
80 Jacobs, *Incidents*, 38.
81 Ibid., 56.

sight of himself and his wife. Of a man who was not my master I could ask to have my children well supported; and in this case, I felt confident I should obtain the boon ... With all these thoughts revolving in my mind, and seeing no other way of escaping the doom I so much dreaded, I made a headlong plunge.[82]

She would not have children by Flint, she'd decided; but perhaps, if she had children by another, she could find some solace.

It offered her little. After letting Flint know, she felt humiliated.[83] But she was committed. And while that commitment sealed her fate in Flint's eyes – he resolved he would never sell her to anyone else – dialectically, philosophically, materially, her decision laid the groundwork for Flint's subjective diminishment. The *only* thing he could do was keep her. Her grandmother may have been disappointed, and Harriet may have felt shame, but Flint's selfhood was exposed. Her body may not have been hers, but she could, and did, decide who would have access to it intimately.

There was no punctuated moment when Harriett transitioned from a slave to a woman. The conflicts between Harriett and Flint were not fisticuffs. Though he hit her, she did not hit back. There was no moment of release – no punctuation in the dialectic that marked the shift toward something else. There was only the slow and tedious practice of evasion. This practice – or, perhaps, *praxis* – of evasion, of 'retreat', signals a different modality and a critique of both Hegel's dialectic and Douglass's masculinity.[84] Normative manhood – which Douglass sought to live by – was pugnacious. It was about the fight, and about conquering in the fight. It was about honour. Douglass and Hegel share this preoccupation with honour. But for some, the very possibility of freedom hinges on doing the dishonourable thing. For some, the very possibility of self-recognition and self-determination hinges upon disrupting the normative conventions of what constitutes 'proper' resistance. This comes at a cost. Harriet did not leave this confrontation unscathed. She was cramped. She resisted indirectly, fugitively.

---

82 Ibid.
83 Ibid., 57.
84 See Hartman, *Scenes of Subjection*, 110.

She moved differently. And yet, perhaps she – *she* – is the one who announces the most capacious and generative example of the master-slave dialectic in this phenomenology of Black spirit.

Transition to Stoicism

We see the turn inward that characterises the shift from the slave to the stoic not so much in Douglass as in Harriett. Once Douglass discovers he is a man by standing up against Covey, he undertakes a movement of reflection through which he recognises himself as an independent object, free from external determinations, through writings, speeches, and images. Douglass articulates his sense of self, beyond the touch of slavery, to others, and he reintegrates this self back into himself. This is akin to Hegel's sense of the slave discovering himself in the external world, in the objects that he fashions. Jacobs, however, cannot experience this sense of discovery of self or self-relation in external things. Rather than standing up to her master, she withdraws into herself. Given her lack of physical strength, at least compared to Douglass and many men, she turns inward. This inwardness, to which we now turn, was enforced by the confines of the small attic and other confined spaces in which she hid. For seven years, confined to the attic, she enacts an interiority that marks the transition from slave to stoic. For seven years, she discovers a sense of self within. For seven years, she reconfigures her life according to the slope of the roof, the press of the ceiling. She hid *in* on her way *out*. She turned inward. While this inward turn was inevitably brutal, she nevertheless moved beyond the 'lifeless mirror' that was the position of the slave.

2

Stoicism

Booker T. Washington and Ida B. Wells

She turned inward. She had to. The cramped space allowed for little else, but it secured something for her, something that would, in the end, enable her to understand her*self*, to gain a sense of self independent of Dr Flint's desires. Harriet Jacobs was enslaved, but she also expressed something beyond the slave's logical dependence. So too did Booker T. Washington and Ida B. Wells. They had different senses of what this self-fashioning meant. Washington turned to education; Wells took to the pen. They were different and those differences matter. They even tell us something about Hegel. They expose his preoccupation with the movement of the *slave*. Like the other thinkers in this text, they announce a nagging Blackness at the heart of Hegel's dialectic.

In this chapter, we sit with Wells and Washington. Hegel might have called them stoics, though we know that this interpretation (or interpellation) is not fully accurate. In sitting with them, we realise that they expose the Blackness of the stoic; in so doing, they also expose how the turn 'inward' is not the turn of a singular subject. While Washington's philosophy has been much maligned in the history of Black Thought, we recognise that, as Kevin K. Gaines says, Washington's 'broader vision of uplift signifying collective social aspiration, advancement and struggle [which] had been the legacy of the emancipation era' is a turn inward to a community.[1]

Wells offered something similar, even as she did it differently. Her vision was one in which Black life could thrive – without

---

1 Kevin K. Gaines, *Uplifting the Race: Black Leadership, Politics, and Culture in the Twentieth Century* (Chapel Hill: University of North Carolina Press, 1996), xv.

the violent interference of whiteness. Her mission is clear: 'The Afro-American is not a bestial race', she writes; 'if this work can contribute in any way toward proving this ... I shall feel I have done my race a service'.[2] The turning 'inward' was a turn away from whiteness, but it was also a turn outward toward others. This stoicism may resonate with Hegel's, but it is not so simple. To think with Washington – and perhaps more so with Wells – is to turn toward Black life as a form of communal commitment.

Stoicism

We are not saying that Hegel was not concerned with something bigger than the individual subject. He was, but he framed it in terms of universals – logical and cultural ones. One of them was freedom. Hegel writes that the stoic consciousness has a 'negative attitude towards the lord and bondsman relationship' (PS 199). It is not a master because its being is not dependently determined as the master *of* the slave, and it is not the slave because its being is not dependently determined by the master's 'will and in his service' (PS 199). To be a stoic is to be indifferent to being a master or a slave. In the context of the Roman Empire, the Emperor Marcus Aurelius is as much of a stoic as the slave Epictetus. '[W]hether on the throne [*Throne*] or in chains [*Fesseln*]', Hegel writes, the stoic's 'aim is to be free, and to maintain that lifeless indifference which steadfastly *withdraws from the bustle of existence ... into the simple essentiality of thought* [*einfache Wesenheit des Gedankens zurückzieht*]' (PS 199). The goal is to be free, and this goal drives the stoic into themselves.

Withdrawing into the calm interiority of the mind, stoicism marks the emergence of a new kind of freedom, corresponding to 'self-consciousness in a new shape': the freedom of thought (PS 197). For Hegel, stoicism inevitably rises out of the collapse of the master-slave dialectic. 'Stoicism', he claims, 'is the freedom which always comes directly out of [though without fully escaping]

---

2 Ida B. Wells, *Southern Horrors: Lynch Law in All Its Phases* (Auckland: The Floating Press, 2013), 5.

bondage' (PS 199).[3] Orlando Patterson describes this as 'the principal means of motivating the slave, who desires nothing more passionately than dignity'.[4] Though still a slave, the rising stoic discovers a freedom in himself, an inner freedom. As Douglass overcame his fear of death, turned away from the object, and faced up to Covey, he discovered the means to free himself from his dependence on the master by turning within. He did this by vacating the thing-like character of his subjectivity within the institution of slavery and 'return[ing] [*zurückkommt*] into the pure universality of thought' (PS 199). Though still a slave, the stoic becomes indifferent to his status as a slave. After all, though Douglass felt himself to be a man after fighting with his master, he remained enslaved. For a 'whole six months afterwards' he remained part of Covey's enslaved labour; it was just that Covey 'never [again] laid the weight of his finger upon me in anger' (NL 65). What leads the post-fight slave into stoicism is that their external self, the subjugated body labouring for the master, decreases in importance at the same rate as their sense of an internal self increases. The stoic is a slave yet free insofar as they no longer see themselves in the enslaved part of them – their body – and now identify with what is more free and less material: their capacity for thought. The stoic is free in thought because the authority of the master applies only to the body, not the mind. The slave, then, has an interiority inaccessible to the master. Gaining freedom is a matter of cutting off as many ties to the world of slavery as possible. Stoicism is a way of denying the significance of the work of the slave.

If Hegel's stoic turns to disembodied thinking as a way of moving toward subjective freedom, however, Blackness – and therefore Black Thought – does not turn away from the body. Often, Black freedom occasions a turn to the body, or perhaps better put, to *embodiment*. Disembodied freedom offers little for one who is emancipated but not liberated. The significance of the slave's work is denied, but the problematic of Black embodiment – what Black

---

3   Though Hegel is clear that it is the slave who becomes the stoic, it is less clear what happens to the master.
4   Patterson, *Slavery and Social Death*, 101.

flesh can and cannot do, what it can and cannot mean – becomes central to the way Black thinking engages with the notion of freedom. Washington thinks this through with his commitment to work; Wells does so through her militant commitment to pushing against the manifold violations of Black flesh. Both deny the significance of the slave's work, but they do so in and through a turn *to* Black flesh, to the embodiment of Black people.

Hegel identifies two conditions for the rise of stoicism: 'Stoicism could only appear on the scene [1] in a time of universal fear and bondage, but also [2] a time of universal culture which had raised itself to the level of thought' (PS 199). Washington's stoicism responds to both of these, and here his focus becomes clearer. Addressing the first condition, he seems to suggest a way in which what he calls the 'school of American slavery' will ultimately, in the end, lead to an overall improvement in the condition of Black people and of the country as a whole:

> when we rid ourselves of prejudice, or racial feeling, and look facts in the face, we must acknowledge that, notwithstanding the cruelty and moral wrong of slavery, the ten million Negroes inhabiting this country, who themselves or whose ancestors went through the *school of American slavery*, are in a stronger and more hopeful condition, materially, intellectually, morally, and religiously, than is true of an equal number of Black people in any other portion of the globe. (UP 8; emphasis added)

Rather than trying to justify slavery, he instead articulates a stoic principle: even 'in the midst of what sometimes seem hopelessly discouraging conditions', like the brutality and inhumanity of American chattel slavery, Washington sustains his faith in the ideal and the possibility that America will one day rise above its sordid existence and fulfil the promise of the universal, or what he calls 'Providence' (UP 8).

In response to the second condition, stoicism is defined in terms of rising out of a concrete and particular slavery into the level of thought and universals. This is the movement from the body-as-enslaved to the *idea* of freedom. With his commitment to providentialism, Washington is convinced of the inevitability of this progress:

> One might as well try to stop the progress of a mighty railroad train by throwing his body across the track, as to try to stop the growth of the world in the direction of giving mankind more intelligence, more culture, more skill, more liberty, and the direction of extending more sympathy and more brotherly kindness. (UP 99)

Washington was after progress. His work was toward uplift – of his race. And though 'racial uplift' can and does have its problems, we nevertheless heed the advice from Fred Moten and Kevin K. Gaines, who give us reason to think that Washington did not necessarily mean well. Moten stresses both of the limitations present in the debate between what Gaines calls 'two general connotations of uplift'.[5] On the one hand, there is Washington's stoic; on the other (as we will see in the next chapter) Du Bois' scepticism. For Du Bois, 'Black elites made uplift the basis for a racialized elite identity claiming Negro improvement … which entailed an attenuated conception of bourgeois qualifications' coming from white 'power, [and] Black vulnerability', rather than from the 'motives or complicity of Black elites'.[6] We must take Washington seriously, and here, we do.

From Slave Fight to Stoic Struggle

While Douglass in his battle with Covey sought simply to overcome enslaved life, to make his master recognise that he was more than a merely corporeal and productive body, the stoic struggle has in mind a meaning, a purpose, that guides the struggle. Douglass's fight with Covey did not have a clear goal in mind; death was accepted as a likely outcome. By contrast, Washington's struggle for education was guided by clear goals: to 'secure and eat ginger cakes', to attend the 'Hampton School', to become like 'General C. Armstrong', amongst other things (UP 5, 20, 26). To make this conceptually clear, we might distinguish Douglass's *fight* with the master from Washington's *struggle*. The slave's fight was an utter

---

5   Gaines, *Uplifting the Race*, xv; quoted in Moten, *Stolen Life*, 121.
6   Gaines, *Uplifting the Race*, xv.

risk; Washington's struggle was a teleological movement toward an ideal.

This teleological movement reveals a different kind of work, a work that does retain significance for the slave, which we might call 'work on the self' or 'self-fashioning'. We see this in Black enslaved people's desire for and access to literacy. One of the most effective strategies for keeping Black people enslaved was to ensure they remained illiterate and uneducated. Once they learned to read – so the thought went – they would be taking the first steps toward sculpting their subjectivities, toward living lives that exceeded the overdetermination of their bodily production, of labour.

With Douglass, the first step toward freedom was learning to read, a path that led directly to the fight with Covey and eventually to his escape from bondage and life as a free man. Such work did not retrench Douglass into slavery, as is the case with labour on the plantation or in the Great House, but instead acted as the very condition for the possibility of the fight with Covey. Self-fashioning is a sort of work that belongs to the slave, not the master, because the product of the labour has no tangible value for the master. The work of reading and writing was Douglass's first step toward the fight with Covey and subsequent escape from slavery because it was the way in which he first encountered himself as an external object in written form.

Douglass's self-fashioning through reading and writing was the condition for the fight with Covey because it was the means by which Douglass formed a self independent of his body as an instrument of chattel slavery. In this sense, reading allowed him to see not just himself, but also his place in the world and the system of slavery, contrary to Hegel's narrative, in which the slave apparently experienced a pre-slavery state and knew the conditions of their own enslavement.[7] It is this sense of an internal self, a robust idea of self, which allows Douglass to risk his life similar to how Hegel's master risked his life in the first fight. Through reading and

---

7   We thank Kwesi Thomas for feedback on this point.

writing, Douglass was able to understand himself as an independent self-consciousness, as more than merely a living tool. Such an understanding shifts the metric by which one moves through the world. Douglass would no longer be bound to Covey's whims; he had, as we said, transitioned ontologically from 'brute' to 'man'.

Washington offers a further development on this theme of self-fashioning through a distinct kind of meritocracy. His stoicism furthers this developing sense of subjectivity rooted in what he calls 'the great human law, which is universal and eternal' (UP 20). If reading and writing uncovered a larger sense of the world for Douglass, Washington takes this larger sense and runs with it, finding a universal in 'merit'. Washington assumed (perhaps falsely) that work – one's *own* work – produces the possibility of further development of self and community. This is the universal law of providence: 'merit, no matter under what skin found, is, in the long run, recognized and rewarded' (UP 20).

Here is a new form of recognition. It is not the recognition of another self-consciousness, directly in the form of a self-consciousness, but that of a future self-consciousness, a higher form of self, or perhaps the promise of being recognised by a truly fair, just, and impartial form of subjectivity, above and beyond any particular determination of race, gender, age, etc. 'No man whose vision is bounded by color can come into contact with what is highest and best' (UP 111). The recognition that the stoic seeks is not simply another person's recognition, not just recognition from this white man or Black man, but a general recognition, a recognition from an ideal person. It is recognition of a hard-earned merit that is *mine*.

With this belief in the promise of merit, Washington was perhaps more Hegelian than we might have thought, and it is perhaps easy enough to see how this very predilection toward universals does not stem the tide of antiblack violence. Thinking ahead to Wells, we want to note here that she does not share Washington's desire for transcending Blackness. We will say more about this later, but for now, we must sit with Washington's thinking.

The way to get such recognition is, for Washingtonian stoicism, to turn inward, meaning away from skin colour. As Washington writes, 'the mere connection with what is known as a superior race will not permanently carry an individual forward unless he has individual worth, and mere connection with what is regarded as an inferior race will not finally hold an individual back if he possesses intrinsic, individual merit' (UP 20). This great, universal, and eternal law entails several particular duties that all are called to fulfil. While individual merit is intrinsic for Washington, it must still be developed through self-fashioning, for which he set out various duties or rules, most of which clearly express his stoicism. Let us list a few.

First, the importance of cleanliness. This is 'the most valuable lesson I got', writes Washington, 'at the Hampton Institute … the use and value of the bath', which lies 'not just in keeping the body healthy, but in *inspiring self-respect and promoting virtue* (UP 28; emphasis added). A daily bath became a necessity for Washington's stoic life, and he wrote that he 'always tried to teach my people that some provision for bathing should be a part of every house', perhaps due to the association between the cleanliness of the body and the purity of virtue (UP 28).[8] A second rule was that getting an education was not simply a matter of self-improvement but of helping others. The 'great prevailing idea' of attending the Hampton Institute 'was to *prepare himself to lift up the people at his home*' (UP 30; emphasis added).

Third, the value of work. While undertaking cleaning duties at the Hampton Institute before the start of school, Washington worked side-by-side with Miss Mackie, a member of one of 'the oldest and most cultured families in the North', doing the most mundane and lowest of activities, who nevertheless 'took delight in performing such service' (UP 35). Through this Washington learned that it was as essential to devote oneself to the basest of tasks – e.g. cleaning windows – as to the highest – e.g. founding

---

8   A related example is Washington's appreciation for tooth brushing. 'In all my teaching I have watched carefully the influence of the tooth-brush, and I am convinced that there are a few single agencies of civilization that are more far-reaching' (UP 36).

a university. Washington 'learned to love labor, not alone for its financial value, but for labor's own sake and for the independence and self-reliance which the ability to do something which the world wants done brings' (UP 35).

Fourth, the need for a strong foundation. When he first travelled to Washington DC and witnessed many Black people who sought only luxury, prestige, and leisure, Washington was deeply disturbed. They had either forgotten or skipped over, he thought, the most important condition of personal growth and improvement: 'beginning at the bottom, on a real, solid foundation' (UP 42). Washington often fantasised that, 'by some power of magic, I might remove the great bulk of these people into the country districts and plant them upon the soil, upon the solid and never deceptive foundation of Mother Nature' (UP 43).[9]

We can summarise these duties thus: 1) cleanliness is the condition of virtuousness; 2) 'those who are happiest are those who do the most for others'; 3) 'dignity of labour'; 4) starting from a solid, real foundation and never getting too soft (UP 32, 35).

Abstract Freedom

The stoic's freedom of thought, however, is an abstract freedom, and thus both similar to and dissimilar from the master's freedom. Stoic freedom is abstract, not concrete, because it is partially modelled on the authority of the master, which shows us how Washington's assimilationist thinking mirrors that of Hegel. For Hegel, the slave gains a sense of independence from the formative activity of work, while Douglass gains it from his fight with Covey. But this sense is still derived from, and thus modelled on, the master's freedom of self-consciousness. Like the master's freedom, the slave's freedom is order-giving, though with an

---

[9] Washington repeatedly emphasised the importance of self-made foundations, as when he described the initial struggles involved in founding the Tuskegee Institute: 'It means a great deal, I think, to start off on a foundation which one has made for one's self' (UP 78).

important difference: the stoic gives orders to himself, not to another, enslaved, self-consciousness. The slave frees himself from the 'master' in order to become, as Washington puts it, a 'mister'.[10]

The slave is dissatisfied with the world because it does not immediately obey orders but instead resists the slave's desires, requiring work. The interior world, however, does obey the slave's will. The slave learns of their independence through labouring on an object, and since this labour requires reflection and deliberation about how to best perform the work, the slave also acquires the capacity to form concepts through this labour. Though the master owns the object, insofar as the slave's labour is not his own (the slave's labour belongs to the master), the master does not own the concept. This is why there emerges in the slave a freedom of thought, while the master remains unthinkingly immersed in his desires and immediate satisfactions. The slave thus gains a power that the master lacks: the power to make and use concepts, the power *to think* (*Denken*).

Emphasising that the slave is as much a logical position as it is an existential disposition, the slave has the capacity to think, to make sense of concepts, to find freedom within itself. This freedom is not absolute, to be sure, as it does not afford the slave the capacity for pure mobility or unfettered expression. But it *does* afford the slave a capacity for a kind of development, a movement beyond the violent and overdetermined desires of the master. *This* movement is what the stoic takes up. While the master is free to express and fulfil his desires through the slave, the (slave-turned-)stoic is free to think about the world and imagine unrealised possibilities.

We see the difference in the slave's and the stoic's respective kinds of freedom in terms of the difference in the types of models that Douglass and Washington respectively encountered. Since Douglass was, while enslaved, prevented from living a different type of life, the life of a free Black man rather than mere chattel,

---

10 'It has been a matter of deep interest to me', writes Washington, 'to note ... the number of people who have come to shake hands with me after an address, who say that this is the first time they have ever called a Negro "Mister"' (UP 120).

he was never able to encounter an example of an ideal he could hold up as something to aim for. Chattel slavery withered the soul; Douglass witnessed how the threat and enactment of violence endemic to slavery had turned older Black folk into meek and subservient shells of themselves. Antiblack chattel slavery was predicated on destroying the mind as much as it was organised around constraining and overdetermining the meaning of the body.

Washington, by contrast, since he spent the formative years of his life, in the aftermath of the Civil War, as a free young Black man, was able to witness and hold up to himself, as an ideal, a real person: 'the late General Samuel C. Armstrong' (UP 26). In General Armstrong, Washington encountered a man he calls 'the noblest, rarest human being that it has ever been my privilege to meet ... I do not hesitate to say that I never met any man who, in my estimation, was the equal of General Armstrong' (UP 26). Washington said that there was something 'superhuman about him', and that it 'never occurred to me that General Armstrong could fail in anything he undertook' (UP 26, 27). The ideal type of education Washington envisioned was to spend time with the General every day, rather than pour over books.

Part of the reason why Washington embodied a new form of subjectivity was because he witnessed, in person, an ideal type of Black man, and then internalised this external form of the 'perfect man', which enabled him to direct his own development toward this concretisation of the universal (UP 26). Similar to how Douglass shaped himself according to the external, enduring, and coherent self he encountered in his reading, writing, and fighting, Washington fashioned himself according to the model of General Armstrong.[11]

This self-fashioning through ideals leads to an ideal sense of self. Stoicism is a more developed form of self-consciousness insofar as it involves an 'I' that experiences itself as an 'I' that is an

---

[11] It is thus not surprising that the 'kind of reading' Washington had 'the greatest fondness for' was biography, because he found in these narratives examples of ideals and virtues lived out by real people (UP 129).

otherness *for* it; but since it experiences this 'I' only 'in the form of thought ... its essence is only an *abstract* essence [*abstracktes* Wesen]' (PS 200).[12] The very thing that allows the slave to discover a new form of freedom – a freedom from bodily enslavement, a freedom within – is also the stoic's limitation. Stoic self-consciousness is free insofar as it *thinks* itself free.

The central thought here is the 'I' which has two simultaneous senses. First, this 'I' has the 'significance of *intrinsic* being, of having itself for object' (PS 179). The stoic has a sense of self insofar as it takes itself as an object originating from itself, not from another person. The stoic is a 'subjective I' insofar as it takes itself as an 'objective I'. Second, the stoic 'I' relates itself 'to objective being in such a way that its significance is the *being-for-itself* of the consciousness for which it is [an object]' (PS 179). Insofar as the stoic 'I' takes itself as an object, it sees its 'objective I' whose being is its own *because* it is an object for the 'subjective I'. The stoic's characteristic act is 'conceptual thinking', thinking in concepts, and as such it is 'a movement within myself' (PS 179). In short, the stoic is 'an "I" which has an otherness within itself', and one that recognises it as *its* self (PS 200).

The stoic's abstract conception of itself means that its sense of self is also abstract. Remaining indifferent to particularity, to the life of a slave or a master, the stoic turns to universals, and thus turns the self into a universal too. The stoic self is a general self, not *my* particular self. Since it deals with universals only, the thought of the 'I' or the self also becomes a universal. Put differently, the 'I' is free from or deprived of all content (*Inhalt*), thus becoming merely the empty form of subjectivity. We see this 'I' in Washington's stoicism insofar as he constantly advocates for a cultivation of the self beyond race, neither Black nor white, a pure, universal 'I'. This indicates what is perhaps the foremost dimension of Washington's stoicism: unselfishness.

It is clear that Washington values this virtue very highly because he talks about it continuously. He repeatedly expresses

---

12 As Hyppolite puts it: 'stoic liberty remains abstract, not vital, a liberty in thought but not in actuality'. *Genesis and Structure*, 182.

admiration for it in the types of individuals he most respects, from General Armstrong to his fellow founders and leaders of the Tuskegee Institute, including Miss Olivia A. Davidson, who led 'a life of unselfishness that I think has seldom been equaled', and 'Mr. Warren Logan ... the treasurer of the Institute, and the acting principal during my absence' (UP 60, 77). While it might initially seem paradoxical to say that the stoic, who differentiates himself from the slave because he was the first to formulate a coherent and enduring sense of self, also indefatigably pursues the virtue the unselfishness, on reflection this makes perfect sense. The vice of selfishness is tied to the particular self, the actual person who lives and breathes in the world, not the higher self, characterised by 'that lifeless impassiveness ... so much admired in the Stoic sage'.[13] The stoic self is one that aims to be unselfish, an aim that is only possible once an enduring form of self has emerged from slavery. To be unselfish means to deny the particular content of the self and to retreat into the pure form of the universal 'I'. For Washington, losing one's particular self and developing one's higher self is the secret of what we can call stoic happiness:

> In order to be successful in any kind of undertaking, I think the main thing is for one to grow to the point where he completely forgets himself; that is, to lose himself in a great cause. In proportion as one loses himself in this way, in the same degree does he get the highest happiness out of his work. (UP 88)

This stoic principle also applies to stoic freedom: the form of the abstract universal entails abstract universal content because the stoic 'freedom of self-consciousness is *indifferent* to a natural existence' – that is, living as a slave – it 'has therefore *let this equally go free*' (PS 200; emphases added). As Washington says of the 'verses of the plantation songs' sung by the slaves: though they were about freedom, they were 'careful to explain [to the masters] that the "freedom" in these songs referred to the next world, and had no connection with life in this world' (UP 10).

---

13 Ibid., 183.

We can – and should – be wary of Washington's interpretation here. After all, enslaved Black folk were quite adept at 'putting on' for slaveholders as a survival tactic. Saidiya Hartman alerts us to the fact that performances of meekness and joy – particularly in the form of dance – cannot be taken at first glance because the meaning of these performances was steeped in the overwhelming violence of slavery itself.[14] In this regard, Washington's reading of the 'freedom' of the slaves as merely otherworldly is *his* reading.

But that is the point: it is *Washington's* reading, and one that connects with the flaccid freedom of the post-emancipation era. Even more to the point, it is Washington's *stoic* reading. The goal of stoicism is the freedom of another world. 'Freedom in thought', Hegel writes, 'has only *pure thought* as its truth' (PS 200). Stoic freedom is not a true freedom; it is just the thought or 'Notion of freedom, not the living reality of freedom itself' (PS 200). Since stoic freedom is a universal – Freedom-in-itself – it has little or no connection to the particularity of the world; its freedom is a completely self-enclosed narcissism. As Hyppolite puts it, 'free thought remains formal ... in the sense that having disengaged the essence of pure thought from all the difference within life, it is able to surmount all those differences and rediscover in them the essentiality of thought'.[15]

Such merely universal, abstract freedom lacks all determinations insofar as it is, as Hegel might put it, an incomplete negation. Stoicism assumes that it will get content from freedom. Yet since its freedom lies merely in abstract cognition, thinking in (empty) universals, it ends up shuffling around empty categories. If one withdraws into oneself, emancipates oneself from the world, one is merely left to think about oneself over and over – I am I am I am I am ... forever – the empty repetition of empty concepts. The 'self identity of thought', writes Hegel, 'is again only the pure form in which nothing is determined' (PS 200). One gains self, freedom, truth, goodness, wisdom, virtue, etc., only by losing the world, and thus one creates a radical dualism between the inner

---

14 Hartman, *Scenes of Subjection*, 47.
15 Hyppolite, *Genesis and Structure*, 183.

citadel of the self and an utterly indifferent and meaningless world. Though these notions are 'in a general way uplifting [*erhebend*] ... since they cannot in fact produce any expansion of content, they soon become tedious [*Langeweile*]' (PS 200). The stoic life, in a sense, becomes stale and boring; it ends up repeating empty mantras and platitudes.

Washington describes many instances of such a faith in universals – the *idea* of truth rather than concrete truth, the *idea* of trust rather than actual trust, the *idea* of goodness rather than genuine good actions. He claims that 'there are few instances, either in slavery or freedom, in which a member of my race has been known to betray a trust', and points to many places where slaves responded with kindness and support to their masters who had returned from the Civil War wounded and pitiable (UP 7). The best illustration of this, Washington recalls, is 'the case of an ex-slave from Virginia' who 'had made a contract with his master, two or three years previous to the Emancipation Proclamation', which allowed the slave to earn his own wages on a better paying farm in Ohio (UP 14). When the war ended and the slave was freed, he felt the call to fulfil his obligation to pay back his white slave owner, and so 'this Black man walked the greater proportion of the distance back to where his old master lived in Virginia, and placed the last dollar, with interest, in his hands', because he 'felt that he could not enjoy his freedom till he had fulfilled his promise' (UP 8). Clearly, he felt more obliged to the idea of duty and was indifferent to the racist contract by which he had found himself enslaved and from which he had been freed.

Lacan and White Misrecognition

At this point we find it helpful to approach Washingtonian and Wellsian stoicisms through Lacan's 'mirror stage'.[16] Lacan, we should recall, was partially inspired to write on this topic by

---

16 Jacques Lacan, 'The Mirror Stage as Formative of the *I* Function as Revealed in Psychoanalytic Experience', in *Écrits*, trans. Bruce Fink (New York: W.W. Norton, 2007), 58–74.

Alexander Kojève's seminars on Hegel's *Phenomenology*, which stressed the master-slave dialectic as the most important part of Hegel's text.

According to Lacan, the infant recognises itself in the mirror before it is able to control its body. Since the image reflected back to the infant is a coherent whole, while their internal experience is fragmented and incoherent, the mirror stage introduces a disturbing tension between the subject and its external image. While the infant, according to Lacan, eventually feels joy in identifying itself with the coherent external body image, there is inevitably a misunderstanding of the self, a self-misrecognition (*méconnaissance*). It is at this mirror stage that the subject first becomes alienated from itself, thus entering the imaginary and symbolic orders. This is not, however, what Douglass or Washington describe.

Born into slavery, they were told from birth that they were incoherent, subordinate, more beast than human. Slaves were not told their dates of birth, their age, their real name, the identity of a parent, or anything beyond their being the chattel of a white master who was endowed with absolute power. Thus the minimal sense of self that slaves saw reflected back on them was never the coherent whole that Lacan describes. It was not until they undertook formative work akin to Douglass's reading and writing lessons or Washington's drive for education that these Black slaves had reflected back to them the holistic self that Lacan identifies as arising in the mirror stage. Moreover, the self that is reflected back to Black subjects is not as immediate and transparent as the image in the clean surface of a mirror. It is opaque. Black knowledge, and therefore Black spirit, always sees through a mirror darkly. It is a slowly unfolding reflection in an object produced by one's labour. Black knowledge is never just (a) given. It is lived. It is worked out. It is worked *for*.

The white person's misrecognition points to something important about the logic of recognition, especially when viewed through the institution of American slavery. Typically, the explanation of what is problematic about relationships of domination – such as that of the master and the slave, or Covey and

Douglass – is that there is an instance of *mis*recognition. Slavery is wrong, so the logic goes, because the master does not recognise the humanity in the slave. The master only views the slave as an object, a farm animal, a tool for fulfilling his desires. Hence, there is assumed to be a cognitive error on the part of the master: Covey fails to notice a fact about the worth or value of Douglass.

But this misses something essential about slavery and other forms of domination. It is not that the master misrecognises the slave because he does not acknowledge that the slave too possesses the same humanity that the master simply assumes is in himself. In fact, as Zakiyyah Jackson writes, it might be that the master recognises something like humanity *in* Blackness, in the figure of the slave.[17] Denying slaves access to the written text, preaching sermons to them about their otherworldly salvation, and even sending them to jail – all of these instances articulate an implicit recognition that Black (or Black(ened), as Jackson puts it) people are, in fact, human.[18] The violence comes in light of – not in spite of – their humanity.

Suggesting that slavery involves merely a 'dehumanisation' or a misrecognition of Black humanity is, then, a flawed analysis. Perhaps the misrecognition – the misrecognition that produces violence – is located elsewhere. Perhaps, instead of thinking about slavery as a misrecognition of the humanity of the slave, we might suggest that the master *misrecognises himself*.

One condition for the possibility of slavery is the failure of the masters to recognise the full significance of their fundamental and inescapable dependence on the other. In our terms, the white master does not fail to see the worth in the Black slave; the condition for the formulation of Blackness as a problem is exactly that the Black person *lives*, that they live as something upon which the world depends, and without which the world – and, in this case, the master – would cease to exist. In short, the white master does not notice that he is himself the blemish, that he – and again, we gender this term intentionally – is the parasitic

---

17 Jackson, *Becoming Human*, 1.
18 Ibid.

entity, deriving his life and his value from the work, body, and productivity of the slave.

It is not simply that Covey overlooked something about Douglass, but that he overlooks something about himself. Covey does not miss Douglass's humanity; he is, in fact, *unsettled* by it, disturbed by the presence of a being whose life is, as Fred Moten might say, *fugitive*.[19] Douglass was sent to Covey because his other master, Master Thomas, had failed to fully constrain him. 'I had lived with [Master Thomas] nearly nine months', Douglass writes, 'without any visible improvement of my character, or my conduct; and now he was resolved to put me out – as he said – "*to be broken*"' (BF 256; emphasis added). What the master wanted to break was precisely Douglass's humanity. But in attempting to do this, Thomas and Covey end up exposing the brutality of their own humanity in the first place. Covey 'enjoyed the execrated reputation, of being a first rate hand at breaking young negroes' (BF 256). What Covey discovered, however, was that Douglass was resilient and irrepressible; hence, Douglass's escape from slavery led to a new form of Black subjectivity: Washington's stoicism.

The Reality of Southern Horrors

But all is not what it seems in stoicism. At first glance, Washington appears to be the logical heir apparent to Douglass's legacy, but there was someone else who perhaps exemplified the next development in a phenomenology of *Black* spirit, of *Black* breath, of *Black* life.[20] Washington's stoicism is, well, *too* stoic; in his yearning for universals, he sought to 'transcend' difference. In so doing, he

---

19 Fred Moten, 'The Case of Blackness', *Criticism* 50:2 (2008): 179.
20 Linda McMurry Edwards claims that, 'When Douglass died in 1895, Wells was his logical heir apparent; they had closely collaborated on several projects. She was better known than W.E.B Du Bois and more ideologically compatible with Douglass than Booker T. Washington – the two men who eventually became the main contenders to fill Douglass's shoes. However, Wells had a major problem: She was a woman.' Linda McMurry Edwards, *To Keep the Waters Troubled: The Life of Ida B. Wells* (New York: Oxford University Press, 2000), xiv.

assumed that struggle, or a certain kind of work, could free Black people from their suffering *as Black*. He, like Hegel, placed too much faith in universals, and, also like Hegel, he found freedom in thinking – a kind of thinking that ultimately sought to move away from the concrete situation of Blackness itself.

The truth, however, is that such cognitive freedom did not stop the antiblack violence. Emancipation did not stem the tide of white supremacism. Though slavery formally ended, Black subjection did not. It transformed into a new monster. The lynching tree replaced the auction block.

Ida B. Wells knew this. She was not a stoic in the Hegelian and Washingtonian sense, but of a different, more developed kind. While she was, to be sure, committed to an ideal, this ideal was neither abstract nor universal. It was grounded on the concrete realities of Black death, on the fact that Black flesh, Black bodies, were always and already slated for death. Her ideal was *life* – Black life; her commitment was to writing and acting against Black death. She may have been a stoic, but not all stoics are the same.

If Hegel and Washington approach stoicism as a kind of longstanding commitment to abstract ideals, then Wells had no such imperative. Her stoicism didn't emerge from an externalised ideal: she had no General Armstrong, and she prescribed no rules for living. She lived out her stoicism in her commitment to her family, friends, and community. When both of her parents died from yellow fever, she had to take care of her seven younger siblings when she was just sixteen years old. Given these very material responsibilities, her writings betray no yearning for transcendence, no sense of freedom in *mere* thinking. Wells offers a militant defence of Black life and a profound criticism of Black death, forged out of the need to care for and tend to her family. Her stoicism is thus steeped in her turn *toward* her community, and particularly toward preserving that community. Rather than abstract freedom or merit, living was her ideal, and lynching was a concrete hindrance to that ideal – a hindrance that neither work nor cleanliness nor education could mitigate.

Wells did not arrive at her anti-lynching work right away. Initially, she went along to get along. 'Like many another person who had read of lynching in the South, I had accepted the idea ... that although lynching was irregular and contrary to law and order, unreasoning anger over the terrible crime of rape led to the lynching.'[21] This made her assume that 'perhaps the brute deserves the death anyhow and the mob was justified in taking his life'. Thomas Moss's death changed her perspective. Moss and his wife Betty were 'the best friends I had in town', and perhaps more to the point, they were people of exemplary morals.[22] Moss 'was well liked, a favorite with everyone', Wells wrote, 'yet he was murdered with no more consideration than if he had been a dog'.[23] Her eyes were opened to 'what lynching really was ... An excuse to get rid of Negroes who were acquiring wealth and property and thus to "keep the [N-word] down".' Wells then began 'an investigation of every lynching I read about'.[24]

In thinking about the lynching of her good friend Thomas Moss, she recognised what Washington did not (and perhaps could not): 'neither character nor standing avails the Negro if he dares to protect himself against the white man or become his rival'.[25] Moss was a Black grocer, who had taken seriously the very duties Washington prescribed – education for oneself and others, cleanliness (which we might also think of as upright moral character), and work. Hard work. In 1889, Moss, along with a few other Black people in Memphis, had formed the collective People's Grocery Company, a business whose clientele was primarily Black. Moss, along with his co-founders, had done the work. They had clearly demonstrated their merit. According to Washington, that should have been enough.

But W.H. Barrett, a white grocer, could not abide such merit. 'Providence' didn't hold in Memphis; there was no transcending 'colour'. Linda McMurry Edwards makes this clear: 'The elevation of educated African Americans meant the degradation

---

21 Ida B. Wells, *Crusade for Justice: The Autobiography of Ida B. Wells*, ed. Alfreda M. Duster (Chicago: University of Chicago Press, 1992), 64.
22 Ibid.
23 Edwards, *To Keep the Waters Troubled*, 135.
24 Wells, *Crusade for Justice*, 64.
25 Edwards, *To Keep the Waters Troubled*, 135–6.

of poor, ignorant whites.'[26] Washington's stoic ideal of universal providence steeped in merit carried no weight in the post-reconstruction South. Differences – racial differences – mattered, and such differences could and would engender violence.

Barrett was exemplary of this. He engaged in a long series of legal and physical attacks on the People's Grocery Company, which ended with Moss and two others being imprisoned and then brutally murdered in the middle of the night. This was Wells' undoing.

She discovered a new kind of white misrecognition, one that emerged in the wake of slavery. While the 'rape of helpless Negro girls and women' was a normalised practice in slavery, it 'continued without let or hindrance, check, or reproof from church, state or press' in slavery's wake.[27] The white man's violence against Black female bodies did not end after the Civil War, but continued without pause.

What was new, though, was an intensified focus on Black male bodies. In slavery, white people could enact whatever type of force or violence on Black bodies they wanted. Since the enslaved were property, no justification for such violence was needed. Post-slavery, however, white people sought to control Black bodies in new ways, ways that pivoted on an important misrecognition. '[W]hat the white man of the South practiced as all right for himself, he assumed was unthinkable in white women.'[28] While white men considered it perfectly acceptable to sexually violate Black women,

> they professed an inability to imagine white women doing the same thing with Negro and mulatto men. Whenever they did so and were found out, the cry of rape was raised, and the lowest element of the white South was turned loose to wreak its fiendish cruelty on those too weak to help themselves.[29]

---

26 Ibid., 144.
27 Wells, *Crusade for Justice*, 70.
28 Ibid.
29 Ibid.

Since such 'cold-blooded savagery' was committed or approved by the 'white men who controlled all the forces of law and order in their communities and who could have legally punished rapists and murderers', there was basically nothing that Black communities could do to stop it.[30]

Of the multiple instances of white misrecognition, one is that while white people demanded a fair and balanced application of law and order for themselves, they were even more eager to exercise a feverish extrajudicial violence against Black people. Another is that while white men took a devilish pleasure in sexually violating Black women, they were driven to the most extreme violence whenever there was a hint of romantic relations between Black men and white women.

Wells identifies the fuel for this misrecognition as a carryover from the slave master's subjectivity into post-bellum whiteness. She became increasingly convinced that the 'Southerner had never gotten over his resentment that the Negro was no longer his plaything, his servant, and his source of income'.[31] During slavery, masters became almost addicted to inflicting violence on their slaves. For some, this was a source of perverted pleasure; many masters, overseers, slave breakers, and so on must have savoured the legal sanction to attack and destroy Black bodies. For others, the violence against slaves was not seen as pleasurable but as an uncomfortable yet necessary evil. It was accompanied by the justification that this violence was actually beneficial to the slaves. The racist account of Black subjectivity held that Black people naturally tended toward violence, rage, and animality because of a supposedly innate lack of temperance, self-discipline, and impulse control. It thus was thought necessary to tame Black bodies with calculated acts of violence.

Although slavery had ended, the master's subjectivity, strongly structured by the acts of violence that had become habitual in slavery, continued. Former slave masters and other white people retained the drive to continue such racial violence, and so needed

---

30 Ibid.
31 Ibid.

a new way to satisfy that drive. White misrecognition – that white men could have sexual relations with Black women while simultaneously being appalled at any hint of intimacy between Black men and white women – enabled the violent drives still lurking in former slave masters to be not only expressed but even protected by the law. The terror and fear that had been omnipresent on the plantation re-emerged with lynching. This misrecognition was occluded by the attempt to 'justify these horrible atrocities to the world' by 'branding [Black men] as a race of rapists, who were especially mad after white women'.[32] With this justification, the 'blood lust' that entailed the murder and torture of Black bodies was 'openly admitted and gloried ... as if it were something to be proud of' rather than something to elicit shame.[33]

With this diagnosis of white misrecognition, Wells saw something that Washington likely did not see, and there is some reason to think that he wilfully chose not to see it.[34] When the Afro-American Council (in which Wells and her husband were active leaders) met in Indianapolis in the summer of 1900, 'Booker T. Washington had called a meeting of the businessmen of the country to be held in Boston, Massachusetts at the same time', likely in order to prove to the white funders of the Tuskegee Institute that their financial support was justified.[35] This might be why the meeting of the Afro-American Council was not as well attended that year. Wells reports that Washington had 'given us the impression that he could not ally himself with us because we were too radical'.[36] Washington was so desperate to appear moderate and sympathetic to whiteness that, when he was around influential white people, he would tell jokes that affirmed racial prejudices. We see this in Wells' response to a Jewish gentleman

---

32 Ibid., 71.
33 Ibid., 85.
34 Hubert Harrison's description of the assimilationism that he saw in the NAAAP is also fitting here: 'Many Negroes ... have a wish-bone where their back-bone ought to be.' *A Hubert Harrison Reader*, ed. Jeffrey B. Perry (Middletown, CT: Wesleyan University Press, 2001), 144.
35 Wells, *Crusade for Justice*, 264.
36 Ibid., 265.

who reported one such joke: 'a great many of us cannot approve of Mr. Washington's plan of telling chicken-stealing stories on his own people in order to amuse his audiences and get money for Tuskegee'.[37]

While Washington went to great pains not to offend white people in order to keep their financial and political support, Wells and the Council's 'policy was to denounce the wrongs and injustices which were heaped upon our people, and to use whatever influence we had to help right them. Especially strong was our condemnation of lynch law and those who practiced it.'[38] Rather than insisting that segregation should be abolished, Washington argued that Black people should spend their energies 'trying to be first-class people in a [J]im [C]row car'.[39] Even more obvious than Washington's reluctance to engage in radical political action was his blocking of a resolution, issued at the Council's annual meeting in 1901, which was intended to condemn a recent lynching wherein 'a human being was burned alive in Alabama' during the session of the Business League that same summer.[40] Washington quashed the resolution in order not to offend white sentiments.

While Washington claimed that white people would naturally respect anyone who worked hard and earned what was meritoriously theirs, Wells saw that the success of Black people – including her friend Thomas Moss – only led to a new kind of racist violence. Just as Jacobs showed us that Hegel was wrong to think that work will set slaves free, Wells shows Washington that industriousness is not only incapable of securing white respect and recognition, but that it also occludes gender considerations that Washington never sufficiently acknowledged. What Brittney Cooper says of Pauli Murray can be traced backs to Wells, who likewise revealed 'the ways in which respectability politics has played a role in constructing Black gender performances of manhood and womanhood,

---

37 Ibid., 331.
38 Ibid., 265. Hubert Harrison would deem Washington's 'good white people' guilty of a 'frightful friendliness'. *A Hubert Harrison Reader*, 145, 147.
39 Wells, *Crusade for Justice*, 265.
40 Ibid., 266.

and the extent to which the regime of respectability circumscribed and limited the strategies of political resistance available to those in the broader African American freedom struggle'.[41]

Why, then, do we think of Wells as a stoic? She did not, after all, seek to transcend the body, and had no predilection for mere freedom in thought. Yet she is a stoic, we argue, because she articulated a commitment, lifelong in its duration and expansive in its scope, to Black life. For Wells, what mattered was the concrete, existential – which is to say, embodied – lives of the people in her community. What she had externalised was not the attempt to think freely, given that she, like Douglass, had long begun to do so. In a different way to Douglass, Wells had not found full freedom in her capacity to think because death remained. Lynchings were everywhere. Thinking was not enough. Throughout her lifelong anti-lynching campaign, Wells remained clear-eyed and laser-focused. While she 'was not the first to expose rape as a mythical cause of mob action', she nevertheless 'became the loudest and most persistent voice for truth' on the issue.[42] She did not stop and would not be stopped.

We see her unflinching commitment to Black life in her 1892 editorial for the Memphis newspaper *Free Speech*. Having had enough of the mendacious claims that the lynchings were responses to sexual violence, she did not mince her words:

> Nobody in this section of the country believes the old threadbare lie that Negro men rape white women. If Southern white men are not careful, they will over-reach themselves and public sentiment will have a reaction; a conclusion will then be reached which will be very damaging to the moral reputation of their women.[43]

She called them liars. She told them the truth. She was letting them know that their 'threadbare lies' had nothing to do with

---

41 Brittney C. Cooper, *Beyond Respectability* (Urbana: University of Illinois Press, 2017), 96.
42 Edwards, *To Keep the Waters Troubled*, 146.
43 Wells, *Southern Horrors*, 7.

'southern outrages', but had everything to do with their own misrecognition.[44]

In this case, 'misrecognition' may be the wrong word. Wells herself does not use it, and neither does she operate in light of it. Washington certainly did; in fact, Wells knew that his operations were part of the ruse, and that his stoic emphasis on work would not stem the tide of violence, let alone create the possibility for something like freedom. She recognised the lie, and she exposed it.

> This gospel of work is no new one for the Negro. It is the South's old slavery practice in a new dress. It was the only education the South gave the Negro for [the] two and a half centuries she had control of his body and soul. The Negro knows now, as then, the South is strongly opposed to his learning anything else but work.[45]

Wells knew better. She knew that, even if Washington thought that work was the best way to upward mobility – to freedom – there was no evidence for the effectiveness of his stoicism.

> Mr. Washington says in substance: give me money to educate the Negro and when he is taught how to work, he will not commit the crime for which lynching is done. Mr. Washington knows when he says this that lynching is not invoked to punish crime but color, and not even industrial education will change that.[46]

White misrecognition might well be misrecognition – a mistake in perception and cognition – but it can also come in the form of an active untruth, of lies. As his form of stoicism demonstrates, Washington capitulated to the lie that Blackness was only good insofar as it could work. But in Wells we find a different kind of stoic commitment that was neither to universal values nor to meritocracy. Instead, she committed to the prophetic role of speaking truth to power, to exposing the lie and the violence of white misrecognition. She called them liars. Even if they believed

---

44 Edwards, *To Keep the Waters Troubled*, 212.
45 Ida B. Wells, 'Booker T. Washington and his Critics', *World Today*, April 1904, 519.
46 Ibid., 520.

their lies, even if their misrecognition was *really* a misrecognition of the state of affairs, Wells knew and showed that it was still a lie. She wrote against that lie with unrelenting courage.

And not without consequence. Her 1892 op-ed won her no friends in Memphis, and became the catalyst for the destruction of her newspaper offices. She was in New York when this happened, and eventually realised that Memphis was no place to return to. She went to Chicago.

But she still wrote.

And she still spoke.

While Wells' stoicism was not the abstract stoicism of Washington or Hegel, it was nevertheless a commitment to an ideal. This ideal was not abstract, but instead housed in the very bodies of those living and dying. To sit with Wells, then, is to sit with a stoicism that is critical of both the abstraction and the idealisations promised by the Hegelian and Washingtonian traditions. It is to expose the fact that, within a phenomenology of Black spirit, there are always other philosophical, ethical, and political possibilities. Always.

Conclusion

Southern trees
Bear strange fruit
Blood on the leaves
And blood at the roots ...

Wells was run out of town in 1892. But she kept writing, and she kept speaking truth to power. This commitment was stoic, even if it did not adhere to the strict abstractions of Washington and Hegel. In Wells, the phenomenology of Black spirit *moved*. It *breathed*. It kept breathing, even as Black breath was being siphoned from Black flesh with lynch rope.

In fact, Wells' stoicism kept breathing after she died in 1931. It continued not through the pen, but through song. Just eight years later, Billie Holiday would also take up a kind of stoic work reminiscent of Wells as she sang 'Strange Fruit' for the first time. She, too, was committed. To the detriment of her career and her well-being, Holiday would sing that song for twenty years, expressing a commitment to Black flesh, to reminding the world of the violence that it enacts against Black life in the name of its own comfort, its own safety. She would die in 1959, her career in shambles – in part because of her commitment to performing a song that many did not want to hear.

And yet, this spirit of stoicism would keep breathing. In 1965, Nina Simone would cover the song, imbuing it with even more of a haunting tone. That year was, of course, the year Malcolm X was killed, and the height of the Civil Rights Movement. Though lynchings had decreased by this time – but had by no means been completely done away with – Black people were still being maligned, mutilated, brutalised, and disrespected by the violence of white supremacy. Simone – like Holiday, like Wells – would remain committed to raising awareness of the physical violence of white supremacist antiblackness.

While Washington and Hegel were committed to abstract ideals of freedom, work and uplift, Black women like Wells, Holiday, and Simone expressed a commitment to the enfleshed and grounded ideal of Black life. This was no mere abstraction; it was, instead, founded in and upon their own practices. They *fleshed out* their commitments, departing from what might be understood as the vacuous idealism of the Hegelian and Washingtonian stoic disposition. In other words, they *filled out*, and therefore moved forward, a dialectical phenomenology of Black spirit. They did so by committing to and working for their people.

We do not mean to romanticise or lionise these women (or maybe we do – just a bit). Our point here is that the stoic commitment they embodied required something different – and perhaps something more – than what Hegel's and Washington's stoicism offered. In these women, and surely many others, we find a commitment to *telling the truth* – a truth that always and already required them to point out the unsightly *problems* in their society. Part of their work, then, was to *negate* what might be understood as the optimism of the stoic. In this way, their work anticipates the scepticism to which we turn in the next chapter.

3

Scepticism

W.E.B. Du Bois and Anna Julia Cooper

'Stoicism', Hegel writes, 'is the freedom which always comes directly out of bondage and returns into the pure universality of thought' (PS 200). Refracted through Booker T. Washington's hyper-pragmatist lens, stoicism becomes the disposition of those who come 'up from slavery'. From Washington's perspective, those who have experienced bondage in all of its concrete and symbolic violence must come out of slavery into what could only be understood as the colourless – and therefore purely universal – ideals of work, discipline, and cleanliness.

As we saw with Ida B. Wells at the end of the last chapter, however, such ideals – perhaps in and through their figuration as 'pure' – offered little solace for those kissed by the sun, the dark incarnate. Slavery may have ended in legal name, but the violence of antiblackness persisted. Wells knew this; she knew *better*; she knew that antiblackness would not release its grip on Black life so easily. She therefore committed to her own brand of stoicism, one in which Black life would be the ideal. She wanted Black people to *live* – or at least to *not die* – and this motivated the continuous fury of her pen. She was a stoic in commitment, not content, because, again, *she knew better*. Knowing better, she did better.

In doing better, Wells inaugurated a transition from Washington's sterile stoicism to what we might call a more grounded stoicism characterised by the practical commitment to preserving Black life. And it is precisely Wells' stoicism – not Washington's – that provides the opening for considering of the next phase in a phenomenology of Black spirit: scepticism.

This chapter takes up scepticism in a sustained fashion. W.E.B. Du Bois, the sharp, slightly younger critic of Washington, is the protagonist here. While Hegel provides a conceptual scaffolding for scepticism, Du Bois embodies it. This chapter considers Du Bois' sceptical take on what we call stoicism's Warring Ideals and Triple Paradox, through concepts that resonate as much in Hegel as they do in him: second-sight, afterthought, and of course double consciousness. With these concepts, Du Bois shifts the character of Hegelian scepticism, providing flesh to the phenomenological bones of Hegel's logic.[1]

As with last two chapters, as much as Du Bois expands and transforms Hegel's sceptic, it is his contemporary, Anna Julia Cooper, who raises Du Boisian scepticism to its logical and embodied extreme by considering a category that Du Bois never sufficiently addresses: gender. Du Bois' scepticism is most clearly defined by the divided nature of double consciousness, but Cooper shows that here gender, specifically female, needs to be added in order to produce what we might call a 'triple consciousness'. Yet more than just adding a third cut to Black subjectivity, Cooper's scepticism gestures not merely to another gender but to what Hortense Spillers might call 'ungendered female flesh'. Reading Cooper through Spillers, we glimpse a kind of freedom that exceeds both the stoic's ideal and the sceptic's negative freedom, revealing their rootedness in a fraught masculinity. The only way to this kind of freedom, Cooper's scepticism shows, is through Black women. Cooper eviscerates a hope that things could be better; her appeal instead is grounded in her *knowledge* that Black women are the condition of possibility for Black life in general. As we will see her repeat below, 'the whole Negro race enters with me'.

---

[1] We must point to the excellent recent work of Kimberly Ann Harris and Elvira Basevich on Hegel and Du Bois, much of which is forthcoming and for which we are very excited. Until then, see Kimberly Ann Harris, 'Du Bois and Hegelian Idealism', *Idealistic Studies: An Interdisciplinary Journal of Philosophy* 51:2 (2021), Special Edition: '"Philosophical Idealism as Anti-Racism" on the Occasion of Hegel's 250th Anniversary', 149–71; and Elvira Basevich, 'W.E.B. Du Bois's Critique of Radical Reconstruction (1865–77): A Hegelian Approach to American Modernity', *Philosophy and Social Criticism* 45:2 (2019): 168–85. For earlier work, see also David Farrell Krell, 'The Bodies of Black Folk: From Kant and Hegel to Du Bois and Baldwin', *boundary 2* 27:3 (2000): 103–34.

Dusk of Dawn

In 1940, two years after turning seventy, Du Bois' published *Dusk of Dawn*, his second (of three) autobiographical books.[2] More autobiographical than *The Souls of Black Folk*, the subtitle of this book is *An Essay Toward an Autobiography of Race*, which leads Chandler to cast it as very reminiscent of Hegel's *Phenomenology*: 'Is it possible', Chandler asks, 'for the most particular or "subjective" history to tell the most general truths, perhaps precisely because such histories do distort, or magnify, and so on in particular sorts of ways?'[3] More than the *Phenomenology*, however, the title *Dusk of Dawn* also evokes imagery from Hegel's *Elements of the Philosophy Right*: 'When philosophy paints its grey in grey, a shape of life has grown old, and it cannot be rejuvenated, but only recognised, by the *grey in grey* of philosophy; the owl of Minerva begins its flight only with the onset of *dusk*.'[4] Connecting Du Bois' dark dawn to Hegel's grey dusk demonstrates that Hegel is mistaken about the supposed ease with which Black and white fade to grey.

To see how Du Bois theorises the dusk of a coming dawn, note how he compares *Dusk of Dawn* to two of his previous books: Written earlier in his life, *The Souls of Black Folk* was 'a cry at midnight thick within the Veil, when none rightly knew the coming day'. Later, *Darkwater*, which was critiqued as having

---

[2] Thomas Holt says that all readings of Du Bois must reckon with Du Bois' insistence that his 'own life became the text, the point of departure, for each of his major explorations of race, culture, and politics'. Thomas C. Holt, 'The Political uses of Alienation: W.E.B. Du Bois on Politics, Race, and Culture, 1905–1940', *American Quarterly* 42:2 (1990): 307.

[3] Chandler says this in his chapter 'Elaboration of the Autobiographical Example in the Thought of W.E.B. Du Bois', where he characterises Du Bois' writing strategy as a 'hesitant' yet 'insistent' 'apology' (in the Socratic lineage), noting its complication of Enlightenment assumptions about objective truth through a 'subjective genesis' and a variation on Derrida's insistence on the interplay between history and *logos* in his 'tracing of the problem of genesis' in Husserl's phenomenology. Nahum Dimitri Chandler, *X: The Problem of the Negro as a Problem for Thought* (New York: Fordham University Press, 2014), 777.

[4] G.W.F. Hegel, *Elements of the Philosophy of Right*, trans. Allen W. Wood (Cambridge: Cambridge University Press, 1991), 12; emphases added.

'too much Hegel' in it, 'was an exposition and militant challenge, defiant with dogged hope'.[5] In *Dusk of Dawn*, later still, he 'started to record dimly but consciously that subtle sense of coming day which one feels of early morning even when mist and murk hang low'.[6] Notice the three moments here. While dusk is the descent into the terror of the darkest darkness of night, and dawn is the promise of rising reds, purples, oranges, and yellows – that hazy dawn rainbow – emerging from night clouds, the *Dusk of Dawn* is that unstable balance between the two, that contradictory, double, and divided position between night and day, dark and light.

While Hegel sees philosophical thought as painting grey on grey, as the sun sets at dusk and Minerva's owl takes flight, Du Bois is very clear that Blackness and whiteness do not easily mix when presented together, just as dusk does not dissipate at dawn but remains in its difference. We will now see that Du Boisian scepticism dwells in this unstable balance that is neither dusk nor dawn.

Saying No: Who Is Hegel's Sceptic?

Scepticism has a structural analogical relation with the previous moments in the *Phenomenology*: stoicism is to scepticism as the master is to the slave. While the master, as Hyppolite puts it, 'was only the *concept* of independent self-consciousness ... the slave was its actual realization'.[7] Similarly, the stoic is the withdrawal into thinking. The emptiness of the stoic is akin to the status of the master insofar as both are static, immobile, and vacuous. Just as everything the master desires must be fulfilled – 'I want this!' says the master – everything the stoic says is true – 'I am I', says the stoic. And just as there is nothing against which the master can measure his desire, there is nothing against which the stoic can

---

5 David Levering Lewis, *W.E.B. Du Bois: A Biography* (New York: Henry Holt and Company, 2009), 395–6; W.E.B. Du Bois, *Dusk of Dawn*, in *Writings: The Suppression of the African Slave-Trade, The Souls of Black Folk, Dusk of Dawn, Essays*, ed. Nathan Huggins (New York: Library of America, 1987), 551.
6 Du Bois, *Dusk of Dawn*, in *Writings*, 551.
7 Hyppolite, *Structure and Genesis*, 184; emphasis added.

verify his truth. A desire that meets no resistance is as unsatisfying as a trivial truth. By contrast, just as the slave is in actuality what the master is in concept, the sceptic is the actuality of what stoicism is in idea. The abstractness of the merely conceptual 'I' in stoicism produces a separation between two sides – the *form* of thought and the *content* of lived experience – that are only superficially related. Since stoic liberty is merely the thought of liberty, it is impotent and ineffectual. In short, stoicism is the *idea* of the freedom of self-consciousness, and scepticism is the *work* of the freedom of self-consciousness – just as the master is independence in concept, and the slave is independence at work.

While stoicism determines, in thought alone, that the world beyond its control is meaningless, the sceptic does the work of stripping the world of meaning. As the sceptic undertakes the labour of negating the worldly particulars it encounters, it brings its own self-consciousness into the actual world. Scepticism is the actual experience of freedom, while stoicism was the merely the concept of freedom. This is considered *work* because the sceptic does not negate the whole world simultaneously but instead performs the laborious process of negating every particular thing. Put differently, the stoic rejects all particulars at once; the sceptic negates each particular in turn. Through scepticism, the infinite nature of stoic subjectivity connects to finite determinations. Scepticism is the actual connection of infinity and finitude.

This emphasis on the sceptic's work shows us that Hegel is thinking less of the modern type of scepticism (e.g. that of Descartes or Hume), where the whole of metaphysics is rejected, and more of the deliberate and focused scepticism of the ancient world, such as we see in Pyrrho or Sextus Empiricus. The latter, for example, details the precise, often tedious, steps he takes in order to refute every argument he encountered. By going through these argumentative moves with such laborious precision Sextus shows that he cannot simply reject the world in general; instead, every particular must be negated in its specific particularity. In order to negate each determinate thing, the sceptic follows a distinct path, as Sextus explains: 'Scepticism is an ability to set out opposition among things which appear and are thought of in any way at all, an ability by which, because of the equipollence in the opposed objects and accounts, we come first to suspension of judgment and afterwards to tranquillity.'[8] Scepticism demonstrates, through various argumentative modes, that for each and every claim, belief, position, or determination, there is also an equally valid and opposed claim, belief, position, determination, etc. With the oppositions established and the justifications for each rendered equally convincing, *equipollency* is achieved. The plausibility of the original claim is thereby annihilated. More simply, for any argument offered in support of a proposition P, there is a conflicting argument (with the conclusion: $\sim P$) that is equally convincing. Whatever question one may ask, there is always a problem. As we will soon see, Du Bois, sceptic that he is, shows that to be Black is to be a problem.

The Sceptic's Experience of Freedom

Sceptical work, however, does not change the world but merely changes our relationship to it. In order to 'annihilate [*vernichtenden*] … the being of the world in all its manifold determinateness', in order to make the otherness of the world 'vanish', the sceptic learns that worldly things are only 'others' *for it* (PS 202, 204). Hegel's stoic mistakenly thinks that the world that he rejects outright is completely separate from him, which is what allows the world to be judged meaningless. Put differently, the stoic judgment that only what is subject to its will is under its control presupposes that what is not subject to its will or out of its control is completely independent of stoic self-consciousness.

The sceptic, however, recognises that it is itself the source of the world; the meaning of the world comes from the sceptic's relationship to it. Each particular thing can only be negated because the meaning of each particular comes from the subject. Every epistemic and evaluative distinction is relative to cognition. The world has no value independently of the sceptical subject.

---

8   Sextus Empiricus, *Outlines of Scepticism*, ed. Julia Annas and Jonathan Barnes (Cambridge: Cambridge University Press, 2009), I.iv.

While the stoic negates the world, guilt-free, in one fell swoop, the sceptic tracks down the genealogies of the particulars in order to annihilate them at their source. The stoic thinks he has killed the weed because he has pulled the leaves; but since he has left the taproot, it comes right back. The sceptic, however, follows the weed to its source in order to do the dirty work of destroying the root itself. The trick is: the source is *consciousness itself*. To negate the world the sceptic follows a belief or opinion back to its source in the mind. The sceptical negation thus includes the particular thing *and* the subject's relationship to it. 'What scepticism causes to vanish', writes Hegel, 'is not only objective reality as such, but *its own relationship to it*, in which the "other" is held to be objective and is established as such … and the truth it has itself determined and established' (PS 205; emphasis added). Scepticism actualises its freedom by demonstrating that the determinacy of each thing comes from the mind of the sceptic, and thus it has no independent determinacy.

There is little doubt that Du Bois' own formulations were inspired, in part, by Hegel's dialectical thinking. Du Bois advocates the work of negating concrete worldly particulars rather than a general rejection in light of the ideal. In fact, it was the various and variable particular reasonings – evolutionary, biological, geographical, cultural, historical, etc. – offered for the supposed inferiority of Black folk that first awakened Du Bois, during his education, to the contradictions in racism. 'I was skeptical about brain weight', he writes, 'I was not sure about physical measurements and social inquires … I lived to see every assumption of [Frederick K.] Hoffman's *Race Traits and Tendencies* contradicted; but even before that I doubted the statistical method' until 'I was in outright revolt' against all forms of racist proofs and arguments.[9]

Du Bois would eventually develop the process of negating each particular on its own as central to his sociological method. From his early *The Suppression of the African Slave-Trade to the United States of America, 1638–1870*, through his city-focused analyses such as *The Philadelphia Negro* and his 'study of a Black Belt

---

9   Du Bois, *Dusk of Dawn*, in *Writings*, 626.

Community ... Lowndes County, Alabama', to the later, more global studies such as the aborted *Encyclopedia of the Negro* and *The World and Africa, an Inquiry into the Part Which Africa Has Played in World History*, Du Bois undertook careful and systematic scientific studies of particular concrete cases in which 'the complete Negro problem' appeared, first in the United States and later globally.[10] He painstakingly employed scientific models, tables, charts, diagrams, interviews, reports, etc., to organise data in order to account for each and every particular.

The meaning of progress for Du Bois is not measured simply by the ideal, because the ideal alone will not save Black people. The path to freedom remains a real question: 'How shall man measure progress?' he asks (SBF 58). Du Boisian scepticism openly confronts, in all its material complexities, 'the sudden transformation of a fair far-off ideal of Freedom into the hard reality of bread-winning and the consequent deification of Bread' (SBF 63).

Through the work of negating the world, particular-by-particular, the allegedly independent world reveals its dependence on self-consciousness. As the world slowly vanishes before the sceptic's eyes, it 'generates the experience of that freedom' that was previously only the thought of freedom (PS 204). As they pursue the work of negating each particular thing, the sceptic acquires a sense of independence, similar to how the slave began to discern its independence by working on the world and shaping it according to its will. The world is *for us*, not *in itself*. 'The sceptical self-consciousness', writes Hegel, 'thus experiences in the flux [*der Wandel*] of all that would stand secure before it its own freedom as given and preserved by itself' (PS 205). This experience of freedom entails the sense of self-certainty. Scepticism discovers, Hyppolite writes, 'the self-certainty obtained through the annihilation of all the determinations of existence; it is the exploration in depth of subjectivity'.[11] Thrown into the world through the need to negate all particulars, the sceptic earns the

---

10 Ibid., 597.
11 Hyppolite, *Structure and Genesis*, 187.

certainty of itself as an independent thing as the fruit of its labours. This hard-won certainty, however, is unstable.

Caught between competing claims, the sceptic realises itself as an unstable entity, in what Hegel calls '*absolute dialectical unrest* [Unruhe]', insofar as it forces together two incompatible and contradictory states without resolution (PS 205). On the one hand, the sceptic is bound up with the merely contingent, unessential twisting and turning of the empirical world. On the other hand, the sceptic 'converts itself again into a consciousness that is universal and self-identical; for it is the negativity of all singularity and all difference' (PS 205). Insofar as the sceptic needs the world to be there to negate it, the sceptic is both the self-certainty it achieves through negating the contingent particulars in the world and yet is dependent on those same contingent particulars. 'At one time', Hegel writes:

> it recognizes that its freedom lies in rising above all the confusion and contingency of existence, and at another time equally admits to a relapse into occupying itself with what is unessential. It lets the unessential content in its thinking vanish; but just in doing so it is the consciousness of something unessential. It pronounces an absolute vanishing, but the pronouncement *is*, and this consciousness is the vanishing that is pronounced. (PS 205)[12]

Scepticism here invokes the problem of consumption. The sceptic shows the meaninglessness of the worldly object by consuming it; yet this very consumption is unsatisfying because the desire to consume it ever returns. The desire for the object was dependent on it in order to consume it. Similarly, scepticism cannot deny (consume) the givenness of the world except by taking the world as given and then denying that givenness. Scepticism is thus the continual movement between the object, the negation of that object, and then the negation of the negation

---

12 As Hyppolite puts it, 'By lowering himself he rises, but as soon as he rises and claims to reach that immutable certainty he descends anew. His immutable certainty is in contact with ephemeral life and the eternity of his thought is a temporal thought of the eternal.' Ibid., 188.

of the object, which is the object's return. The sceptic must thus separate itself into two selves insofar as it 'does not itself bring these two thoughts of itself together' (PS 205). Hyppolite claims that scepticism thus entails the 'double feeling of its nothingness and its grandeur'.[13]

This is the trick of scepticism: though it is an unstable, restless, and contradictory form of self-consciousness, it is not only aware of this but also 'itself maintains and creates this restless confusion [*bewegende Verwirrung*]' (PS 205). The sceptic does not try to resolve the tensions but finds stability in its very instability. This is precisely the structure of sceptical subjectivity. The task of the sceptic is to not to resolve equipollency among conflicting appearances but to remain right there, amid the tension and instability. Because of equipollency, because two equally convincing arguments stand before it, the sceptic must suspend judgment (*epochê*). It neither confirms nor denies, 'neither reject[s] nor posit[s] anything'.[14] Unable to decide, it suspends and is suspended. This suspension of judgment, which Sextus calls 'a standstill of the intellect', entails tranquillity (*ataraxia*), understood as 'a freedom from disturbance or calmness of soul'.[15] The sceptical self is a divided self, and the sceptic delights in this very dividedness. While the dialectical movement was unknown to the master, the slave, and the stoic, it is now the very being and activity of the sceptic.

Warring Ideals

What Hegel describes as the 'doubly contradictory consciousness [*gedoppelte widersprechende Bewußtein*]' (PS 205) of the sceptic, Du Bois calls 'double consciousness' (SBF 7).[16] But it would be rash to read these two labels as direct parallels.[17] There are resonances,

---

13 Ibid., 187.
14 Sextus, *Outlines*, I.iv.
15 Ibid.
16 To emphasise its active nature, Ibram X. Kendi calls it 'dueling consciousness'. Ibram X. Kendi, *How to Be an Antiracist* (New York: One World, 2019), 24.
17 Elvira Basevich is especially good in her elegant reading of the ways in which

to be sure, and Du Bois' disposition maps quite well on to that of Hegel's sceptic. But, precisely where one sees resonances, Hegel makes a claim – albeit an apparently throwaway one – that throws the harmonic resonances between his thought and Du Bois' into its own kind of dialectical unrest.

For Hegel, the sceptic is thoughtless – or at least confused: the wavering, the instability, in which the sceptic takes delight turns out to be little more than the rambling of someone unable to think clearly:

> This consciousness is therefore the unconscious, thoughtless rambling [*bewußtlose Faselei*] which passes back and forth from the one extreme of self-identical self-consciousness to the other extreme of the contingent consciousness that is both bewildered and bewildering [*verworren und verwirrenden*] … It affirms the nullity of seeing, hearing, etc., yet it is itself seeing, hearing, etc. It affirms the nullity of ethical principles, and lets its conduct be governed by these very principles. (PS 205)

For all of the movement that Hegel's sceptic inaugurates, for all of the clarity that comes from dispelling the sterile and ultimately ineffectual abstraction of the stoic, Hegel's sceptic cannot properly think. The split is too much; the doubleness ends up looking like that of small children who have just learned the word 'no': 'Its talk is in fact like the squabbling of self-willed children, one of whom says *A* if the other says *B*, and in turn says *B* if the other says *A*, and who by contradicting *themselves* buy for themselves the pleasure of continually contradicting *one another*' (PS 205). Hegel's sceptic, then, is not just confused; it is immature, childish in its disposition, contradicting for the sake of contradiction itself.

We know why Hegel says this. He recognises that the sceptic is, like all the phases of the dialectic, a moment in the development of consciousness. And yet, it is precisely with this last treatment of scepticism (Hegel devotes only two more paragraphs to scepticism in the *Phenomenology*) that Hegel and Du Bois part ways.

Du Bois elaborates, appropriates, and critiques central Hegelian notions. See Elvira Basevich, *W.E.B. Du Bois: The Lost and the Found* (Cambridge: Polity Press, 2021).

Du Bois was a lot of things, but confused and immature he was not. If he took 'delight' in the dialectical unrest of living (and dying) as Black in the United States, that delight came from the knowledge he had acquired in diagnosing *the United States itself* in terms of the antiblack violence it enacted and enacts. Du Bois' 'no' wasn't just a 'no for no's sake'. His enactment of negation had existential weight. It came from a mature and thoughtful reflection on the plight of Black folk who had suffered under the weight of slavery and its legacies.

We call this mature because Du Bois knew *why* he was saying no. More to the point, his 'no', his enactment of the negation of the particular, preserved the possibility that the very thing that caused him and his people violence could also be a site of profound generativity. 'This, then', Du Bois writes, 'is the end of [the Negro's] striving: to be a co-worker in the kingdom of culture, to escape both death and isolation, to husband and use his [*sic*] best powers and latent genius' (SBF 9).

The doubleness to which Du Bois points is therefore *not* confused or immature. To put it differently, the very confusion Hegel derides in the sceptic is precisely the portal, the pathway, the opening to a greater sense of clarity about the state of affairs. Yes, the Black soul 'ever feels his twoness, – an American, a Negro' (SBF 7), but at the same time, Black people know that they are compelled to be both at once – even as there is an unresolved tension between the two ideals – *because their existence as a problem throws the possibility of resolution into default.*

Since being Black is being non-white, and being American apparently entails whiteness, the Black soul must manage the impossible: the compulsion to be white and yet remain Black, to become American, even as they know they are non-American (African). The Black soul thus strives 'to merge his double self' and in 'this merging he wishes neither of the older selves to be lost' (SBF 7). This unstable merging does not 'Africanise America' and neither does it 'bleach his Negro soul in a flood of white Americanism' (SBF 7). Hence the logic of double consciousness is: '*neither and both*' (SBF 67; emphasis added). Du Bois is *neither* simply American *nor* African, *and* yet he is *both* African *and* American.

This 'longing to attain self-conscious manhood' is a longing to make the impossible possible, 'to make it possible for a man to be both a Negro and an American without being cursed and spit upon by his fellows, without having the doors of Opportunity closed roughly in his face' (SBF 7). He cannot just be white because he is Black, yet his very Blackness is dependent on whiteness for its determination as Black. This internal contradiction splits Blackness in two, which is why the Black soul is structured like the sceptic: 'In scepticism', writes Hegel, 'consciousness truly experiences itself as internally contradictory [*in sich widersprechendes Bewußtein*]' (PS 206). Du Bois puts it thus:

> What, after all, am I? Am I an American or am I a Negro? Can I be both? Or is it my duty to cease to be a Negro as soon as possible and be an American? If I strive as a Negro, am I not perpetuating the very cleft that threatens and separates Black and White America? Is not my only possible practical aim the subduction of all that is Negro in me to the American?[18]

Thus a Black soul is cut into '*two* souls, *two* thoughts, *two* unreconciled strivings, *two* warring ideals *in one dark body*, whose dogged strength alone keeps it from being torn asunder' (SBF 7; emphases added). In the Black soul, like in the sceptic, 'the duplication which formerly was divided between two individuals, the lord and the bondsman, is now lodged in one' (PS 206).

Scepticism is the first explicit acknowledgement of the divided character of the self, that it is both dependent and independent, both changeable and unchangeable, sensuous and intellectual. It is not wrong to think of Kant's subject as an unstable combination of transcendental and empirical egos. The problem is that the two parts that I am are not structured and ordered, but are 'a purely casual, confused medley, the dizziness of a perpetually self-engendered disorder' (later, the unhappy consciousness will bring order to the sceptic's chaos) (PS 205). As with all hyphenated identities, the two parts of the sceptic's self are determined and

---

18 W.E.B. Du Bois, 'The Conservation of Races', in *Writings*, 821.

affirmed, but not reconciled. Since there is no reason to affirm any particular determinacy (given equipollency), scepticism allows all determinations to run free. The sceptic 'keeps the poles of this its self-contradiction apart, and adopts the same attitude to it as it does in its purely negative activity in general' (PS 205). Whatever one puts forward, the sceptic says the opposite. If one claims P, the sceptic claims $\sim P$; if one claims $\sim P$, the sceptic claims P.

There is no possibility of resolution here. Hence 'the Black man's turn[ing] hither and thither in hesitant and doubtful striving', without a clear path to success and respect (SBF 8). Similarly, the sceptic 'passes back and forth from the one extreme of self-identical self-consciousness to the other extreme of the contingent consciousness that is both bewildered and bewildering' (PS 205). Yet what appears to be a fault of the Black soul, this turning hither and thither, is really the 'waste of *double aims*, this seeking to satisfy *two unreconciled ideals*' (SBF 8; emphases added).

The transition from the slave to the stoic, from Douglass to Washington, was marked by the emergence of ideals toward which the stoic aimed. At the same time, though the ideal of America was cast as an 'homage to civilization, culture, righteousness, and progress', it was, in actuality, used to render the Black soul that aimed for it 'helpless, dismayed, and well-nigh speechless' (SBF 11). Despite the purity of Washington's vision, despite his stoic intentions, his ideal was white. Though 'free', Black Americans felt 'the stain of bastardy, which two centuries of systematic defilement of Negro women had stamped upon [their] race' (SBF 11). Though 'free', their Black 'voting is vain' (SBF 11). Though 'free', Black education is wasted. Though 'free', the ideal was all but accessible to Black souls. All of this was intentional and structural, and marked the fall of the stoic ideals. As Du Bois writes: 'the bright ideals of the past ... all these in turn have waxed and waned, until even the last grows dim and overcast' (SBF 12). Du Bois is not saying these ideals are wrong, for a sceptic would not fall prey to the simple trick of assuming the opposite. Instead, he is simply showing that 'each alone is over-simple and incomplete' (SBF 12). To fail to recognise this incompleteness and one-sidedness, the implicit whiteness of the ideal, risks what Du Bois calls 'a second slavery' (SBF 12). To stave off 're-enslavement', scepticism was necessary (SBF 23).

Here we see the essential difference between Washington's and Du Bois' respective accounts of ideals.[19] Washington's stoic ideals belong to an *idealised* world; Du Bois' account responds to the concrete context of the American South. We see this when Du Bois sets out to 'study the condition of the Negro to-day honestly and carefully' by 'turn[ing] our faces to the Black Belt of Georgia and seek[ing] simply to know the condition of the Black farm-laborers of one county there' (SBF 104–5). This is why Du Bois rejects Washington's deferral of progress and quieting of strivings for equality, which he instead demands immediately. Political, economic, and educational advancement are inseparable from the raising of Black souls to equal status. Though they conflict, the ideal of the American and that of the African rise and fall together. The problem of the colour-line is the problem of the entirety of the United States of America. The colour-line creates 'two separate worlds' that are oriented by two opposing ideals (SBF 75). This 'separation is so thorough and deep' that no part of the nation is left whole, even though it appears as whole to the white world on the one side of what Du Bois calls *the Veil*. As we will see below, the Veil cuts through 'the higher realms of social intercourse … in church and school, on railway and street-car, in hotels and theatres, in streets and city sections, in books and newspapers, in asylums and jails, in hospitals and graveyards' (SBF 75).

In the eyes of a sceptic, Washingtonian stoicism fails because its ideals are unstable. This instability comes from the unacknowledged logic of stoic idealism: ideals compete. Since they are created *by* humans, since they are *for* humans, they reflect the humans who create them. If the humans who create them are raced, then the ideals too have a race. In short, the mark of the

---

19 Shortly after receiving a job offer to be the 'chair of classics' at Wilberforce University, Ohio, Du Bois received a terse job offer from Booker T. Washington to teach mathematics at Tuskegee. Reflecting on the various possibilities for his life trajectory, Du Bois said, 'It would be interesting to speculate just what would have happened, if I had accepted the last offer of Tuskegee instead of that of Wilberforce.' Du Bois, *Writings*, 589.

creators transfers to their creations. Caught between two ideals, souls that aim at both are made to feel 'ashamed of themselves' (SBF 8). Like the soul of the sceptic, the unreconciled and unstable nature of competing ideals reflects and substantiates the unreconciled and unstable nature of the Black soul. '[S]eeking to satisfy two unreconciled ideals', 'often wooing false gods and invoking false means of salvation', writes Du Bois, 'has wrought sad havoc' on the lives of Black Americans (SBF 8). His description is clear:

> From the double life that every American Negro must live, as a Negro and as an American, as swept on by the current of the nineteenth while yet struggling in the eddies of the fifteenth century – from this must arise a painful self-consciousness, an almost morbid sense of personality and a moral hesitancy which is fatal to self-confidence. (SBF 151)

The Black soul, whose being is divided, is a single thing split in two. A complete existential doubleness: 'a *double* life, with *double* thoughts, *double* duties, and *double* social classes, [which] must give rise to *double* words and *double* ideals' (SBF 151; emphases added). Such a double life catches Black souls in a 'peculiar ethical paradox', though there is power in this paradox (SBF 151).[20] Rather than ignore or conceal the paradox of the Black soul, Du Boisian scepticism asks: 'Why not then flatly face the paradox?'[21]

Stoicism's Triple Paradox

Du Boisian scepticism begins where Wells left off – by locating the failure of Washington's ideal. Washington's faith in the capacity of the free Black population, once educated as stoics, to win over the

---

20 We find a seed of Du Bois' concept of double consciousness in his essay 'Conservation of the Races'.
21 Du Bois, 'Sociology Hesitant', *boundary 2* 27:3 (2000), 42. To be fair, while Du Bois is here talking about the paradox that arises in sociological theories from the tension between the law-like nature of human action and the 'evident incalculability in human action', his strategy in debates about sociological methodology extends to his larger strategy beyond the discipline of sociology.

hearts and souls of white people should have withered when faced with the concrete particularities of the post-slavery South. This was a South, we should remember, that had no qualms producing strange fruit on those poplar trees. No matter how hard they might work, how high they might aim, or how close to the ideal they might think they were, that ideal was not for Black souls. Wells may have had a stoic commitment to writing about lynching, but it is her prophetic criticism of the practice that most anticipated Du Bois' scepticism.

Consider, for example, Wells' words that we heard in the last chapter: the 'Southerner had never gotten over his resentment that the Negro was no longer his plaything, his servant, and his source of income'. Now hear this resonate in Du Bois: 'There was scarcely a white man in the South', he writes, 'who did not honestly regard Emancipation as a crime, and its practical nullification as a duty' (SBF 32). Wells may not have overtly expressed the dividedness of a sceptic's consciousness, but she *did* negate Washington's own brand of naive idealism. While a different political-social-economic situation might have perhaps allowed Washington's ideals to amend the evils of chattel slavery, Wells understood that the lack of real change in the overall structure of the nation after the war solved nothing. It was Wells' critique of stoic ideals that led to the sublation of stoicism and the emergence of scepticism.

Beginning with Wells' recognition, Du Bois developed her insight into scepticism. While Wells critiqued Washington for his sycophantic performances in front of whites, Du Bois carried this critique to Washington's work as a whole: 'Mr. Washington', Du Bois wrote, 'represents in Negro thought the old attitude of adjustment and submission', though now with an 'economic cast, becoming a Gospel of Work and Money' (SBF 40). Du Bois argues that, with its total faith in the promise of the ideal, 'Mr. Washington's programme practically accepts the alleged inferiority of the Negro races' and so quiets, if not silences, demands for equality (SBF 40). Despite the effects of centuries of chattel slavery, Washington's unwavering belief in the Gospel of Work and Money led him to conclude that equality itself must be earned rather than gifted. For Du Bois, Washingtonian stoicism was 'a policy of submission' insofar as it asked Black folk to relinquish, at least temporarily, three things: 1) political power; 2) insistence on civil rights; and 3) higher education of Negro youth (SBF 40, 41).

Du Bois therefore reveals in Washington's stoic programme a 'triple paradox' (SBF 41). First, though Washington preaches industry, capitalist competition prevents working people from defending their rights without suffrage. Second, though Washington 'insists on thrift and self-respect ... silent submission to civic inferiority' shrinks the sense of self until there is basically nothing left to respect (SBF 42). Third, though Washington promotes technical and vocational training above 'institutions of higher learning', the very existence of schools such as Tuskegee depends on teachers who are trained in universities and revered centres of scholarship (SBF 42). Since 'Southern whites would not teach' Black students, and 'Northern whites in sufficient numbers could not be had, it was left to the Black population to train Black teachers to teach Black students' (SBF 75). Hence there must first be colleges to train 'teachers of teachers', because trying 'to establish any sort of a system of common and industrial school training, without *first* (and I say *first* advisedly) without *first* providing for the higher training of the very best teachers, is simply throwing your money to the winds'.[22] Without such higher institutions of learning, Tuskegee would have been impossible. Thus, Du Bois points out, the 'demand for college-bred men by a school like Tuskegee, out to make Mr. Booker T. Washington the firmest friend of higher training'.[23]

To the triple paradox of Washington's stoicism, Du Bois sees two responses, which we can call cynical and sceptical. First, the cynical response. Stemming from the revolutions of Toussaint and Nat Turner, some find 'the Negro's only hope in emigration beyond the borders of the United States' (SBF 42). This 'attitude of revolt and revenge' completely rejects whiteness and all white people (SBF 42). Second, the sceptical response assumes a quieter

---

22 Du Bois, 'The Talented Tenth', in *Writings*, 852, 854.
23 Ibid., 860.

attitude, one rooted in 'conscience' rather than 'a general discharge of venom' (SBF 42). It asks America for three things: '1. The right to vote. 2. Civic equality. 3. The education of youth according to ability' (SBF 42). While sceptics do not excuse Black folk completely, and shun 'pampering', they seek the reduction of the barbarism of deep-seated racism (SBF 43). In addition to Washington's call for the construction of vocational training schools, they demand universities and colleges for Black students that are equal to and 'in close connection and co-operation with Harvard, Columbia, Johns Hopkins, and the University of Pennsylvania'.[24]

Contrary to Washington, Du Bois claimed that 'from Academus to Cambridge, the culture of the University has been the broad foundation-stone' for the education of both white and Black folk (SBF 65). While recognising the stoic ideals Washington set up high in the sky, the sceptics argue that the path toward them cannot succeed by willingly relinquishing claims to the same rights and opportunities afforded to white folk. Without well-educated and well-prepared leaders, the 'Negro would have to accept white leadership', for the 'function of the college-bred Negro ... [is that of] the man who sets the ideals of the community where he lives, directs its thoughts and heads its social movements'.[25] University is where Black students learn how to create ideals that are appropriate to Black communities as well as so-called universal ideals.

Rejecting Washington's stoic submissiveness, sceptics see that 'it is the duty of Black men to judge the South discriminatingly' (SBF 44). Neither outright rejection nor smiling approval of the Reconstruction Period are justified. Open-eyed scepticism is the only cure for a nation lost and broken. 'Discriminating and broad-minded criticism is what the South needs', for the souls of Black folk and white folk alike (SBF 45). Importantly, the burden of this problem belongs not on 'the Negro's shoulders', as Washington claimed; instead, it 'belongs to the nation' as a whole. America will not be healed by 'plastering it with gold ... by diplomacy and suaveness, by "policy" alone'; the sceptics' 'candid and honest

---

24 Du Bois, *Dusk of Dawn*, in *Writings*, 599.
25 Ibid., 604; Du Bois, 'The Talented Tenth', in *Writings*, 851.

criticism' is needed (SBF 45). The stoic's general rejection of the whole situation does nothing but leave the world exactly as it is; only the work of the sceptic, negating each particular wrong one-by-one, will address the concrete context composing the nation.

It is not that the sceptic rejects the stoic outright, for the sceptic does not simply abandon all ideals.[26] Du Bois clearly states that 'to make men, we must have ideals', and he acknowledges 'the need of broad ideals and true culture' (SBF 67, 66). Like the stoic, the sceptic proclaims the sway of Truth, Beauty, and Goodness (SBF 62, 63). The sceptical move is, first, to uncover the contradictions between these ideals, and, second, to reveal the divisions those contradictions create in Black souls. The 'danger is that these ideals, with their simple beauty and weird inspiration, will suddenly sink to a question of cash and a lust for gold' (SBF 63).[27] With this focus on ensuring that ideals are used properly, the debate between Washingtonian stoicism and Du Boisian scepticism is a matter of what constitutes proper education. It is not simply that Washington advocated for vocational schools and Du Bois for more scholarly and intellectual universities, since Du Bois highly valued both. 'Teach workers to work', he wrote, and '[t]each thinkers to think' (SBF 67). Which one is more important? 'Neither and both', for their shared goal was to 'develop men' (SBF 67, 83). 'These two theories of Negro progress', Du Bois emphasises, 'were not absolutely contradictory'.[28] While the

---

[26] In many other writings, Du Bois repeatedly emphasises the importance of ideals, but it is essential that such ideals 'be placed there by Black hands, fashioned by Black heads, and hallowed by the trail of 200,000,000 Black hearts beating in one glad song of jubilee'. Du Bois, 'The Conservation of Races', in *Writings*, 820.

[27] A different reading of the implication of the effect of competing ideals on the Black soul is what Du Bois considers the only 'patent defense' left to Black communities: 'the defense of deception and flattering, of cajoling and lying' (SBF 153). Stripped of physical, political, and economic defences, the only way to survive as a Black person was through prevarication and duplicity. Notice that here too the Black soul must be double, as the only way for a Black person to defend himself is to be two-faced, to engage in double-dealing and two-timing. To be accepted as American, Black people had to pay a fee, and the 'price of culture is a Lie' (SBF 153).

[28] Du Bois, *Dusk of Dawn*, in *Writings*, 605.

oneness of stoicism demands prioritisation of its ideal alone, the doubleness of scepticism insists on both.

We should note that 'beyond this difference of ideal', as Du Bois wrote, 'lay another more bitter and insistent controversy' with Washington.[29] It concerned what Du Bois calls the 'paradoxes' in 'Washington's undisputed leadership of the ten million Negroes in America'.[30] Echoing Wells' critique, Du Bois rejected Washington's 'decry of political activities among Negroes' – especially since 'Negro civil rights called for organized and aggressive defense' – as well as his advice of 'acquiescence or at least no open agitation'.[31] For Du Bois, this only allowed or enabled antiblack violence and racist exclusion, while also 'putting the chief onus for his condition upon the Negro himself'.[32] Given the near universal influence of what Du Bois called 'the Tuskegee Machine', Washingtonian stoicism concealed paradoxes that damaged, rather than encouraged, the progress of Black folk.[33] This was particularly damaging to Black Thought. Washington's grip on economic, political, social, and educational forces involving Black folk was so strong that, 'when any Negro complained or advocated a course of action', especially one that did not align with Washington's principles, 'he was silenced with the remark that Mr. Washington did not agree with this'.[34] Hence the 'young Black intelligentsia of the day declared, "I don't care a damn what Booker Washington thinks? This is what I think, and *I* have a right to think."'[35]

More than the difference in educational emphasis, it was this censorship of Black Thought that eventually led Du Bois to various processes, actions, and organisations intended 'to oppose firmly present methods of strangling honest criticism; to organise intelligent and honest Negroes; and to support organs of news and

---

29 Ibid.
30 Ibid., 606.
31 Ibid.
32 Ibid.
33 Ibid., 607. Du Bois later echoes this characterisation: 'Tuskegee became the capital of the Negro nation' (609).
34 Ibid., 685
35 Ibid., 609.

public opinion'.[36] Denouncing Washington's policies of accommodation and conciliation, as depicted in the Atlanta Compromise, Du Bois launched a series of organisations and publications such as the Niagara Movement, the National Association for the Advancement of Colored People (NAACP), *The Crisis*, etc.[37] Thus began a lifelong career of fighting, in his words, to secure 'every single right that belongs to a freeborn American, political, civil, and social; and until we get these rights we will never cease to protest and assail the ears of America ... lest [it] become in truth the land of the Thief and the home of the Slave'.[38] Through it all, though, Du Bois' clashes with Washington and other Black leaders were less ego-driven, and more the 'development of larger social forces beyond personal control', more 'the expression of social forces than of our minds'.[39] Hence Washingtonian stoicism and Du Boisian scepticism were names for larger forces in the whole dialectic of Black Thought.

Second-Sight and Afterthought

According to Du Bois, the Black soul, because it is double and divided, is 'gifted with a second-sight' (SBF 7). This sight is called 'second' for two reasons: first, because it begins as dependent on a primary sightedness, the vision of whiteness; second, because 'second-sight' is a metaphor for a kind of mystic seeing, a clairvoyant mode of perception, that allows one to see more than what others might perceive. In African American folk culture, children who are born with the placenta covering their face are considered to be gifted with psychic, if not prophetic, capacities.

---

36 Ibid., 618.
37 The Atlanta Compromise followed from a speech Washington gave to the Cotton States and International Exposition in Atlanta, Georgia, on 18 September 1895, in which he promoted what he saw as the keys to Black uplift – vocational training and practical trades rather than higher education or integration, and so on. For more, see Louis R. Harlan, *Booker T. Washington: The Wizard of Tuskegee, 1901–1915* (Oxford: Oxford University Press, 1986), 71–120.
38 Du Bois, *Dusk of Dawn*, in *Writings*, 619.
39 Ibid., 623.

At first sight, whiteness is prior to Blackness insofar as it is what problematises, in the etymological sense of *throwing-forth*, Blackness. Blackness comes second in 'a world', Du Bois writes, 'which yields [the Black soul] no true self-consciousness' (SBF 7). Independent self-consciousness appears to belong only to the first-sight of the white soul, and thus 'only lets [the Black soul] see himself through the revelation of the other world' (SBF 8). Hence a second meaning of the second-sight: the Black soul sees second insofar as it finds itself in a world already cloaked white. Every Black soul 'remember[s] well when the shadow swept across' it, when it discovered that it was 'shut out from [the white soul's] world by a *vast Veil*' (SBF 6; emphasis added). Without an opportunity for having a say, the 'shades of the prison-house closed round us all', Du Bois writes, rendering him 'an outcast and a stranger in mine own house' (SBF 6). Hence a third meaning of the second-sight: the 'sense of always looking at one's self through the eyes of others' (SBF 7). Not only does the Black soul find itself imprisoned in a world made by and for white souls, it must also see itself *through* the white gaze. The white world and the souls of the Black folk that are forced to live there are predetermined by white determinations. Black souls must see themselves as Black because that is what the white gaze compels them to do. The Black soul thus sees itself second, in a second-sight that does not allow for much self-evaluation or self-determination because it entails 'measuring one's soul by the tape of a [white] world that looks on in amused contempt and pity' (SBF 7).

All of this might suggest that second-sight is overdetermined by whiteness, by the supremacy of the white gaze. But this would be to misunderstand Du Bois here. While secondary or dependent according to the measure of the white world, the Black gaze, Du Bois writes, can still be seen as a gift. As noted above, Du Bois is not using the phrase 'second-sight' simply because of the philosophical order of operations it engenders; he is also showing that this form of seeing provides a more expansive – and therefore more powerful – perspective on the world. Second-sight is not an 'absence of power … it is not weakness', but 'the contradiction of double aims' (SBF 8). Alongside the capacity to see through two sets of eyes, there is a second-thought, an afterthought – a *nachdenken*, to use Hegel's cherished term.

Du Bois repeats this phrase on one page: 'behind the thought lurks the afterthought' (SBF 70). What produces this second-sight and 'brutal afterthought' is the 'Veil of Race' that obscures the vision (SBF 70, 61). The point is – and it is here that second-sight takes on its meaning as clairvoyance – that it is only possible to notice the obscurity created by the Veil from one side. To white eyes, the Veil is invisible.[40] To white eyes, there is just one ideal – American Freedom – and there is only one path toward this ideal. White eyes 'have never been able to see why the Negro ... [is] infected with a silly desire to rise in the world, and why their fathers were happy dumber, and faithful' (SBF 118). The reason is that the Veil winds so tightly through the entire structure of the South that 'there almost seems to be a conspiracy of silence' (SBF 136). Antiblack racism is one with the 'atmosphere of the land, the thought and feeling, the thousand and one little actions which go to make up life' (SBF 136).

Though the Veil is basically invisible to white eyes, if one 'lingers long enough there comes the awakening ... Slowly but surely his eyes begin to catch the shadow of the color-line' (SBF 136–7). Once seen, the Veil cannot be unseen. Silently, the Veil sets out separate paths: one for whites and one for Blacks. Along the path toward American ideals, Du Bois knows, 'all that makes life worth living – Liberty, Justice, and Right – is marked "For White People Only"' (SBF 154).[41] Yet from the white side of the Veil, this sign isn't visible; it doesn't even register to their cognition. 'We must not forget', Du Bois reminds us, 'that most Americans answer all queries regarding the Negro *a priori*', that is, before experiencing both sides of the Veil and the instability of the conflicting ideals (SBF 76–7).

---

[40] On the theme of invisibility as an opportunity to gesture toward other encounters between Black thinkers and Hegel, see Jack Taylor, 'Ralph Ellison as a Reader of Hegel: Ellison's Invisible Man as Literary Phenomenology', *Intertexts* 19:1 (2015): 135–54.

[41] See Liam Kofi Bright, 'Du Bois' Democratic Defense of the Value Free Ideal', *Synthese* 195:5 (2018): 2227–45.

The Souls of White Folk

While the Veil divides Black and white souls in every aspect of American life, only Black souls see both sides. Here the second-sight and afterthought of Black eyes and Black souls show us something white eyes cannot see and white souls cannot know about themselves. Hence Du Bois' claim that he was 'singularly clairvoyant' of white souls because he could 'see in and through them' (SBF 227). In a pre-emptive inversion of Ellison's *Invisible Man*, here white souls become translucent to Blacks.

While white souls are bound to the immediacy of a single consciousness, Du Bois' double consciousness allows him to 'view [white souls] from unusual vantage points', perspectives that white souls cannot see because of the structure of whiteness itself (SBF 227). As *neither and both* African and American, Du Bois is not foreign to white America but 'bone of their thought and flesh of their language', even though he is stuck on one side of the Veil (SBF 227). Cedric Robinson and (following him) Fred Moten call this the status of being an 'internal alien'; we call it *inner exclusion*.[42] Inner exclusion means being part American but *not* a part *of* America – a part yet apart. Such a perspective allows Du Bois to see the inner 'workings of their [the white souls'] entrails'.[43] 'I see', he writes, just an 'ugly human' (SBF 227).

Such a perspective embarrasses white folk, and they resent those who see such things. Black souls have witnessed white people intimately, when they are most vulnerable and cruel, and this humiliates them. When Black souls point out the Veil, when they reflect back to white folk their whiteness, their words sound, to white ears, full of 'bitterness' and 'pessimism' (SBF 227).

---

42 Cedric J. Robinson, *Black Marxism: The Making of the Black Radical Tradition* (Chapel Hill: University of North Carolina Press, 2000), 182; Moten, *Stolen Life*, 135. Ernesto Laclau and Chantel Mouffe's theorisation of a 'constitutive outside' resonates with this paradoxical locality. See Laclau and Mouffe, *Hegemony and Socialist Strategy* (London: Verso, 1985) for the origin of this concept.

43 When describing the emergence of Black American religion, Du Bois echoes this point: Black Americans are 'sharing, although imperfectly, the soul-life of that nation' (SBF 151).

Yet despite the best efforts of white souls, whiteness cannot be unseen. The more they try to silence Black perspectives to hide their shame, the clearer it becomes.

Such clarity affords a kind of stance that, while it may not practically change the world as such, allows one to diagnose its violence with incisive sharpness. From beyond the Veil, white people are, in fact, 'ugly humans', as those born behind the Veil know so well. They also know and recognise the feeble and limited attempts by the white world to hide this ugliness. They recognise the violence of a white(ned) God, of a white(ned) heaven. After a while, those behind the Veil see the farce of industriousness, recognising the absolute falsity in the admonition to work hard 'in your lowly sphere, praying the good Lord that into heaven above … you may, one day, be born – white!' With this, both human and divine decrees are made to agree that 'whiteness is the ownership of the earth forever and ever, Amen!' (SBF 228). Having painted the world white from top to bottom, success, in this world and the next, equals white success. Hence 'every great soul … every great thought … every great deed … every great dream' was bleached (SBF 253). A mockery of Washingtonian stoicism if there ever was one.

Those behind the Veil know it is all a lie. They recognise the falsity of this claim; they feel the violence of this 'bleaching' of the world. And yet, lie though it may be, the world still functions this way, encouraging – demanding – that the colour-line not only be reinforced, but that Black people be called upon to do the impossible: to be incorporated into a world that can only look upon them with 'amused contempt and pity'. As Du Bois repeats, the problem of the colour-line is an enduring one. At the same time, even as it endures, so does the clairvoyant perception of second-sight afforded to those beyond the Veil.

In a 2003 interview with Frank Wilderson, Saidiya Hartman extends Du Boisian scepticism by discussing the problematics of freedom. Putting her own gift of second-sight and second-thought to work, Hartman tells Wilderson that slaves (and we will add, their afterlives) occupy 'the position of the unthought'. She puts it this way:

> On one hand, the slave is the foundation of the national order, and, on the other, the slave occupies the position of the unthought ... So much of our political vocabulary/imaginary/desires have been *implicitly integrationist* even when we imagine our claims are more radical ... ultimately the metanarrative thrust is always towards an integration into the national project, and particularly when that project is in crisis, *Black people are called upon to affirm it*.[44]

To feel one's twoness, to be a sceptic in the way Du Bois was, is not simply to see the dividedness of oneself. It also allows one to see *through* the ruse of national myths of freedom and liberty, and to be made acutely aware that one's role in the world is to *affirm* the myths when crises arise. It is to see from the position of the unthought. What Du Bois offers, by way of Hartman, is a sceptical awareness of the *necessity of the Black person*.

If the slave recognises their necessity in their struggle with the master, then the Black sceptic recognises how necessary their existence is to the maintenance of the world. When we discussed Hegelian scepticism earlier, we noted that the sceptic perceives that the independent world is dependent on the sceptic's self-consciousness. Read through Hartman, Du Bois' sceptical double-consciousness affords the insight that the world – even the white one – is dependent upon *Black* life. This, in turn, announces the absolute necessity of Black people to the construction and maintenance of the world within which they find themselves, even as they are framed and treated as objects of subjugation. No Negro, no world, so the saying goes.

Hartman does more than extend Du Bois' sceptical reflections. In her work, and other Black feminist works, we find a third dimension of dependence, one that operates within and beyond Black life.[45] This is the social-ontological dependence of Black life on what Hortense Spillers might call 'ungendered female flesh'. Spillers puts it this way:

---

44 Saidiya Hartman and Frank Wilderson, 'The Position of the Unthought', *Qui Parle* 13:2 (2003): 184–5; emphases added.
45 For more of Hartman's critique of Du Bois, see the chapter 'An Atlas of the Wayward' in her *Wayward Lives, Beautiful Experiments: Intimate Stories of Upheaval* (New York: W.W. Norton, 2019).

the African female subject ... is not only the target of rape – in one sense, an interiorized violation of body and mind – but also the topic of specifically *externalized* acts of torture and prostration that we imagine as the peculiar province of *male* brutality and torture inflicted by other males. A female body strung from a tree limb, or bleeding from the breast on any given day of field work because the 'overseer', standing the length of a whip, has popped her flesh open, adds a lexical and living dimension to the narratives of women in culture and society.[46]

'This materialized scene', continues Spillers, 'of unprotected female flesh – of female flesh "ungendered" – offers a praxis and a theory, a text for living and for dying, and a method for reading both through their diverse mediations'.[47] What Spillers and other Black feminists point out is a 'no' to even the sceptic's habit of no-saying. This move pushes the phenomenology of Black spirit forward, but in unanticipated, more complex ways.

What emerges on the other end of this Black feminist double negation is, yes, an affirmation of *something*, but the meaning of this something is – in perhaps an even more sceptical affirmation than that of Du Bois – simultaneously determinate and indeterminate: Black female flesh is indeed *female*, but it is also *ungendered*. It is precisely in ungendered female flesh that someone like Spillers finds a kind of a sceptic freedom. Because the Black female is ungendered, she calls the very 'matrix' of gender into question. It is precisely this calling into question – this negation of the *logic* of gender – that opens out onto new 'insurgent ground'.

> This problematizing of gender places her, in my view, *out* of the traditional symbolics of female gender, and it is our task to make a place for this different social subject. In doing so, we are less interested in joining the ranks of gendered femaleness than gaining the *insurgent* ground as female social subject.[48]

Perhaps most importantly, this insurgent ground is not simply available for Black women. The freedom Spillers announces and

---

46 Spillers, 'Mama's Baby', 68.
47 Ibid.
48 Ibid., 80.

anoints through ungendered female flesh is also a possibility for freedom for Black males. 'It is the heritage of the *mother*', Spillers writes, 'that the African-American male must regain as an aspect of his own personhood – the power of "yes" to the "female" within.'[49]

We are turning to Hartman and Spillers here in order to transition from Du Bois' masculine scepticism to Anna Julia Cooper's Black feminist scepticism. This transition can be articulated by leaning into a classic sceptical term: *if*.

If Du Bois inaugurates and develops a disposition of Black scepticism in the phenomenology of Black spirit; *if* he announces an unsettled double consciousness at the heart of the souls of Black folk; *if* he announces a 'cut' in the consciousness of Blackness, then Black feminists like Spillers announce a *cut of the cut*, an originary unsettling of Black life not merely at the level of race, but also at the level of *gender*. *If* Du Bois' double consciousness produced a clairvoyant mode of perception that allowed him to see white folks in ways they could never see themselves, then thinkers like Spillers and Hartman develop an even more clairvoyant mode of perception that sets in sharp relief the manifold modalities of violence that an antiblack world – especially one like that of the United States – enacts. Our point is that we must not simply listen to anyone who is behind the Veil. We must listen, above all, to those who have experienced the Veil and its legacies in deeper, even more complicated cuts: Black women.

While Hartman and Spillers provide contemporary intellectual and historical analyses of the cut of the cut, they are prefigured by another Black woman – one who was Du Bois' contemporary, and who knew, long ago, that we must start with Black women.

The Cut of the Cut: Cooper's Radical Tripartite Scepticism

Du Bois located a single cleavage in the Black soul. Perhaps partially due to his masculinity (if not misogyny), he sometimes overlooked the other divisions in his soul.[50] Anna Julia Cooper,

---

49 Ibid.
50 To be fair, Du Bois does gesture toward this occasionally: 'The uplift of

however, knew of these divisions because she lived them. In living them, she articulated in *A Voice from the South* an early version of what we now know as the intersectionality of race and gender oppression.[51] For Cooper, compounds of inequalities and oppressions operate together and exacerbate each other.

We can, furthermore, connect Cooper's proto-intersectional thinking to the importance of embodied perspective, which later becomes theorised as 'standpoint theory'.[52] Cooper shows that in Du Bois' account of the 'Negro Problem' '[o]ne important witness had not yet been heard from ... the open-eyed but hitherto voiceless Black Woman of America'.[53] The standpoint of the American Black woman is essential because she brings a unique perspective: 'not many can more sensibly realize and more accurately tell the weight and the fret of the "long dull pain"' that is a history of violence.[54]

Just as Du Bois recognised that he had to preserve, even if in a critical fashion, the ideal of America, Cooper presented her thought as uninterested in a wholesale negation of masculinity. Just

---

women is, next to the problem of the color line and the peace movement, our greatest modern cause. When, now, two of these movements – woman and color – combine in one, the combination has deep meaning.' W.E.B. Du Bois, *Darkwater* (London: Verso, 2016), 105.

51 Other Black female contemporaries of Cooper also theorised intersectionality. Mary Church Terrell, for example, writes in her self-published autobiography: 'This is the story of a colored woman living in a white world. It cannot possibly be like a story written by a white woman. A white woman has only one handicap to overcome – that of sex. I have two – both sex and race. I belong to the only group in this country, which has two such huge obstacles to surmount. Colored men have only one – that of race.' Mary Church Terrell, *A Colored Woman in a White World* (Amherst, MA: Prometheus Books, 2005), 29.

52 It is not surprising that some feminists locate the seeds of standpoint theory in Hegel's *Phenomenology*. See J.T. Wood, 'Critical Feminist Theories', in L.A. Baxter and D.O. Braithwaite (eds), *Engaging Theories in Interpersonal Communication: Multiple Perspectives* (Thousand Oaks: Sage, 2008), 323–34; and Emily Griffin, *A First Look at Communication Theory: Standpoint Theory* (New York: McGraw-Hill Higher Education, 2009), 441–53.

53 Anna Julia Cooper, *Voice from the South* (Lanham, MD: Rowman & Littlefield, 1998), 51.

54 Ibid.

as white men 'are not to blame if they cannot *quite* put themselves in the dark man's place, neither should the dark man be wholly expected fully and adequately to reproduce the exact Voice of the Black Woman'.[55]

Cooper's scepticism goes even further than a preservation of her (white and Black) male counterparts. She, too, negates (and preserves) other particulars. She begins *A Voice from the South* with an extended meditation on the history of Christendom and the barbaric actions of the Germanic peoples, finding problems and promises in both. Even though the Germanic peoples were violent and brutal, Cooper argues, they nevertheless revered their women. Even though many Catholic bishops were abusive sexually, Cooper sees in Jesus – not Christendom – the resources for recognising the centrality and importance of women.[56] If *The Souls of Black Folk* begins with a meditation on the history of cultures *in general*, situating Black people as split in their consciousness, *A Voice from the South* begins with a meditation on the history of cultures as they treat and understand women, underscoring women's importance, while simultaneously highlighting their mistreatment. We might see Cooper here as extending Du Bois' approach but with a twist: there aren't two, but three axes – Black, Woman, and American. In so doing, Cooper discloses the unique combinations of discrimination, exclusion, and violence that build up at those exact axial intersections. Du Bois might have coined the notion of double consciousness, but in Cooper's work we already see the beginnings of what we might call 'triple consciousness'. *The cut of the cut.*

Unlike the stoic Washington, Cooper never wrote from a place of abstraction. She, like Wells, lived and experienced the intersectional violence about which she wrote. We can discern this in Shirley Moody-Turner's reading of Du Bois' regular rejection of Cooper's work for publication in *The Crisis*. Reading the thirty-three letters they exchanged between 1923 and 1932, Moody-Turner finds 'evidence of what Joy James has identified as

---

55 Ibid., 52.
56 Ibid., 14–21.

"profeminist politics'".[57] Profeminist politics enabled Du Bois to 'advocate for Black women's liberation while failing to recognize adequately Black women's intellectual contributions to the very causes he championed ... as editor of *The Crisis*, for instance, he offered his general support to Cooper, but time and again he resisted, neglected, or otherwise failed to assist Cooper in the actual publication of her writing'.[58] Even through these rejections, Cooper is unnecessarily generous in her refusal to blame men, writing that it 'is no fault of man's that he has not been able to see truth from her standpoint', because he is 'absorbed in the immediate needs of [his] own political complications'.[59] Cooper's standpoint endows her with an even greater clairvoyance because she 'is confronted by both *a woman question and a race problem*, and is as yet an unknown or an unacknowledged factor in both', while Du Bois' confronts only the race problem.[60]

When discussing the importance of her standpoint, Cooper emphasises the image of the Black woman as a 'seed' or 'germ', as the 'life-blood from which the race is to flow'.[61] The implication is that real progress is a matter of slow and well-tended growth rather than 'spasms' of revolt or momentary bursts of strength.[62] 'Only the Black woman', Cooper writes, 'can say "when and where I enter, in the quiet, undisputed dignity of my womanhood, without violence and without suing or special patronage, then and there the whole *Negro race enters with me*"'.[63]

---

57 Shirley Moody-Turner, '"Dear Doctor Du Bois": Anna Julia Cooper, W.E.B. Du Bois, and the Gender Politics of Black Publishing', *MELUS: Multi-Ethnic Literature of the U.S.* 40:3 (2015): 48; Joy James, 'Profeminism and Gender Elites: W.E.B. Du Bois, Anna Julia Cooper, and Ida B. Wells-Barnett', in *Next to the Color Line: Gender, Sexuality, and W. E. B. Du Bois*, ed. Susan Gillman and Alys Eve Weinbaum (Minneapolis: University of Minnesota Press, 2007), 70.
58 Moody-Turner, '"Dear Doctor Du Bois"', 48.
59 Cooper, *Voice*, 107, 113.
60 Ibid., 112; emphasis added.
61 Ibid., 61.
62 Ibid.
63 Ibid., 63.

We should tarry here a moment longer in order to pick up on the resonances between Cooper and Spillers. Can we detect Cooper's influence when Spillers says that the 'African-American male has been touched ... by the mother, *handed* by her in ways that he cannot escape'?[64] Cooper's affirmation of the epistemological, ethical, and political centrality of Black women's perspectives prefigures Spillers' claim that, irrespective of what Black men may want to believe about themselves, they are always and already brought into being by *the mother*. When Cooper says that 'the whole Negro race enters with me', she is not speaking in hyperbole. She is adopting a more radically sceptical – and therefore radically free – stance than that of her male counterparts and contemporaries, including Washington, Du Bois, and, as we will see in the next chapter, Marcus Garvey.

What, then, does it mean to claim that Cooper was a sceptic? Quite simply, it means she was unwilling to engage in a wholesale adoption of abstract ideals. She did not deal in consciousness or character; she dealt with *cases*.[65] Women are central to the world's development, she argues, 'not because woman is better or stronger or wiser than man, but from *the nature of the case*, because it is she who must first form the man by directing the earliest impulses of his character'.[66] For Cooper, it is the case, in its triply determined particularity, that women are called upon to form not only themselves, but men, too. In this way, but certainly not only in this way, women are the primary pathway through which culture, politics – *life* – unfold and develop.

We might want to detect in this a kind of 'domestication' of the woman by Cooper, but that would be to miss her point. Her claim about her standpoint arises out of a grappling with cultural history, wherein women emerge as the mediators in relation to a

---

64 Spillers, 'Mama's Baby', 80.
65 Looking for resourceful resonances in Hegel, the German for 'case, cases' is *der Fall, die Fälle*, which can mean fall (falling down, a fall from power, waterfall, fall of the Berlin wall or *Mauerfall*) and case, both in the sense of a case, event, or matter (a legal case, a detective's case) and a grammatical case (nominative, genitive, accusative, dative).
66 Cooper, *Voice*, 21.

brutal and barbaric violence, where they are the ones who better embrace and embody the ideal of peace. It is not about raising children. It's about the moral and ethical contributions of women, especially Black women.

Even this, however, might miss the force of the consideration of gender in Black feminist scepticism, because the category 'woman' is not stable. 'Woman' does not produce a firm ethical and moral ground for all of those who fall under its name. Cooper knew this. She knew that Black women are 'dispirited and crushed down by' an 'all levelling spirit in America which cynically assumes "A Negro woman cannot be a lady".'[67] Prefiguring Spillers, she already knew that Black women were ungendered. She knew that Black women were and are:

> so full of promise and possibilities, yet so sure of destruction; often without a father to whom they dare apply the loving term, often without a stronger brother to espouse their cause and defend their honor with his life's blood; in the midst of pitfalls and snares, waylaid by the lower classes of white men, with no shelter, no protection nearer than the great blue vault above, which half conceals and half reveals the one Caretaker they know so little of.[68]

For Cooper, Heaven seemed the only reprieve, though even here her scepticism runs deep. Heaven is only half-known, and the 'Caretaker' in Heaven is known even less. To occupy Black womanhood is to not even be assured of the promise *of the afterlife*. Talk about unstable.

All this being said, it is precisely *through* Cooper's scepticism that we find her most heartfelt plea: 'Oh, save' Black women, she writes, 'help them, shield, train, develop, teach, inspire them! Snatch them in God's name, as brands from the burning! There is material in them well worth your while, the hope in germ of a staunch, helpful, regenerating womanhood on which, primarily,

---

67 Ibid., 32.
68 Ibid., 25.

rests the foundation stones of our future as a race.'[69] Cooper's appeal, sceptical as it is, is steeped not merely in a hope that things could be better; her appeal is grounded in her *knowledge* – restless and unstable as it is – that Black women are, indeed, the primary site of possibility for Black people in general. Let us repeat her words: *'the whole Negro race enters with me'*.

We emphasise that this is not hyperbolic. Cooper's claim about Black women's centrality and importance echoes throughout the history of Black life. Even the most cursory and standard treatment of Black history will disclose that it was Black women who led the charge for change and liberation, even if they were not credited. Harriet Tubman was a 'Moses of her people'; Sojourner Truth proclaimed the incredible capacities of Black women to do the work of their male counterparts; and in the two previous chapters we encountered two Black women – Harriet Jacobs and Ida B. Wells – who, in different ways, never lost sight of their families and communities. Jacobs constantly makes overtures to her cousins, her grandmother, and her children, and Wells writes against the lynching of Black men as she tends to her large family and precarious community. With Cooper, it is *the case* that Black women are central to Black life not because of some moral, ethical, or political superiority, but because their ungendered vulnerability affords them an epistemological stance that clarifies the existential, political, ethical, and moral stakes of living while Black. Beyond the Veil, there is yet another cut, one that provides an even more heightened clairvoyance than the one acquired and deployed by Du Bois.

Perhaps this is why *A Voice from the South* reads as a plea for education. After all, Cooper does not seem to advocate for a liberal feminist politics of parity. Her appeal is not grounded in a claim about the equality of the sexes – a claim that would, in the end, mirror the colour-blindness of Washington's scepticism. Her voice instead finds its ethical and political thrust in *the case* that Black women are, on the one hand, uniquely perceptive about the state of affairs, and, on the other, are *already tasked* with doing the

---

69 Ibid.

work – without the accolades or training of their male counterparts – of uplifting the race:

> With all the wrongs and neglects of her past, with all the weakness, the debasement, the moral thralldom of her present, the Black woman ... stands mute and wondering at the Herculean task devolving upon her. *But the cycles wait for her. No other hand can move the lever. She must be loosed from her bands and set to work.*[70]

Misogynoir took its toll. In doing so, Black women found – and continue to find – themselves in a position of *epistemic* authority, able to assess the possibilities and limitations of the current state of affairs more accurately. Cooper's 'standpoint' approach, importantly, is not ideological, but grounded in the particular *case*, the determinate situation, in which Black women find themselves. Ungendered by past and present violences, called upon – often without their consent – to uphold and shape not simply themselves but also their counterparts, Black women, Cooper argues, *require* education, attention, training.

As we have said, Cooper's work is, in a way, updated by Spillers. Though Spillers makes no appeal to or plea for education, she does insist upon the centrality, importance, and primacy of Black women in the development of Black life more generally, even in the lives of Black men. Spillers turns to motherhood, but – akin to the scepticism we are tracing in this chapter – through a negation of its normativity. After all, Spillers is the one who coined – or at least popularised – the term 'ungendered', and in so doing, called the normative logic of motherhood into question.

> Even though we are not talking about *any* of the matriarchal features of social production/reproduction – matrifocality, matrilinearity, matriarchy – when we speak of the enslaved person, we perceive that the dominant culture, in a fatal misunderstanding, assigns a matriarchist value where it does not belong; actually *misnames* the power of the female regarding the enslaved community. Such claiming is false because the female could not, in fact, claim her child, and false, once again, because 'motherhood'

---

70 Ibid., 28; emphasis added.

is not perceived in the prevailing social climate as a legitimate procedure of cultural inheritance.[71]

Augmenting Cooper's claim that Black women's importance does *not* stem from their maternal capacities, Spillers goes a step further and suggests that Black women, ungendered as they are, do not carry the capacity to *legitimately* 'pass down' an inheritance. Spillers' 'Mama's Baby, Papa's Maybe' is a critical reflection on Daniel Patrick Moynihan's famous report, which essentially claims that Black people are situated in a 'tangle of pathology' because Black men are absent from Black homes.[72] This pathology, according to Moynihan, has resulted in Black people's inability to be fully incorporated into normative US social and political structures, and therefore hindered their progress.

The truth is, Black men themselves have not been able to occupy the patriarchal position afforded to their white male counterparts. Cooper tells us that 'There has been no disposition, generally, to get the Black man's ideal or to let his individuality work by its own gravity, as it were', which we read as a profound claim about Black men's lack of access to the benefits of patriarchal structures – Black men are ungendered, too.[73] Dispossessed by a gendered matrix that renders Black flesh ungendered, Black men have been denied the capacity to sustain family lines. In the end, *the case* shows that Black women occupy the central role in Black families – even as they are denied legitimate access to the 'procedure of cultural inheritance'. What this means, then, is that:

> The African-American male has been touched, therefore, by the mother, *handed by* her in ways that he cannot escape, and in ways that the white American male is allowed to temporize by a fatherly reprieve. This human and historic development ... takes us to the center of an inexorable difference in the depths of American women's community: the African-American woman,

---

71 Spillers, 'Mama's Baby', 80.
72 Daniel Patrick Moynihan, *The Negro Family: The Case for National Action* (Office of Policy Planning and Research United States Department of Labor, March 1965), 29.
73 Cooper, *Voice*, 37.

the mother, the daughter, becomes historically the *powerful and shadowy evocation of a cultural synthesis long evaporated.*[74]

Spillers' point is that it is precisely in and through Black women that any kind of generative possibilities arise. Perhaps departing here from Cooper, Spillers knows that such possibilities will not come through incorporation into normative frameworks, but instead through an embrace of the 'monstrosity ... which her culture imposes in blindness'.[75] Possibilities emerge in the very symbolic site where violence occurs. This kind of scepticism doesn't delight in the unsettled nature of consciousness itself but instead in the wholehearted embrace of what shakes out of this unsettling, namely, an acute capacity to understand and diagnose our condition, perhaps even to produce a different way to live. This, we argue, is a radical Black feminist scepticism that pushes Du Bois' further than he could ever go. Black feminist scepticism experiences the cut of the cut, the split behind the split figured by the Veil. From this double cut, triply conscious position, Black feminist scepticism – inaugurated, or at least popularised, by Cooper – offers a different modality of engagement, and thereby moves the phenomenology of Black spirit forward by further diagnosing the pitfalls and promises of one's particular case.

Conclusion

In her 1892 essay, 'The Gain from a Belief', Cooper directly replies to a sort of intellectualised scepticism that we might (though she does not explicitly) consider akin to that of Du Bois. She imagines that a 'solitary figure stands in the marketplace ... A strange contrast his cold intellectual eye to the eager, strained, hungry faces that surge by in their never ending quest of wealth, fame, glory, bread.'[76] She names this figure 'Earth's skepticism'.[77] In response she aims 'neither to argue nor to refute' but only 'to utter

---

74 Spillers, 'Mama's Baby', 80; final emphasis added.
75 Ibid.
76 Cooper, *Voice*, 188.
77 Ibid.

just one truth: The great, the fundamental need of any nation, any race, is for devotion, heroism, sacrifice; and there cannot be devotion, heroism, or sacrifice in a primarily skeptical spirit.'[78]

While Cooper herself expresses many key sceptical notions, especially intersectional articulations of triple consciousness, her critique of extreme scepticism pushes beyond the limitations of Du Bois and into the three moments of unhappy consciousness that we will consider momentarily. The key for Cooper is that it is 'faith', not scepticism, that 'is particularly urgent in a race at almost the embryonic stage of character building'.[79]

We will soon see how striking it is how clearly these three terms – devotion, heroism, and sacrifice – parallel not only the three figures of unhappy Black consciousness (Garvey and Hurston's devotion, King and Baker's sacramental work and desire, and Malcolm X's and Davis' self-mortification) but also the precise structure of Hegel's unhappy consciousness: unchangeable universality and changeable individuality. Cooper locates the necessity for admitting both that 'truth must be infinite, and as incapable as infinite space, of being encompassed and confined by one age or nation' and that this infiniteness relates to 'one little creature's finite brain'.[80]

Cooper develops scepticism by recognising the structure of the sceptic's double consciousness and thereby brings to rest the endless fleeing from American to African and back again. The order that she develops within consciousness likely emerges from Cooper's articulation of her triple intersectional consciousness. This third identity – Black woman, ungendered – brings order to a previous disorganised and restless consciousness so that, as Hegel puts it, the 'Unhappy consciousness itself *is* the gazing of one self-consciousness into another, and itself *is* both, and the unity of both is also its essential nature' (PS 207). Cooper articulates this

---

78 Ibid., 193; note that here we have changed the order of 'devotion' and 'heroism' in order to make our argument more streamlined, but without compromising, we believe, Cooper's writing.
79 Ibid.
80 Ibid.

order through what she calls 'a life made true'.[81] Such a life must 'reach out and twine around every pulsing interest within reach of its uplifting tendrils'.[82] While multiply divided, Cooper orients the finite changeable individuality toward the infinite Unchangeable universality within one Black consciousness.

81 Ibid., 194.
82 Ibid.

II. (Un)Happy (Black) Consciousness

4

Devotion

Marcus Garvey and Zora Neale Hurston

> If God is not for us, if God is not against white racists, then God is a murderer, and we had better kill God.
>
> – James Cone

With Hegel's figuration of the 'unhappy, inwardly disrupted consciousnesses [*unglückliche, in sich entzweite Bewußtein*]', which we will call just 'unhappy consciousness', the dialectic of Black spirit moves forward. Having trod through the self-consciousness of bondage; having found – only to disrupt – the idealisation of stoic freedom; having moved through the double- and triple-consciousness of Black scepticism, Black life has found itself internally divided. With the end of slavery and at least a minimal space for self-examination carved out, Black folks strove to reconcile themselves with and through their internal divisions. Chattel slavery had ungendered and unworked any sense of internal coherence, producing a self marked by bondage. But they knew better, for they had heard the stories of Moses and Exodus: Jubilee was possible. Such a possibility was just enough to show a glimpse of a different self, one that might exist beyond subjection and enslavement, a higher sense of self, one that aligns with Hegel's Unchangeable. They may have been forced to reckon with a brutal Christianity that enforced their bondage, but they *knew* better. Though white folk had tried to claim Jesus for whiteness, Black folk knew Jesus was a friend and a liberator. God, as Henry McNeal Turner once proclaimed, is 'a negro'. *This* Christianity – one founded upon folk wisdom as much as upon certain traditional theological doctrines – provided a set of concepts and promises through which Black people could seek to free themselves from a lower self and realise the promise of a higher, more dignified one, concepts that affirmed their existence as the *imago dei*. They were, therefore, initiated 'into a process of seizing the truth, a project of deliverance and healing, in short the promise of a new life'.[1]

This 'new life' would not come overnight, of course. Neither would it involve a wholesale rejection of the religion of the white Protestants, Catholics, and others who enslaved, degraded, and segregated them. But it would bring into sharp relief the fact that they, as *Black* people, could find dignity in their higher selves. In short, as the phenomenology of Black spirit moves forward, so will the development of Black religion. As we explore this twofold development, we will see how Black spirit moves through the twentieth century in a phase that correlates to what Hegel calls the 'unhappy consciousness'. It would make sense for the three movements of unhappy consciousness – devotion, sacramental work and desire, and self-mortification – to show themselves in this and the next two chapters. But a close parallel reading will not do here. Though Hegel appears to mark his unhappy consciousness with a tripartite logic that *feels* Christian, the phenomenology of Black spirit (a spirit that includes what we might call the 'religious', to be sure) does not always proceed in these ways. As we will see in this chapter, Marcus Garvey traffics in Christian tropes and themes as he articulates the African as the 'Unchangeable'. In fact, he encourages people to do the preparatory work of returning to Africa – to a land where, for him, liberation could be possible. But, unlike Hegel's Unchangeable, the 'African' is also geographically and culturally grounded; Garvey knows where (and, to a degree, what) Africa *is*; correlatively, 'Africanness' is derived from his sense of the continent.[2]

---

1   Mbembe, *Critique of Black Reason*, 96.
2   Hegel was ruthlessly racist toward Africa. See, for example, Robert Bernasconi, 'Hegel at the Court of the Ashanti', in Stuart Barnett (ed.), *Hegel After Derrida* (London: Routledge, 1998), 41–63; M.A.R. Habib, *Hegel and Empire: From Postcolonialism to Globalism* (Basingstoke: Palgrave Macmillan, 2017); Babacar Camara, 'The Falsity of Hegel's Theses on Africa', *Journal of Black Studies* 36:1 (2005): 82–96; and Catherine Rooney, *African Literature, Animism, and Politics* (London: Routledge, 2000), 157–85.

And yet, this isn't the only form of devotion. While Garvey traffics in these tropes, despite not fitting neatly within them, Zora Neale Hurston exhibits a different kind of devotion, one wholly uninterested in the Christianity which underpins Hegel's phenomenology of spirit. She instead sees infinite value in the creative mythologies of southern Black communities, in Caribbean hoodoo doctoring and conjuring, and in tall tales of devils and tricksters. As we will see, Garvey extols an 'Africanness' – one that exists out there, across the sea, an empire in reverse – as that to which Black people should be devoted, encouraging them to prepare themselves for a return, or aliya. But Hurston turns to Black communing, even intraracially, to assert the individuality to which she is devoted. This changes the way devotion is understood. With Garvey, devotion is self-preparation, a purifying and reorienting of oneself toward a higher self only obtainable once all Black people return to their origin – in short, back to Africa. But when we sit with Hurston – as she sits on those Florida porches listening to the beauty and joy embodied in those 'lying sessions' – we can hear a mode of devotion in the practice of self-*fashioning*. In Hurston's approach, Black people have all they need exactly where they are. No need to prepare for a beyond; no appeals to Africanness, Christianity, or an unchangeable elsewhere are necessary. The higher Black self is already here, right here and now, if we only hear it in what Fred Moten calls (referencing Hurston) 'the essential drama of Black life'.[3]

Devotion

Devotion (*Andacht*), for Hegel, is the first moment of unhappy consciousness. It is called devotion because it seeks to purify itself so that it is prepared to receive the essential, the Unchangeable, as it is incarnated in a particular form. Put differently, the unhappy consciousness seeks to surrender itself to the immediacy of the Unchangeable or God. In doing so, it prostrates itself before the

---

3 Fred Moten, *In the Break: The Aesthetics of the Black Radical Tradition* (Minneapolis: University of Minnesota Press, 2003), 1.

individual form of the Unchangeable, or Jesus Christ, in the hope of passively receiving it. It is essential that the changeable relation to the Unchangeable is one of passive reception, for it wants to avoid any chance of contaminating the universality of the Unchangeable with the particularity of its unfixed form. The devoted unhappy consciousness views its particularity as soiled and disdained, and sees its true self in the promise of a reunification with God. Unhappy consciousness thus desperately desires to escape from its empirical earthly existence in order to return to 'its own proper nature' in heaven above (PS 215). Unhappiness here is a form of estrangement or alienation. Here on earth, its true self or own proper nature does not exist; bringing it about cannot be the achievement of a particular consciousness but must 'come about from *its* side', that is, the side of the essential, the Unchangeable, the kingdom of God (PS 215; emphasis added). Hence, devotion is the form of relation that seeks to prepare itself so that it can properly passively receive the Unchangeable and thus return to its true self. Devotion is preparation and purification.

We find various examples of such devotion in the history of religious asceticism. Christian ascetics tried to rid themselves of any shred of their particularity, as with mystics like the Desert Mothers or anchoresses like Julian of Norwich. They undertook severe *askeses* that trained into them into virtues of chastity, abstinence, frugality, humility, and purity. Devotion is a practice of renunciation, of surrendering oneself unto God, of preparing the changeable self so as to receive the Unchangeable gifted from above.

We see the practice of devotion in early Black religious communities, especially insofar as their spiritual practices were connected to moral, political, and social development. According to Anthony Pinn, post-emancipation Black religious communities 'never restricted themselves to the realm of spiritual health. On the contrary, Black churches committed themselves to moral reform, sociopolitical change, and mission activity'.[4] Echoing

---

4 Anthony Pinn, *Why Lord? Suffering and Evil in Black Theology* (New York: Continuum, 1995), 39.

Washingtonian stoicism, devotional moral uplift included developing virtues and dispositions through teetotalism and 'thrift and industry', as promoted by the Society for the Suppression of Vice and Immorality.[5] This self-imposed discipline was meant to connect 'moral conduct with the freedom of Black people'. If Black people 'demonstrated themselves to be civilized and moral beings', then 'white Americans would not be able to enslave' them.[6]

For us, Marcus Garvey most embodies the figure of devotion, as we see in his definition of 'faithfulness': 'the state of mind and heart in the individual that changes not' (PO 5). To receive the Unchangeable, one must make oneself, as much as possible, unchangeable, and to be faithful or devoted is to 'serve without regret or disgust, to obligate one's self to that which is promised' (PO 5). Through such spiritual, moral, political, and social development, Black souls would prepare themselves for the coming of their God, a Black God, the God of Africa. After all the resentment, guilt, hatred, and other vitriol sedimented through centuries of chattel slavery, the task of the early Black churches was to purify Black souls so that they were properly disposed to the reception of God, a disposition that Garvey transposed toward political ends. As we will see, Garvey took up the focus on devotional practices in the early Black churches in order to develop a global emigrationist project for the whole African diaspora, though, to be sure, calls for Black separation had been made decades earlier.[7] This project was called by different names – Back to Africa, Black Nationalism, and so on. But whichever name is used, we can see, at its core, the structure of devotion.

The goal of Garveyism, in short, was to unify and empower all African peoples under the name of Africa. Though they were spread around the globe in various countries and cultures, Africa served as a shared, unchanging banner under which all Black persons could find their dignity. It might be hard for us today to

---

5   Ibid., 40.
6   Ibid.
7   See Martin Robison Delany and Robert Campbell, *Search for a Place: Black Separatism and Africa, 1860* (Ann Arbor: University of Michigan Press, 1969).

imagine what *Africa* must have meant to Black folk back then, especially given that our twenty-first-century consciousness of the African continent is flooded with images, sound bites, rhythms, wars, literature, films, and more. Yet to underprivileged and discriminated former slaves and other disenfranchised and segregated Black Americans, the idea of Africa was charged with the possibility and promise of a better life. In the absence of any serious scholarly or scientific attempt to understand Africa's history, geography, societies, and politics, etc., what Africa meant for African Americans followed from what it meant for white European colonisers, slave traders, and slave owners. Mbembe describes this vision of Africa thus: 'From the beginning of the Atlantic trade, the [African] continent became an *inexhaustible well of phantasms*, the raw material for a massive labor of imagination whose political and economic dimensions we can never underscore enough.'[8] Here Black devotion configures these phantasms into an Unchangeable: Africa, the promised land.

The marginalisation and discrimination that Black folk experienced living in civilisations outside of Africa had to be understood, Garvey thought, in terms of what he means by education: the 'medium by which a people are prepared for the creation of their own particular civilization, and the advancement and glory of their own race' (PO 6). Rather than drum up excuses or cast blame on others, Garvey abjures those who seek to shed their Blackness and take on whiteness, those who 'find excuses to get out of the Negro race ... It is [they] who are unworthy, because [they] are not contributing to the uplift and up-building of this noble race' (PO 6). Listen to the notes of Tuskegee: 'As a race oppressed, it is for us to prepare ourselves', writes Garvey, so that 'we may be able to enter into the new era as partakers of the joys to be inherited' (PO 8). Garveyism thus extends the modern notions of autonomy and self-determination to Black bodies, which also meant endowing Blackness with the power of reason. The means for this was geographical. Mbembe puts it this way: 'Blacks became citizens because they were human beings endowed, like all others, with

---

8   Mbembe, *Critique of Black Reason*, 70–1; emphasis added.

reason. But added to this was the double face of their color and the privilege of indigeneity. Racial authenticity and territoriality were combined, and in such conditions Africa became the land of the Blacks.'[9] As Garvey proclaims: 'Let Africa be our guiding star: our star of destiny' (PO 7). 'Nationhood is the highest ideal of all peoples', and Africa was the natural homeland for a nation of Black folk (PO 7). 'Africa for Africans', Garvey wrote, was the goal of 'political re-adjustment of the world', which 'means this – that every race must find a home' (PO 13). This included *all* and *only* Africans, which meant that 'everything that was not Black had no place and consequently could not claim any sort of Africanity'.[10] This is why Garvey claims that the 'leadership of the Negro today must be able to locate the race, and not only for today but for all time' (PO 41). Hence Garvey's Universal Negro Improvement Association (UNIA) was meant for all Africans for all time. Africa for Africans meant the Unchangeable, eternal, universal Africa for all diasporic Africans throughout the world.

The reason Garveyism is a form of devotion, we argue, is because it is an attempt to overcome the divided nature of Black subjectivity and thus to unify Black identify in the figure of Africa. As Fanon put it, this 'plunge into the chasm of the past is the condition and the source of freedom'.[11]

Garvey tried to actualise this star of destiny in the form of the Black Star Line, a concrete, practical step that distinguished Garveyism from previous Back-to-Africa attempts. 'African migration', even Du Bois admits, 'is a century old and a pretty thoroughly discredited dream … But a definite plan to unite Negrodom by a line of steamships was a brilliant suggestion and Garvey's only original contribution to the race problem.'[12] While

---

9 Ibid., 91.
10 Ibid. 'As a result', Mbembe continues, 'it was impossible to conceive of Africans of European origin.'
11 Frantz Fanon, 'Racism and Culture', in *Toward the African Revolution: Political Essays*, trans. Haakon Chevalier (New York: Grove Press, 1988), 43.
12 W.E.B. Du Bois, 'The Black Start Line', in *Writings*, 980. We must temper this, however, given that Du Bois and Garvey's relationship was quite strained, mostly because Garveyism and the NAACP endorsed conflicting strategies.

other Black thinkers discussed and planned a mass exodus from the United States, Garvey and other members of the Universal Negro Improvement Association formed a public corporation, quickly raised massive funds, and bought and refurbished ships to sail African Americans back to Africa.

Black Suffering

Although the Black Star Line only lasted about two years, from 1919 to 1922, and ended with Garvey's conviction for mail fraud and eventual deportation, it is clear to us that Garveyan devotion emerged out of De Boisian scepticism. In a way, both Du Bois and Garvey wrestled with a similar question. Du Bois, in characteristically sceptical fashion, posed it thus:

> Why did God make me an outcast and a stranger in mine own house? The shades of the prison-house close round about us all: walls strait and stubborn to the whitest, but relentlessly narrow, tall, and unscalable to sons of night who must plod darkly on in resignation, or beat unavailing palms against the stone, or readily, half hopelessly, watch the streak of blue above. (SBF 3)

Du Bois' response is a bitter one, but it is the question – how a perfectly good God could allow the brutality and violence of American chattel slavery and its afterlives – that speaks to Garvey's devotion. The history of enslavement could not serve to prove the power and goodness of God, for it implied a contradiction at the heart of the divine. It was therefore necessary to construct an account of God despite and against a history of evil and violence.

The position thus became that any depiction of God as the cause of Black suffering was an *error of depiction* rather an error of God. Slavery was a human stain, not a divine blemish. The Unchangeable is excused; the changeable blamed. Here is how

---

For example, speaking of Garvey's 'personal vituperation of the editor of *The Crisis*', Du Bois writes that 'Marcus Garvey is, without doubt, the most dangerous enemy of the Negro in America and in the world. He is either a lunatic or a traitor.' Du Bois, 'A Lunatic or a Traitor', in *Writings*, 990.

Pinn puts it, discussing the views of the Methodist entrepreneur and activist David Walker: 'Divine sanction of Black oppression was impossible, because he understood God as kind, just, loving, powerful, and righteous.'[13] Garvey later affirmed this: 'That the Negro became a race of slaves was not the fault of God almighty, the Divine Master, it was the fault of the [white] race' (PO 26). Some Black thinkers turned to scripture in order to demonstrate that the Christian God was on the side of those who suffer rather than of those who caused suffering.

Take, for example, how Maria Stewart treated the story of the Hebrew Exodus from Egypt.[14] As 'the first woman of color to lecture publicly on political issues', Pinn points out, she emphasised the importance of the Exodus story as 'a major marker of God's devotion to human freedom'.[15] Since God sided with oppressed peoples, America would suffer the same fate as the Egyptians until it properly dealt with its enslavement and brutal treatment of Black Americans. According to Pinn, 'Stewart assumes both ontologically and epistemologically that God is near to and acts on behalf of the powerless and the disenfranchised in the interests of divine justice.'[16] The way to make a good God consistent with Black suffering was to transform the Christian God into a Black God.

In the early African American churches, one of the most common ways to understand how God permitted Black suffering was to view 'suffering as pedagogical in nature'.[17] Pinn

---

13 Pinn, *Why Lord?*, 41.
14 Looking ahead to Zora Neale Hurston, we note that, in 1939, she rewrote the Exodus story, blending the Moses of the Old Testament with the Moses of Black folklore and song in order to create an allegory of power, redemption, and faith. In mixed voicing of biblical rhetoric, Black dialect, and colloquial English, Hurston narrates Moses' life from the day he is placed in the Nile River in a reed basket, to his development as a magician, to his emergence as a heroic rebel leader, culminating in his becoming a Great Emancipator. See Zora Neale Hurston, *Moses, Man of the Mountain* (New York: Harper Perennial, 2008).
15 Pinn, *Why Lord?*, 46.
16 Quoted in ibid.
17 Ibid., 44.

fundamentally disagrees with this approach on ethical grounds – understanding slavery as pedagogical, and therefore useful, does nothing to alleviate the suffering of Black people. But the unfortunate truth is that many Black people did see it this way.

Nietzsche's thoughts on suffering and early Judeo-Christian thought, then, are helpful here. For Nietzsche, the fact of suffering is not, in itself, the problem. All people suffer, to be sure, so the real problem is when there is no discernible reason for the suffering. As Nietzsche puts it, it is the 'meaninglessness of suffering, *not* suffering itself, [that] was the curse that lay over mankind'.[18] It is no coincidence that, in this same discussion, Nietzsche explains the importance of the 'ascetic priest' and the 'ascetic ideal', given that asceticism is basically a set of devotional practices. To reconcile themselves with a good God and avoid 'suicidal nihilism', suffering had to make sense, to be made sense of, to be justified for the freed Hebrew slaves and for emancipated Black folk in America.[19] An African Exodus from America, akin to the Hebrew Exodus from Egypt, was necessary. The history of chattel slavery had to be interpreted to serve a purpose that was aligned with the good of Black people. Hence slavery came to be viewed as harsh pedagogy.

According to Pinn, 'Stewart claimed that African-Americans had been foolish, and God needed to provide them with a painful education.'[20] Pinn calls this interpretation 'a version of the redemptive suffering argument' because it 'resolves the problem of evil' through 'a reevalution of suffering'.[21] Suffering, for Stewart, was a merely temporary and instrumental evil, one that 'is best resolved by God'.[22]

Stewart reserved a special role for Black women in this redemption story, a role that 'was the result of their strong – tried

---

18 Nietzsche, *Genealogy of Morals and Ecce Homo*, trans. Walter Kaufman (New York: Vintage, 1989), III 28.
19 Ibid.
20 Pinn, *Why Lord?*, 47.
21 Ibid.
22 Ibid., 48.

by fire – character'.[23] The unique role of Black women emerges from the effect of their unique education in slavery. After working in the fields, as painstakingly and agonisingly as the men, Black female slaves also had to raise white children in the Big House, and Black children in the slave cabins. As we saw in Harriet Jacobs' experience, we must not forget the rape and sexual violence that female slaves suffered from cruel white masters. Thus, 'as metal is refined by fire', writes Pinn, 'the ethical and moral fiber of Black women was strengthened by their suffering'.[24] Within this narrative – one that, we must note, is incredibly brutal and violent – slavery was seen as part of divine providence; it could, and would, be understood as part of God's redemptive plan for Black people. Slavery provided what can only be understood as the vilest and most violent of object-lessons, but it was nevertheless a kind of schooling that prepared the enslaved for the realisation of the goodness of God.

Read through this narrative, slavery was a catechism, a propaedeutic process that prepared Black souls to sense the divine, to find the good in the bad, and it therefore paved the way for a kind of devotion that parallels the devotion of Hegel's unhappy consciousness. Abolitionists and 'Black Christians manipulated this theme and combined it with biblical imagery to express a solution to the apparent paradox of their enslavement'.[25] While white Americans used their privileged status to ordain themselves as inheritors of God's plan, Black Americans 'suggested that God has set them apart to be tested'.[26] Pedagogy in slavery thus resonates with the asceticism of the unhappy consciousness's training in devotion. The forging of the Black soul over centuries was a way of testing and training Black people to become perfect devotees of the good God beyond this world – or at least in Africa.

---

23 Ibid.
24 Ibid., 45.
25 Ibid., 51.
26 Ibid.

Feeling

As we said, to receive the Unchangeable or God, unhappy consciousness had to prepare itself properly. This meant rejecting one's earthly individuality and undergoing a rigorous devotional asceticism. To avoid getting its own way, the finite individual turns to a receptive faculty: feeling.

The issue with striving to relate to the Unchangeable through thought was that the form of thinking of a finite being must itself be finite, and since a finite form of thinking cannot handle an infinite being, it cannot think itself into a proper relationship with the infinite, Unchangeable being. Thus devotion, 'where we consider it as pure consciousness … does not *relate* itself as a *thinking* consciousness to its object' (PS 217). Instead, devotion's relationship to the Unchangeable beyond is through *feeling*, *Gefühl*, a lower form of immediacy.[27]

In this moment, then, unhappy consciousness devotes itself to the Unchangeable through a deep feeling, a vague intuition, a profound sensation of the divine presence. Devotion is still pure, it is just a purity of feeling rather than thinking. As Hyppolite puts it, this feeling 'is neither the abstract thought of the stoic nor the pure anxiety of the skeptic'.[28] As Hegel writes, devotion is 'the inward movement of the pure heart which *feels* itself [*innerliche Bewegung des reinen Gemüts*]' (PS 217). Devotion is not truly thinking but rather 'only a movement *towards* thinking' (PS 217; emphasis added). In devotion, thought is reduced to the 'chaotic jingling of bells, or a mist of warm incense, a musical thinking that does not get as far as the Notion, which would be the sole, immanent objective mode of thought' (PS 217). Here Hegel is referring to the Catholic Mass, in which the presence of Jesus is indicated by the *ding!* of a bell and the priest's swinging of the censer with burning incense (PS 217). The divine is also invoked in the Mass through ritual objects (relics and bones of the saints), the consumption of

---

27 The emphasis on feeling in this first moment of unhappy consciousness evokes the chapter on Sense-Certainty.
28 Hyppolite, *Structure and Genesis*, 207.

the Eucharist, rosary devotions, lighting candles, singing hymns, and so on, as well as through the architectural history of cathedrals and other religious sites of worship and observance. Through the design of such spaces for complete sensory immersion, Catholics are made to feel the divine within and without.

Black churches also constructed experiences in order to evoke the feeling of God, perhaps most clearly through music.[29] While music was important for Black churches, and still is today, it was also important for the development of Black people after emancipation in terms of distancing their identity from slavery. To do this, they refused to transfer the 'Negro spirituals' from the plantation fields to the churches. Newly emancipated Black communities wanted to cultivate in themselves a moral disposition and personal character that were free from associations with an enslaved condition. '[M]any Black religious leaders believed "corn field" religious practices [such as spirituals] merely reinforced negative opinions concerning Blacks. Therefore, many Black churches … [replaced] spirituals with hymns.'[30] This might have been a movement toward respectability, but the truth is that the spirituals, though repressed, remained central to Black liturgy – and to Black life more generally. Du Bois put it this way:

> The Music of Negro religion is that plaintive rhythmic melody, with its touching minor cadences, which, despite caricature and defilement, still remains the most original and beautiful expression of human life and longing yet born on American soil. Sprung from the African forests, where its counterpart can still

---

29 For more on this, see Anthony Pinn (ed.), *Noise and Spirit: The Religious and Spiritual Sensibilities of Rap Music* (New York: New York University Press, 2003); James H. Cone, *The Spirituals and the Blues: An Interpretation* (Maryknoll, NY: Orbis Books, 1991); Howard Thurman, *The Negro Spiritual Speaks of Life and Death* (New York: Harper & Brothers, 1947); W.E.B. Du Bois, 'Of the Faith of the Fathers', in *Souls of Black Folk*; and, for a different take on the relationship between Black music and the divine, Alisha Lola Jones, '"You Are My Dwelling Place": Experiencing Black Male Vocalists' Worship as Aural Eroticism and Autoeroticism in Gospel', *Women and Music* 22 (2018): 3–21. This is by no means an exhaustive list, but it helps to underscore the importance of music in Black religious traditions.
30 Pinn, *Why Lord?*, 40.

be heard, it was adapted, changed, and intensified by the tragic soul-life of the slave, until, under the stress of law and whip, it became the one true expression of a people's sorrow, despair, and hope. (SBF 191)

Though Du Bois was a sceptic, he knew well enough that Black music, the music of Black religion, was nevertheless a profound expression of devotion – to *both* freedom *and* their God, to their God *as* the medium through which freedom might be attained. As Douglass also noted, music expressed their feeling, their yearning for something *more*.

For Garvey, the feeling of the divine was the ideal form of devotion. 'The highest compliment we can pay to our creator', he writes, 'the highest respect we can pay to our risen Lord and Savior, is that of *feeling* that He has created us as His masterpiece ... because in us is *reflected* the very being of God' (PO 57; emphases added). To truly reflect God in the soul, one had to prepare oneself through devotional practices, the most important of which was to sense God with the purest possible feeling. This feeling is the realisation 'that there is but a link between them and the creator', and it is this feeling that Garvey sees as the marker of a stronger race (PO 57). For Garvey, weaker races see stronger races as superior, and thus as blocking the path toward God. This is what happened when Black folk were made to view white people as being above them, and so as more closely connected to God. To counter this, Garvey strove to develop Black souls until they could feel that 'there is nothing in the world that is above them except the influence of God' (PO 57). The way to bring the changeable individual Black soul into communion with the Unchangeable God is through pure feeling.

Return of the Body

This turn to pure feeling, Hegel shows, inevitably fails. The ringing of the bell, the burning of incense, the singing of spirituals, and so on show that the unhappy consciousness depends on what is most individual about it: its body, its changeable self. Unfortunately for devotion, feeling leads back into the body, exactly what it tried to escape. As Hegel writes, 'instead of laying hold of the essence, it only *feels* it and has fallen back into itself [fühlt *es nur und ist in sich zurückgefallen*]' (PS 217). In reaching out for the particularised God, unhappy consciousness falls back into its body. The more it devotes itself to escaping its finite, empirical form, the more it tries to merely feel, rather than think, the presence of the unchangeable beyond, the deeper into its body the unhappy consciousness sinks. If we consider Christianity as an example, while Jesus came to earth in human form, he also died. Long dead and gone, it is impossible, on earth, to feel God immediately.

The mistake of devotion, then, is that it promises something it cannot fulfil – the possibility of touching the particularised God, Jesus. What one feels during, say, the Eucharist is not God but oneself. The bread and wine are just bread and wine; the smoke is just incense; the hymns are just human voices. As Hyppolite puts it, the 'God who is dead is no more accessible than the God who never knew life'.[31] Devotion leaves one only with a feeling of *self*, not a feeling of God.

Hegel points to another example of the failure of devotion: when Mary found the empty tomb; Hyppolite adds the Crusaders.[32] Both Mary and the Crusaders set out to meet the missing Jesus. Yet, since he died on the cross, all that was left was an empty grave and abandoned lands. 'Consciousness', writes Hegel, 'can only find as a present reality the *grave* of its life' (PS 217). The Unchangeable promises to save us from ourselves, but when we go looking for it, all we find is 'something that has already vanished' (PS 217). When it tries to find Jesus, God on earth, unhappy consciousness also comes up empty-handed. As Hegel writes, 'this essence is the unattainable *beyond* [*unerreichbare* Jenseits] which, in being laid hold of, flees, or rather has already flown [*schon entflohen*]' (PS 217). The search for the beyond was doomed to fail from the start.

Hyppolite reports something topical from Hegel's early notes: 'either the ideal is within me, in which case it is not an ideal, or it

---

31 Hyppolite, *Genesis and Structure*, 202.
32 Ibid., 208.

is outside me, in which case I can never attain it'.³³ As we will see in the next two chapters, the problem with devotion is the same as the problem with all attempts to relate the changeable to the Unchangeable. The essential, the Unchangeable, must appear to a particular individual in a particular form, which means that the God to which the individual relates 'is not perfect and genuine, but remains burdened with imperfection', contamination, and particularity (PS 215). The Unchangeable's presence is soiled by our changeable presence. Garvey notices something similar: 'even if they outwardly profess the same faith, so we have as many religions in Christianity as we have believers' (PO 5). We get in our own way when trying to relate to God.

Life and Ends in Garveyism

As we are starting to see, Garveyism strongly parallels Hegelian devotion. We can see this even more clearly in his definition of life. 'Life', Garvey claims, 'is that existence that is given to man to live for a *purpose*, to live to his own satisfaction and pleasure, providing he forgets not the God who created him and who *expects a spiritual obedience* and observation of the moral laws that He has inspired' (PO 4; emphases added). In Garvey's definition, the life of devotion, given the tension it entails, cannot avoid ultimate failure in its attempt to bring the individual together with the Infinite beyond. The task: to live an obedient and observant life in accord with the divine plan. The reason for failure: the unwanted importance of bodily feeling.

Garvey locates a higher form of self in all Africans. This higher Black self is an excellent example of what Hegel means by the 'Unchangeable'. For Garvey, these higher selves were distinctly *Black*. Turning to Blackness – or, more precisely, *Africanness* – as the Unchangeable, Garvey's devotion, like Hegel's, entails choosing the correct ends. Correct ends come from something larger than oneself, not from individuality. As Garvey writes, the 'ends you serve that are selfish will take you no further than yourself; but the

---

33 Ibid., 198.

ends you serve that are for all, in common, will take you even into community' (PO 4). Like Hegelian devotion, Garveyism seeks to subordinate personal aims to universal aims, which requires a moral training of affects. Some affects must be expelled, others cultivated, in order to purify the soul so that it may be prepared to receive God's will. For example, fear, which Garvey defines as 'a state of nervousness fit for children and ... los[s] of control of one's nerves', makes the individual concerned with themselves rather than with a larger, more universal – and therefore divine – plan of Black racial uplift (PO 5).

Beyond any individual, pride in Africa must be cultivated and shared among the whole African diaspora. This is how a Black person prepares her or himself for unifying with the Unchanging. For true unification, Garveyism requires 'the honesty of our own souls', earnestness of intent, and respectability rather than hatred and decadence (PO 8, 9). 'I have no time to hate anyone', Garvey writes. 'All my time is *devoted* to the up-building and development of the Negro race' (PO 12; emphasis added). Noting that all great powers fall – from Athens to America – Garvey calls upon all Africans, 'to the four hundred million Negroes of the world, *prepare* yourselves for the higher life' (PO 17; emphasis added). Garvey clearly believed that a life of devotion could successfully achieve its goal of communion with the Unchangeable. As he writes, 'he who lives well, transforms himself from that which is mortal, to immortal', which is precisely the task of devotion (PO 5). Taking up this task is necessary because the Bible *alone*, Garvey claims, cannot save any Black soul.

Racial Purity

Garvey's commitment to not hating, however, does not mean that he did not value racial distinctions. For him, Black and white souls and selves were different in kind. Race assimilation was simply 'preposterous' (PO 20).[34] Garvey thought that 'white men should

---

34 Like Garvey, Fanon sees assimilation as another name for alienation. Fanon, 'Racism and Culture', 38.

be white, yellow men should be yellow, and Black men should be Black' (PO 20). Racial purity was necessary for Garvey, though all races were created equal. To ensure racial purity and to avoid war, prejudice, and oppression, each race should claim a different part of creation: 'If Europe is for the white man, if Asia is for brown and yellow men, then surely Africa is for the Black man' (PO 23). The higher self in Black souls is thus not the same as the higher self in the white soul. Ignoring racial divisions and striving for assimilation inevitably fails, Garvey thinks, because telling a Black individual to aim for a higher form of whiteness necessarily fails.

Though he was highly influenced by Washington, Garvey believed that the 'white man of America will not ... assimilate the Negro, because in so doing, he feels that he will [have] committed racial suicide' (PO 20). To white eyes, the Black soul is, by definition, lowly; it has no higher form. Yet this is as preposterous as assimilation, the result of unjustifiable prejudice.

To clarify Garvey's vision, we can make a terminological distinction: the lower self of Black souls is Black, while the higher self is African. In Hegelese, 'Black' is the changeable and 'African' is the Unchangeable. Africanness is a higher form of Blackness, one that Black souls construct independently of white souls. While Blackness was given to slaves by white people, Africanness is something Black souls give to themselves through devotional rituals of preparation. It is the task of Black souls to actualise their inner Africa through diligent asceticism. As Garvey writes, only 'when the Negro by his own initiative lifts himself from his low state to the highest human standard he will be in a position to stop begging and praying, and demand a place that no individual, race or nation will be able to deny him' (PO 20).

Casting Africanness as the Unchangeable is a form of devotion because it is an attempt to overcome the divided structure of the self that Du Bois identified in double consciousness (I am both African and American, which means I cannot inhabit either position fully) by rejecting the significance of the American sense of self (Blackness) or by casting the Black experience in America as a training in preparation for a reunification with Africa. Black souls, for Garvey, will never be able to call America, or any place outside Africa, home. In order to attain their higher, Unchangeable form, African Americans must reject America and (like all diasporic Africans) return to Africa.

Furthermore, only African leaders – such as Garvey himself – can uplift lower Black selves into their higher African selves. Only when Africans 'have a leadership of our own', Garvey writes, 'will we be able to lift ourselves from this mire of degradation to the heights' (PO 22). Garvey was adamant about the importance of having good African leaders because they were necessary, like bodhisattvas, to uplift Black souls into a higher African self. This was especially important since most Black leaders at the time, in Garvey's view, had betrayed their race and humiliated themselves in order to gain white approval. Here we see a version of the fundamental flaw of unhappy consciousness: individuality, the changeable, is unavoidable. *The biggest impediment to being a leader is that one's individuality can corrupt the higher self.*

Leaders, therefore, must first lift themselves to their higher selves before uplifting others, a difficulty that Garvey well knew: 'few of us [Black leaders] understand what it takes to make a man', what we might call a man of devotion (PO 27).[35] Since the higher self is that with which a leader is meant to uplift others, the task of leadership is endangered if one's individuality gets in the way. True 'leadership means martyrdom, leadership means sacrifice, leadership means giving up one's personality, giving up everything for the cause' (PO 41). In order to become a true leader, Garvey sought to purify himself of his individuality and submit himself to the higher cause.[36]

Hence one of the key teachings of Garveyism: if Black souls 'can only get to know themselves, to know that in them is a

---

35 Garvey writes: the African 'race need men of vision and ability; men of character and above all men of honesty, and that is so hard to find' (PO 31).

36 Garvey even likened himself to Jesus; as Jesus was persecuted by his people, the Jews, so Garvey was attacked and persecuted by Black American leaders (PO 38). 'Radicalism', he writes, 'is a label that is always applied to people who are endeavoring to get freedom. Jesus Christ was the greatest radical the world ever saw' (PO 16, 39). Since return to Africa was the path toward freedom, Africans would walk the same path as Jesus.

sovereign power, is an authority that is absolute', then all Black souls will become African (PO 27). To become African meant repatriation to Africa. Notice how Garvey's devotion steps beyond Washington's stoicism. After having been 'industrially ... trained by the Sage of Tuskegee', writes Garvey, 'the world is having a rude awakening, in that we are evolving a new ideal ... [one that] includes the program of Booker T. Washington and has gone much further' (PO 35). While Washington was necessary for that earlier stage of the development of Black spirit, he 'has passed off the stage of life and left behind a *new problem*' (PO 35; emphasis added).

Recalling Du Bois' identification of Blackness as a problem, Garvey's devotion is the synthesis of the lessons of Washington's stoicism and Du Bois' scepticism. One of the key developments of Garveyism is that the new problem cannot be solved by industry alone, but must be addressed 'by the political and military leaders' (PO 35). Garvey's Black Nationalism was developed in order to guide 'the awakened spirit of the New Negro' so that it might attain this higher form of self: *the African* (PO 35). Taking on the modality of nationalism, however, entails what was perhaps Garveyism's inescapable error.

White God in Blackface (White Empire for a Black World)

If our dialectical parallelist analysis of the devotion section of unhappy consciousness is correct, the central problem of Black devotion was that God was still white. Even though Black thinkers argued that the Christian God was a good, loving, righteous God, it was clear that, for almost two thousand years, that God had been a God allied with whiteness. Heaven might as well have been Jim Crow marked '*for white souls only*'. The God of Black thinkers – the God whose goodness was determined through the pedagogical benefits of slavery and the redemptive suffering of Black people more generally – remained entrenched in white supremacy. Such a God turned Black suffering into a virtue; it called upon Black people to suffer in the name of a goodness they could only ascertain in and beyond death. Henry McNeal

Turner might have claimed that God was a 'Negro', but, given the work of Maria Stewart, David Walker, and others, God's alleged Blackness still justified white violence. That God, then, was a white God in *blackface*, a theological construct that could not shake its embeddedness in a philosophical-theological tradition of white supremacy and white normativity.

As Pinn notes, this interpretation 'was in keeping with notions of American manifest destiny that justified the ill-treatment of and attacks on Native American peoples', as well as the moral framework for the European colonisation of Africa and other continents.[37] Pinn also sees resonances with the 'doctrine of white supremacy and the providential role of white Americans in spreading Western civilization and Christianity'.[38] Though applied to different ends, the form of this interpretation remained racist and colonial.[39]

In his account of the origin of slavery in America, Garvey reports that the reason Sir John Hawkins gave Queen Elizabeth I of England for his attempt to turn Africans into chattel slaves in the Americas was that he was saving them from their supposed natural savagery and barbarism through the blessings of Christianity and European civilisation.[40] Despite the fact that Black folks suffered for hundreds of years under this logic, Garvey redeployed the same reasoning. As Europeans had colonised the globe, Garvey now sought the 'colonization of Africa by the Black race' (PO 41). While we might hope that a Black colonisation of Africa would not entail the kind of oppression and enslavement we see in other colonial projects, this is, and can only be,

---

37 Pinn, *Why Lord?*, 50.
38 Ibid., 51.
39 For Hegel's thinking on world history and colonialism, see Alison Stone, 'Hegel and Colonialism', *Hegel Bulletin* 41:2 (2020), 247–70. See also Teshale Tibebu, *Hegel and the Third World: The Making of Eurocentrism in World History* (Syracuse, NY: Syracuse University Press, 2011).
40 Calling Africa an 'origin' evokes figures of lineage, derivation, evolution, and so on that carry distinct racial and cultural connotations. On a similar note, Moten speaks of 'an engagement with a more attenuated, more internally determined, exteriority and a courtship with an always already unavailable and substitutive origin'. Moten, *In the Break*, 6.

a hope. Casting the Back-to-Africa project in the same colonial *form* means that the violence of (white) colonialist power is still there. A Black coloniser is still a *coloniser*, and Garvey's vision of Africa was steeped in the lessons he had learned from observing the European colonial enterprise.[41] The lens might be different, but the logic remained. As Garvey writes, 'white people have seen their God through white spectacles, we have only now started out (late though it be) to see our God through our own [African] spectacles' (PO 29).

Garvey, like Black religious leaders before him, takes up the God of white people but now sees it through the lens of Africa. 'We Negroes believe in the God of Ethiopia', he writes, 'we shall worship him through the spectacles of Ethiopia' (PO 29). The justification for the Ethiopian spectacles was that the Christian redemption story was the same as Africa's redemption story: 'the doctrine Jesus taught – that of redeeming mankind – is the doctrine we ourselves must teach in the redemption of our struggling race' (PO 39). Just as God's kingdom was corrupted through human action, especially through racial oppression, Africa too, Garvey claimed, was once a great continent. Long before the slave trade, when 'Europe was inhabited by a race of cannibals, a race of savages, naked men, heathens, and pagans, Africa was peopled with a race of cultured Black men, who were masters in art, science and literature; men who were cultured and refined; men who, it was said, were *like the gods*' (PO 48). Pay close attention here to Garvey's language – he merely inverts the terms of colonial logic. He does not challenge the binary structure of savage and civilised, but simply changes who occupies which position.

Garvey advocated for a return to Africa because, he promised, it would reunify all Black folks with a former, higher life, reviving a mythical time when all Africans lived like gods. Yet the problem is that this vision remained colonial in nature; it hinged on the

---

41 This is why Fanon sees such a return to origins movement – where a 'headlong, unstructured, verbal revalorization conceals paradoxical attitudes' – as a response among oppressed peoples to their colonisation. Fanon, 'Racism and Culture', 42.

notion that nations rise and fall, where such rising is predicated on subordinating others. 'Among the first modern African thinkers', writes Mbembe, 'this was simply a way to embrace the teleologies of the period', with the same categories and forms of classification.[42] Eventually becoming Pan-Africanism, Mbembe continues, '[i]t was a discourse of inversion, drawing its fundamental categories from the myths that it claimed to oppose and reproducing their dichotomies: the racial difference between Black and White, the cultural confrontation between the civilized and the savage, the religious opposition between Christians and pagans, the conviction that race founded nation and vice versa'.[43] Du Bois spoke of this inversion when he characterised Garvey as a 'Black Napoleon'; he recognised that Garvey's vision was itself a colonial project, one steeped in the very violence to which Black people were subjected.[44]

For all of Garvey's successes, and notwithstanding the dignity he afforded Black people in the early twentieth century, his devotion remained steeped in discourses of purity and colonialism. Yes, he was unapologetically Black, and in a way that scared white people to their core. To suggest otherwise would be disingenuous. But – and this is a big *but* – his devotion to Africanness as a higher form of Blackness did not necessarily entail a move away from white logics of coloniality and purity. Garvey, like all the thinkers we have traced so far, must be beheld in this tension; he must be acknowledged for the implicit contradiction of his ideals and his programme insofar as it plays a moment in this phenomenology of Black spirit.

Before concluding our discussion of Garvey and turning to Hurston's devotional practices, it will be useful to take a brief look at Henry McNeal Turner's critique of devotion. Born to free parents in 1834, Turner argued that devotion was, in itself, insufficient. More was needed to unify the changeable individual with the Unchangeable universal than merely repainting the

---

42 Mbembe, *Critique of Black Reason*, 88.
43 Ibid., 92.
44 W.E.B. Du Bois, 'Marcus Garvey', in *Writings*, 978.

same concepts, goals, and arguments under the aegis of Africa. It was necessary to create a 'Black God', not just a white God in blackface.[45] Pinn sees Turner's ontological proposition – 'God is Black' – as a 'response to white theologians who portray God as ontologically and epistemologically white – condoning racism'.[46]

Echoing prior attempts to connect African American with Hebrew slaves, Turner claimed that God speaks directly to oppression and suffering, whether that came from being enslaved or from the racist practices that followed emancipation. Indicating a 'relationship between the Hebrews and African-Americans' connects God's covenant to Blackness.[47] Like God's plan for the chosen people, the Jews, the 'teleological nature of events points toward the divine plan of a "civilized" Africa'.[48] The Episcopal priest Reverend Alexander Crummell interpreted the fact that Black people survived chattel slavery as evidence of God's testing or forging of Black souls. 'Their tribulations', writes Crummell, 'were not intended to punish or destroy but to prepare the Black race for a glorious destiny', where this destiny was the spreading of the Gospel to all corners of earth.[49] For Crummell and Turner, slavery was the 'preparation for the task of redeeming Africa'.[50] At the heart of this task, as Mbembe puts it, was 'a category that was at once political and existential ... "the time to come"'.[51] This futural category rested on 'two kinds of capacities and practices: hope and imagination'.[52] Slavery was thus the first stage in a

---

45 Pinn, *Why Lord?*, 54.
46 Ibid.
47 Ibid., 51.
48 Ibid., 52.
49 Quoted in ibid. See also Du Bois' characterisation of a Black Jesus welcoming Crummell to Heaven (SBF 157). As Robert Gooding-Williams puts it: 'Du Bois concludes his narrative [of Crummell's life] by depicting a Black ("dark"), tormented ("pierced"), and Jewish Christ welcoming Crummell to heaven and praising him ... [for h]aving lived and worked his whole life within the Veil.' Robert Gooding-Williams, *In the Shadow of Du Bois: Afro-Modern Political Thought in America* (Cambridge, MA: Harvard University Press, 2009), 100–1.
50 Pinn, *Why Lord?*, 51.
51 Mbembe, *Critique of Black Reason*, 92.
52 Ibid., 93.

longer process of reconstructing the Black self by reconceiving the past and the memory of slavery in terms of a better future in Africa. Thus this task 'consisted of inventing a new interiority'.[53]

An education in slavery served to prepare Black souls for moral development, wherever they may be. The whole purpose of American chattel slavery was to procure, for Africans, Christianity and civilisation. Hence Turner further elaborated an 'emigrationist "theodicy"' that had been initially developed by prominent Black nationalists such as Crummell (and was later taken up by Garvey), but with a new attempt to make God thoroughly Black.[54]

Turner argued that Africa's natural resources were there for Black people to exploit to their own ends, following the return of those educated by American chattel slavery in how to flourish in body and soul. 'The four millions of us in this country [the USA]', Turner wrote, 'are at school, learning the doctrines of Christianity and the elements of civil government.'[55] As soon as we are educated sufficiently to assume control of our vast ancestral domain, we will hear the voice of a mysterious Providence, saying, "Return to the land of your fathers".'[56] More than simply preparing oneself in order to be pure enough to passively receive God's grace, Black people had to do the work of God's plan in order to connect individual Black souls with the Unchanging beyond. Importantly, for Turner, white Americans had failed to work toward divine providence, and thus 'God's ultimate plan did not depend on the cooperation of whites.'[57] Turner believed that American chattel slavery would, in the end, serve as a formative education for Black souls, and that 'the evil deeds of white men

---

53 Pinn, *Why Lord*, 51. See also Alexander Crummell, *Africa and America: Addresses and Discourses* (New York: Negro Universities Press, 1969), 14–36.
54 Pinn, *Why Lord*, 51. See also Henry Blanton Parks, *Africa: The Problem of the New Century; The Part the African Methodist Episcopal Church Is to Have in Its Solution* (New York: A.M.E. Church, 1899); Michelle Mitchell, *Righteous Propagation: African Americans and the Politics of Racial Destiny after Reconstruction* (Chapel Hill: University of North Carolina Press, 2004).
55 Pinn, *Why Lord?*, 51.
56 Turner, cited in ibid., 55.
57 Quoted in ibid., 56.

would not prevent the greatness of Africa'. Further, while the education of Black souls occurred in America, their true advancement 'would only be accomplished in Africa'.[58] Rather than a future in the next life, Turner saw a promise for flourishing on earth. The challenge was just that the land in which that flourishing would take place was not America, where emancipated and educated Black peoples were, but back in Africa. America was and always would be, Turner concluded, a white man's country. The final step of the education in slavery was thus to emigrate back to the homeland. This last step, however, would require more work. Hence, Turner's Black Nationalism required what Hegel calls 'sacramental work', the subject of our next chapter.

Zora Neale Hurston

While Garvey's devotion comes with its own complications, there are other devotees in Black Thought. Zora Neale Hurston (1891–1960) is one. Hurston was devoted to Black people, to be sure. But her devotion was not steeped in externalised unchanging and Unchangeable ideas, ideals, or even gods. While Garvey preached preparation for a unification with an African within and without, Hurston located the Unchangeable wherever Black people gathered, created forms of life, and expressed joy and beauty. Like Wells, Hurston directed her devotion toward the *lives* of Black people, committing to writing about them in ways that spoke to their interiority, to their complex lives. It is precisely the complexity of each individual life that is the object of Hurston's devotion.

If 'Africanness' was Garvey's Unchangeable ideal – an ideal that was itself external to, at least, African Americans – then Hurston commits herself and her writings to the self-determining individual as the site of the Unchangeable exactly where she is. She knows, as Hartman puts it, that the desire for an irretrievable and unknowable African origin 'does not or cannot restore or remedy

---

58 Ibid.

loss, redeem the unceremoniously buried, or bridge the transatlantic divide'.[59] Her commitment, as we will see, changes the content of Black spirit, for it calls our attention toward something else, something other than the violence of white supremacy and antiblackness – it shifts our focus toward the vicissitudes, singular beauty, and genius of Black life. With that shift, we find ourselves in a different modality of devotion – one that discards the catechetical work of preparation in favour of the practice of self-fashioning wherever Black life happens. For Hurston, Black people always and already have all they need within themselves. There is no need to turn to external realities – even (and perhaps especially) to notions of race.

Like all of our thinkers, Hurston's devotion brings its own contradictions. Garvey and Hegel see devotion as a commitment to something that overcomes individuality. But from an early age, Hurston was encouraged to foster her individuality. Lucy Ann Potts, Hurston's mother, 'encouraged [her] to strive continually for individuality and self-expression'.[60] Growing up in an antiblack world, Hurston struggled and suffered. By the time she was fourteen, she had worked multiple jobs. Though she showed writerly and scholarly promise, her assertive demeanour and frankness vis-à-vis her social world prevented her from receiving the attention and accolades in life that she only received decades after her death. She worked incessantly but could not pay the bills. She wrote plays and books that received rave reviews, but that did not bring her comfort or lasting success. Moving from job to job, and becoming increasingly sick, Hurston enjoyed 'brief periods of professional notoriety', but died sick and penniless – died sick *because* she was penniless. As Alice Walker writes:

> Without money, an illness, even a simple one, can undermine the will. Without money, getting into a hospital is problematic, and getting out without money to pay for the treatment is nearly impossible. Without money, one becomes dependent on other

---

59 Hartman, *Scenes of Subjection*, 76.
60 Katie Cannon, *Black Womanist Ethics* (Eugene, OR: Wipf and Stock, 1988), 99.

people who are likely to be – even in their kindness – erratic in their support and despotic in their expectations of return.[61]

We could, of course, see Hurston's story as ultimately tragic. Because the truth is Hurston should not have died the way she did. She should have enjoyed a life filled with the very joy and complexity about which she wrote; she should have had enjoyed longstanding acclaim in and throughout her life. But such a conclusion would not fare well in light of Hurston's own self-identity. She did not want pity – certainly not the kind of pity that would reduce her to an object of white sympathy. 'I am not tragically colored', she once wrote, elaborating:

> There is no great sorrow damned up in my soul, nor lurking behind my eyes ... I do not belong to the sobbing school of Negrohood who hold that nature somehow has given them a lowdown dirty deal and whose feelings are all hurt about it ... No, I do not weep at the world – I am too busy sharpening my oyster knife.[62]

To be fiercely individualist in this way – to hold and behold the individual as the Unchangeable ideal to which she was committed and was always-already enacting – pushed Hurston to adopt a different politics, a different approach to the ways Black collective life could be understood. So, no: we shouldn't pity Hurston – though it is necessary to account for the structural and interpersonal forms of antiblackness (even and especially as they are refracted through gender and class) that led to her anonymous death.

Womanist ethicist Katie Cannon puts it this way: 'Hurston, like Black people generally, understood suffering not as a moral norm nor as a desirable ethical quality, but rather as the typical state of affairs.'[63] In other words, Hurston understood what Christina Sharpe pushes contemporary readers to understand – namely, that

---

61 Alice Walker, quoted in ibid., 116.
62 Zora Neale Hurston, 'How It Feels to Be Colored Me', *World Tomorrow*, 1928, quoted in Alice Walker, 'In Search of Zora Neale Hurston', *Ms.*, March 1975, 88.
63 Cannon, *Black Womanist Ethics*, 104.

antiblackness is the 'ground' upon which we walk.[64] Knowing this, Hurston did not appeal to an external notion for reprieve. She, instead, turned to Black people, individual Black people, as the concrete sites of and for the possibility of meaningful and joyful existence. 'The solace of generalization was taken from me', she once wrote, 'but I received the richer gift of individualism ... All clumps of people turn out to be individuals on close inspection.'[65] Adhering – *devoting* herself – to this truism, she lived, thought, and wrote about Black life in light of the individual Black lives to which she was devoted.

This devotion placed her politically out of step with her contemporaries. It is no coincidence that Garvey and Hurston were both sharp critics of integration. Anticipating Saidiya Hartman's critique of community, Hurston preferred to stay with the nitty-gritty interpersonal dynamics of Black life – of Black lives. Integration, she thought, would starve and eliminate the creativity and vivacity she saw in individual acts of self-formation. In a letter to the *Orlando Sentinel* she wrote in response to the 1954 *Brown v. Board of Education* decision, she said: 'How much satisfaction can I get from a court order for somebody to associate with me who does not wish me near them? ... Since the days of the never-to-be sufficiently deplored Reconstruction, there has been current the belief that there is no greater delight to Negroes than physical association with whites.'[66] As such, she did not adhere to what we might call the 'race consciousness' of her contemporaries, deeming integration 'insulting rather than honoring my race'.[67] Thinking of Black people in generalities, forcing them to integrate into white institutions, erased the rich and complex interior lives they spun in their communities. 'The word "race"', Hurston wrote, 'is a loose classification of physical characteristics.

---

64 Christina Sharpe, *In the Wake: On Blackness and Being* (Durham, NC: Duke University Press, 2016), 7.
65 Zora Neale Hurston, *Dust Tracks on a Road* (New York: Harper Perennial, 2006), 248.
66 Zora Neale Hurston, 'Letter to the Orlando Sentinel', *Orlando Sentinel*, 11 August 1955.
67 Ibid.

It tells nothing about the insides of people. Pointing at achievements tells nothing either. Races have never done anything. What seems race achievement is the work of individuals.'[68]

Consider that last line: *what seems race achievement is the work of individuals*. While Garvey saw 'Africanness' as the Unchangeable to which a *race* of people should be devoted, Hurston thought there was no need for such preparatory work because the Unchangeable is already here. Put differently, the preparatory practice – which is to say, Hurston's devotion – is found in making oneself in community. To live is already to be making life. Hurston's devotion is not aspirational – there is no telos, no place or destination to which the work of self-fashioning points. Instead, according to Hurston, the possibility of and for self-making is already here, it's already happening and happening all the time. It is happening because, for Hurston, Black people are *people*. In our eyes, Hurston shows how the changeable designation 'Negro' is already overcome and the Unchangeable is present whenever and wherever one fashions a life.

> I *do* glory when a negro does something fine, I gloat because he or she has done a fine thing, but not because he is a Negro. That is incidental and accidental. It is the human achievement which I honor. I execrate a foul act of a Negro but again not on the grounds that the doer was a Negro, but because it was foul ... In other words, I know that I cannot accept responsibility for thirteen million people. Every tub must sit on its own bottom.[69]

From our contemporary lenses, Hurston's refusal of race consciousness might seem out of step with a kind of liberatory politics. But if we pay close attention, we see someone who was so devoted to Black lives that she savoured their complexity where others (such as Du Bois with his 'Talented Tenth' or Garvey with his mythic African royalty) denigrated what they saw as a lowly, backwards existence.

For Hurston, Black people were and are *people*; and individual people, no matter what the racial designation, have rich interior

---

68 Hurston, *Dust Tracks*, 249.
69 Ibid.

lives in which they formulate personal and collective narratives. Hurston devoted herself to mining that rich interiority – through anthropological story gathering – for its self-fashioning and self-determining capacities. Neither organisations like the UNIA or NAACP nor charismatic leaders like Garvey or Du Bois could respond to the creative capacities of individual lives. In fact, Hurston was not even concerned with a 'there' – a higher self out there, across the ocean or in governmental institutions. 'There is no single Negro nor no single organization', she wrote, 'which can carry the thirteen million in any direction.'[70] Unlike Garvey with his commitment to taking Black people back to Africa, Hurston was convinced that no one needed to 'steer' Black people in any direction.[71] They did not need to leave their present lives and sail to an Africa they had never known. Freedom and self-determination could and would be cultivated right where people found themselves, from the bayous of Louisiana to the Florida swamps. It would show up in different, complex, and sometimes violent ways.

Hurston's characters attest to this, such as Janie Crawford, the protagonist of *Their Eyes were Watching God*. Having endured marital abuse from her two previous husbands, Janie 'becomes a woman' in search of love and care. She eventually finds it in the arms of Vergible 'Tea Cake' Woods, a man twenty years her junior, who 'makes her feel alive, vital, needed, wanted, loved and unlimited, and she gives of herself freely. The horizon with all its infinite possibilities, is back.'[72] In the end, however, Tea Cake loses his mind and threatens to kill her.

---

70 Ibid., 251.
71 Here Hurston is closer to what Nathaniel Mackey calls a '"broken" claim to connection', which Moten elaborates in relation to the complicated relations 'between Africa and African America that seek to suture corollary, asymptotically divergent ruptures – maternal estrangement and the thwarted romance of the sexes – that he [Mackey] refers to as "wounded kinship" and "the sexual cut"'. Moten, *In the Break*, 6. Referring to Nathanial Mackey, *Bedouin Hornbook*, Callaloo Fiction Series, vol. 2 (Lexington: University Press of Kentucky, 1986), 30, 34–5.
72 Zora Neale Hurston, *Their Eyes were Watching God*, quoted in Cannon, *Black Womanist Ethics*, 135.

> The gun came up unsteadily but quickly and leveled at Janie's breast. She noted that even in his delirium he took good aim ... He steadied himself against the jamb of the door and Janie thought to run into him and grab his arm, but she saw the quick motion of taking aim and heard the click. Saw the ferocious look in his eyes and went mad with fear ... She threw up the barrel of the rifle in frenzied hope and fear ... He paid no more attention to the pointing gun than if it were Janie's dog finger. She saw him stiffen himself all over as he leveled and took aim. The fiend in him must kill and Janie was the only living thing he saw.[73]

But Janie shoots Tea Cake before he shoots her. She kills him to save herself. She kills him as part of her own self-fashioning. Janie enacts violence – even to the point of death, and even against someone she loves – in the name of preserving and fashioning her own individuality. She kills the determinations of others, even a spouse, in the name of her own power of self-creation.

Hurston's novels are filled with characters like Janie – characters whose fierce self-fashioning places them in difficult situations that force them into impossible decisions and actions. The point is that Hurston's devotion appears in her depiction of these characters *as* individuals, as those who find something like a higher self – the Unchangeable – *in* themselves, *in* their actions. What we are focusing on here is not the difficult ethical decisions one has to make in self-*preparation* for a later nowhere, but instead the possibilities and pitfalls of self-*fashioning* a life as it is lived now and here. Hurston attunes us to acts of self-formation by attuning us to individuals' present interiority, to their capacity for sorrow and pain as it is experienced in and from community. Perhaps most of all, such acts of self-formation bring Black joy.

Lindsey Stewart, in her masterful text on Hurston, sees in her a politics of Black joy:

> Politically, the politics of joy includes a shift toward self-determination and a shift away from the pursuit of white political

---

73 Hurston, *Their Eyes were Watching God* (New York: HarperCollins e-book), 264.

recognition; a refusal of assumptions of Black southern tragedy and inferiority; and a keen awareness of racial dynamics that remain intransigent, even while Black representation in the public sphere increases.[74]

While Garvey relied on the language of colonialism and the iconography of empire – which is to say, while he was drawing from white language to articulate his political vision – Hurston was savouring, without elevating, the figurative capacity of Black dialect, the imaginative power of Black folklore, the genius of Black idioms emerging from the countryfolk of the Florida swamps or the Voodoo priests of New Orleans. To find Black life, Hurston did not envision an African Empire but simply listened to the colourful 'lying-sessions' of farmers and countryfolk sitting on the porch of a village store in Eatonville, Florida, or any other rural Southern site of Black gathering, sociality, and creation.[75]

Rather than trying to sculpt a Black identity based on the form of the master, in the form of empire, Hurston saw beauty, life, meaning, and power in Southern Black life that already existed and was already underway. Black expressions of joy have no need of being translated into the King's speech. While Garvey designed a flag, often known as the Pan-African flag, Hurston sought to capture Black language as it exists, without need of translation or so-called refinement. There is no mere respectability politics here. If there must be a comparison with the white measurement of civilisation, Hurston did something closer to Chaucer's identification and celebration of what was the English vernacular. As Chaucer collected tales composing the English identity using the idioms in which they were spoken, Hurston collected folk tales and living mythologies using the idioms in which they were shared.

She found Black life in storytelling.

She did it by writing in the idiom of the people with whom she communed.

---

74 Stewart, *The Politics of Black Joy*, 14.
75 Hurston, *Dust Tracks*, 48.

And she did it by leading a fiercely 'unctuous' life, filled with quiet grace and unshouted courage.[76]

Zora Neale Hurston didn't have to appeal to external notions of an Unchangeable beyond in order to love Black life. She rejected the call to transcend the particularities of individual interiority. Instead, she knew, like all the other Black women we celebrate in this book, that the possibilities for Black spirit are found right here, in this place, in the specifics of Black lives as they are lived, wherever they are found. The work is already being done here and now. It is being written in a Black idiom, and it describes the rich interiority of Black life – of Black lives. While Hurston died sick and penniless, laid in an unmarked grave until Alice Walker discovered it decades later, she nevertheless devoted her life to sitting with the individual lives of Black people. In so doing, she articulated – gathered and savoured – the fact that Black people had, and still have, joy. She wrote of their rhythms; she wrote in their words. She tended to those who were not interested in white recognition. She showed how Black lives were, in and of themselves, already beautiful, bursting with life and meaning.

In short, Hurston devoted herself to the work of showing how Black people fashion lives in this world, throughout the diaspora. As an anthropologist, she did not simply write about this; she herself lived it, lived it with those she studied *as* a Black woman. She may have died in poverty and sickness, but her life was staked on a beautiful commitment to Black life as it is lived. It was work, and it was sacred work. It was *sacramental* work. In the next chapter, will see another version of this work in the lives and labours of Dr Martin Luther King, Jr and Ella Baker.

---

76 For more on this, see Cannon's *Black Womanist Ethics*, chapters 4 and 5.

5

Sacramental Work and Desire

Dr Martin Luther King, Jr and Ella Baker

Hurston left us with the individual. Her legacy was steeped in attention to Black lives as they were lived. She developed rich and complex characters who defied easy moral categorisation. More than this, she critiqued the dominant Black politics of her day, recognising race and racism but not succumbing to it. Her life was marked by a devotion to integrity – to the integrity of making something of oneself, of being a 'tub' that could stand on its own bottom. She took joy in this. And she took joy in expressing this joy in her characters – even as they struggled.

Hurston therefore retained the affective dimensions of Hegelian devotion, but moved beyond it. Her attention to joy speaks to the feeling of that devotion, but it is turned toward the individual – a turn that exceeds Hegel's discussion, and one that pushed beyond and beneath Garvey's commitment to 'Africanness'. It is precisely in this turn that we see the next phase of the phenomenology of Black spirit. And it is this turn toward the single subject who must *do the work* that speaks to Hurston's role as a transitional figure, one who bridges the gap between devotion and the next movement in Black life. We call this next movement 'sacramental work and desire', and here we explore Martin Luther King, Jr and Ella Baker as its exemplars.

King and Hegel

Among all the Black thinkers discussed in this book, Martin Luther King might have the clearest relation to Hegel. Even amid the intensity of the Montgomery bus boycott, King said that Hegel was his favourite philosopher.[1] Reportedly first encountering Hegel during his undergraduate years at Morehouse, when he was only fifteen years old, he 'succumbed to an almost uncritical fascination with the Hegelian dialectic'.[2] Later, as part of his Boston University graduate studies, King studied Hegel more deeply in Edgar S. Brightman's year-long philosophy of religion course.[3] When Brightman died during King's second year at Boston, his protégé L. Harold DeWolf became King's mentor. Under DeWolf's tutelage, King was immersed in rigorous studies of ancient, medieval, and modern philosophy, personalism, Christian ethics, systematic theology, non-western religions, psychoanalysis, existentialism, and Heidegger. All the while, however, 'he turned back to Hegel, reviewing the *Phenomenology of Mind* and poring over *the Philosophy of History* and *The Philosophy of Right*', with W.T. Stace's *The Philosophy of Hegel* being especially formative for his grasp of dialectics.[4] Hegel clearly struck a chord in King's mind, though his feelings toward the German philosopher morphed. He admired Hegel's 'world-historical men' but dismissed 'Hegel's [so-called] "absolute idealism"'; he always venerated 'Hegel's analysis of the dialectical process'.[5] We can only speculate what he might

---

1 Interview with Thomas Johnson, *The Montgomery Advertiser*, 19 January 1956. See also Stephen C. Ferguson, 'The Philosopher King: An Examination of the Influence of Dialectics on King's Political Thought and Practice', in *The Liberatory Thought of Martin Luther King, Jr.: Critical Essays on the Philosopher King*, ed. Robert E. Birt (Lanham, MD: Lexington Books, 2014), 91.
2 David Levering Lewis, *King: A Critical Biography* (Urbana: University of Illinois Press, 1978), 20. Lewis notes that King only earned a 'C' in that class.
3 Ferguson, 'The Philosopher King', 91; see also Stephen B. Oates, *Let the Trumpet Sound: A Life of Martin Luther King, Jr.* (New York: Harper & Row, 1982), 36.
4 Oates, *Let the Trumpet Sound*, 38. The question of Hegel's influence on the early King is unsettled. Stephen C. Ferguson, for example, argues that 'King's *early* conception of dialectics is not Hegelian, but rather reflective in character ... However, after 1965, King as dialectician becomes more Hegelian, approximating ... a regulative dialectic.' Ferguson, 'The Philosopher King', 88. Ferguson notes that 'there is no evidence that King read *Science of Logic*', though he did read the smaller *Logic*.
5 Oates, *Let the Trumpet Sound*, 38. In contrast to Hegel's seeming idealism, King insisted on a kind of 'Realism' that resonates strongly with much of Hegel's *Philosophy of Right* insofar as it embodies a force that 'compels us

have thought of the dialectical parallelism in our *Phenomenology of Black Spirit*.

Through this formative education in dialectical thinking, 'Hegel helped King out of his dilemma over pacifism and neo-orthodoxy'.[6] On the one hand, 'Protestant liberalism was too optimistic about human nature' insofar as it believed a 'false idealism' that had an 'abiding faith to adapt and reform [the individual] so that one might receive God'.[7] This is, in essence, Hegel's devotion. On the other hand, Reinhold Niebuhr 'and the neo-orthodoxists were too pessimistic' insofar as 'they lapsed into a mood of antirationalism and semifundamentalism, which exaggerated the utter hopelessness of the world and man's incapacity to change it or himself'.[8] This is basically what Hegel means by self-mortification. In our parallelism, neither Garvey's devotion nor (what became) X's self-mortification suffice because, in King's eyes, humans are neither simply good nor simply bad. In each individual there is 'an eternal civil war between the two raging within him'.[9] As Hegel might put it, there is an internal strife between the changeable and the Unchangeable in each self-consciousness. The task of sacramental work and desire is, in King's words, to 'appeal to the good in man, by asking him to open himself to the possibility God [the Unchangeable] had given him for brotherhood'.[10] This began, King writes, because of a 'revolutionary change in the Negro's evaluation of himself', one

---

    to admit that the struggle will continue until freedom is a reality for all the oppressed peoples of the world'. Martin Luther King, Jr., *Testament of Hope: The Essential Writings and Speeches*, ed. James M. Washington (San Francisco: Harper, 2003), 7. Elsewhere King pointed out another disagreement with Hegel: 'his absolute idealism was rationally unsound to me because it tended to swallow the many in the one'. Martin Luther King, Jr. *Stride toward Freedom* (New York: Harper & Row, 1958), 100–1.

6 Oates, *Let the Trumpet Sound*, 39.
7 Ibid.
8 Ibid. In his 'Letter from Birmingham Jail', King characterises this dialectical tension thus: 'we need emulate neither the "do-nothingism" of the complacent nor the hatred and despair of the Black nationalist' (WW 75).
9 Oates, *Let the Trumpet Sound*, 39.
10 Ibid.

that sparked a 'determination to struggle and sacrifice until the walls of segregation have been fully crushed by the battering rams of justice'.[11] Here we might hear Hurston echoing in King's words: while she wasn't interested in integration (and neither was Garvey, for that matter), Hurston and her characters speak to an openness to the possibilities of selves-in-community – they are individuals with integrity, people who try to live joyous and worthwhile lives.

King's ethical impulse was still toward the collective, but, as we will show, he knew that the success or failure of realising this collective ethical vision depended on the actions of each person. To achieve the beloved community, people had to put in the work. But they had to do it with an eye toward the Unchangeable (which, in King's case, was God). King therefore saw nonviolent direct action as this work – this sacramental work – that navigated the middle ground between the pure passivity of devotion we saw in the last chapter and the pure activity of self-mortification we will see in the next chapter. The importance of nonviolent direct action is not merely what it does to white folk, but also what it does to Black folk. Nonviolence brings about 'the revolutionary change in the Negro's evaluation of himself' by 'demonstrating to the Negro, North and South, that many stereotypes he has held about himself and other Negroes are not valid'.[12] We might therefore call nonviolent direct action a kind of work that has the Unchangeable as its object of desire but is nevertheless enacted *through* individuals. Though this work happens in the concrete context of human action, it is nevertheless a thankful work, a pious praxis. Because it is steeped in and yearns for the Unchangeable, this work is sacred. It is sanctified. It is sacramental.

Sacramental Work and Desire: Returning to Hurston on the Way to King

Sacramental work and desire [*Begierde und Arbeit*] is the second moment in unhappy consciousness insofar as it emerges out of the

---

11 King, *A Testament of Hope*, 6.
12 Ibid., 76.

moment of devotion. Despite its purest intentions, devotion failed to unify the changeable individual with its Unchangeable essence because its relation was through feeling or sensation and therefore failed to eliminate the individual. Unhappy consciousness resorted to feeling because it needed to avoid the inevitable failures that come with a purely cognitive relation to the Unchangeable. As Hegel puts it, '*the return of the feeling heart into itself* is to be taken to mean that it has an *actual* existence as an *individual*' (PS 218). Feeling was meant to eliminate any trace of individuality, and thus purify the changeable individual so that it may receive the Unchangeable, essential being, or God.

But, as Zora Neale Hurston knew, feeling wouldn't suppress the individual's prominence; it would only heighten it. We return to Hurston here because she is a transitional figure in every sense of the word: her life exemplifies the transition between devotion and sacramental work and desire. In her life's work, we find ourselves hearing Black speech, moving to Black rhythms, and witnessing Black feelings – not in an attempt to prepare oneself for some external Unchangeable (like Garvey's Africanness) but instead because those feelings were *good unto themselves*. Hegel tells us that 'in its feeling the essential Being is separated from it, yet this feeling is, in itself, a feeling of *self*', which means that the devotional unhappy consciousness ends up only touching itself: 'it has felt the object of its pure feeling and this object is itself'. Devotion leads only to 'self-feeling' (PS 218). More than simply thinking of or feeling the actual world, unhappy consciousness' relation to it 'is the *changing* of it or *working on it*' (PS 220). The individual makes its mark on the external world, not (like the sceptic) only to negate it, but to come into communion with the Unchangeable *in* the world – and here, we again hear Hurston's words reverberating through Hegel: *I do not weep at the world – I am too busy sharpening my oyster knife.*

With the failures of devotion, unhappy consciousness recognised that it could not avoid individuality. Earthly life is not only unavoidable, but is God's gift, the gift of life. Seeing this life as a gift allows us to think of everyday desire and labour as the fulfilment of and thanksgiving for this gift. Receiving this gift, we try to give back, to give in return. My work is thus not a form of self-*re*nunciation but of self-*an*nunciation. As such, it is a kind of thanksgiving, wherein the ability to work is a gift that must be appreciated and returned.

The trouble, though, is that work, like devotion, reasserts rather than renounces individuality; Hurston knew this. She had no truck with eternal and external ideals; she was content with self-*an*nunciation. She preferred the richness and complexity of Black individuals who spoke differently, moved to different rhythms, and yes – even practised a different kind of magic. On this reading, Hurston was not simply a devotee; she was more than the passive recipient of a catechetical work that would make her ready for communion with an external and eternal reality. She renounced the Unchangeable (as something in the) beyond and asserted the individual self – both *her* individual self, and the individual selves of her characters – because there is a moment of unsurpassable enjoyment and satisfaction in a work well done. *What seems race achievement is the work of individuals.*

And yet, 'race achievement' is still a *thing*, an *idea*, a reality with which many contended. Garvey might have called it 'Africanness'; others might call it God; and though she certainly wouldn't frame it this way, Hurston might have called it the individual. Self-fashioning might have been a gift that Hurston gave herself and her characters, but it is still a gift. The changeable individual approaches the world as 'a *gift* from an alien source, which the Unchangeable makes over to consciousness to *make use of*' (PS 220; emphases added). As Hyppolite puts it, the 'world exists only to provide it with the occasion to discover itself and to pose itself for-itself as it is in-itself'.[13] And such a gift is so vast that a finite being cannot ever fully repay it.

Hurston would not have called the gift of individuality an 'alien' gift. It was something *she* cultivated. It was something she *worked* at. And yet, in order to do her work, Hurston still relied upon others: she worked odd jobs and she depended upon the beneficence of others. In turn – though not necessarily in repayment – Hurston

---

13 Hyppolite, *Structure and Genesis*, 209.

devoted her life to telling Black stories. Or, more precisely, she devoted her life to telling the stories of Black people. She wrote for *them*. And in so doing, she expressed her own desire – fulfilled at times and disappointed at others – to be in communion with the other individuals to whom she was committed. 'The meaning of [unhappy consciousness's] labor', writes Hyppolite, 'is to reach ... communion'.[14] Hurston wrote, thought, and engaged in the name of making an individual life-in-community. Her life was marked by her commitment to those with whom she communed. Her work was a labour of self-fashioning; it was also a labour of love. But more to the point, it was *labour*.

Hurston thus enacted a different form of labour – one not overdetermined by the desires of the master in the master-slave dialectic, but instead understood as a response to a gift that she appreciated. And, just as she is not a pure devotee, neither should her work be understood solely in terms of this next moment of this phenomenology of Black spirit. Hurston is a profoundly transitional figure since she announces the limitations of devotion through her movement beyond it. She was committed to the individual as the Unchangeable, but this Unchangeable is still immanent, still situated within, not beyond, the individual. Hurston's individual is not Garvey's Africanness, and because of this, her work pushes us beyond the self-negating work of devotion into the powerful praxis of self-affirmation.

For Hurston, this kind of self-affirming and self-fashioning work was sacred. It marked her life and her legacy. And, perhaps more to the point, Hurston's life and its legacy powerfully, *powerfully*, speak to and express what King called 'the revolutionary change in the Negro's evaluation of himself'. Hurston knew better; Black people were – and are – complex. And while we might disagree with her politics, she charted a path of and for Black self-dignity and determination that can neither be overstated nor overlooked.

Why do we say all this? Because, in the phenomenology of Black spirit, *Martin Luther King, Jr is logically impossible without*

---

14 Ibid.

Zora Neale Hurston. King embodies and extends the work of self-fashioning to which Hurston devoted her life. But there is a difference – slight as it may seem – that makes *all* the difference. King embraced the sacramental work and desire of the determinate, changing individual, but he did so with an eye toward the Unchangeable, toward God.

This eye toward God *is* the difference that makes all the difference: Hurston will signal how the master-as-desire and the slave-as-work return in one self-consciousness; she worked on what she wanted *how* she wanted, and in this regard, her work is a form of self-sacrifice and thanksgiving. This work is sacred, but it is not *sanctified*.[15] Hurston's work needs neither the approval nor the teleological necessity of an external, transcendent Unchangeable like God. Her work is important in itself; her commitment to individuality was steeped in her assumption that Black people have all they need.

But King's work *is* sanctified. He did not share the pessimism of the neo-orthodox theologians, and neither did he share the unbridled optimism of his liberal Protestant counterparts. Here we can see even better why King appreciated Hegel: in Hegel, we find a world that is not *merely* fallen, but is an expression of the Unchangeable. Knowing the divided nature of the world – a theme to which we will return in a moment – King therefore *finds* himself committed to individuality *in spite of himself*. King was *called*, by God, to do his work. While Hurston willingly, cognitively, and devotionally committed herself to individuality, King's 'descent' (if we may call it that) into his individuality wasn't (fully) intentional; it happened because his calling was suited to his individual talents; it reinforced his uniqueness, his brilliance, his charisma. And it was precisely his fitness for his calling that allowed him to see his influence, his oration, and his effectiveness

---

15 We are aware of the work Hurston did in her book *The Sanctified Church*. But we know that, first, that work is an ethnographic study, and second, that Hurston was not particularly invested in theistic paradigms. That's the difference we want to signal here – namely, the divine as an external and Unchangeable referent to which one's life is devoted and around which one's work is oriented.

as good. In King's life and work, then, labour becomes sanctified, as it works on a sanctified world. Hence, we call this moment of unhappy consciousness – a moment that Hurston logically inaugurates and King fully embodies – *sacramental work and desire*.

Shaky Goods, Divided Selves, and Divided Worlds: King, the Law, and Justice

Having been called, King understood his work as good. This good however, is a shaky good; effective, brilliant, and charismatic, King nevertheless made what we might understand as ethically dubious decisions, like his overcited infidelity. It is here that we can see, in part, what makes the unhappy consciousness 'unhappy'. On the one hand, unhappy consciousness recognises that its actuality and individuality are unavoidable, and so it starts to view its earthly existence as meaningful because it derives from the Unchangeable. As Hegel writes, the 'world of actuality to which [sacramental] desire and work are directed is not for this consciousness something *intrinsically null*, something merely to be set aside and consumed' (PS 219). On the other hand, while unhappy consciousness might find meaning in its existence, it also discovers that it cannot be *fully* good – which is to say, it cannot completely become the Unchangeable. As Hyppolite puts it, 'self-consciousness remains unhappy because its essence – the unity of the immutable and the specific – remains a beyond for it, a truth which it does not find within itself and with which it cannot coincide'.[16]

Unhappy consciousness, then, is divided, struggling between various poles of existence – 'good' and 'bad', 'passive' and 'active', and so on. And here's the thing: the one who engages in sacramental work and desire sees this dividedness, but recognises that *the world is just as divided as it is*, recognises that the world is 'an *actuality broken in two*' (PS 219). Just as unhappy consciousness is a divided self, with one half the changeable unessential and the other the Unchangeable essential, so too the world is in 'one aspect intrinsically null, but from another aspect is also a sanctified

---

16 Hyppolite, *Structure and Genesis*, 208.

world' (PS 219). The world is imbued with the essentiality of the Unchangeable; it just requires the work and the desire to bring it out. Perhaps King knew, better than anyone else, that the external and internal 'civil war raging within' humanity produced a striving toward a good – one that could always be thwarted.

But the divide exceeds the internal struggles of each individual. Sometimes, it shows up in laws, in the notions of 'justice' to which we are all encouraged to assent. King knew this: evoking Aquinas, he knew there were two types of laws: unjust and just laws. Unjust laws appear when, through one aspect, the world is deemed intrinsically null; just laws appear when, through another aspect, the world is deemed a sanctified world. An unjust law is 'out of harmony with the moral law' of the Unchangeable; it is a 'human law that is not rooted in eternal law and natural law' and so 'degrades human personality' (WW 70). Therefore, according to King, 'one has not only a legal but a moral responsibility to disobey unjust laws' (WW 70).[17]

By contrast, a just law is a 'man-made code that squares with the moral law or the law of God', the Unchangeable (WW 70). In harmony with God's law, a just law 'uplifts human personality', and thereby compels not only a 'legal but a moral responsibility to obey' (WW 70).[18] King argues that an 'individual who breaks a law that conscience tells him is unjust, and who willingly accepts the penalty of imprisonment in order to arouse the conscience of the community over its injustice, is in reality expressing the

---

17 Here King locates the inverted moralities of integration and segregation. The civil disobedience in the name of integration and desegregation obligates following just laws but not unjust laws, while what King calls the '"uncivil disobedience" of the segregationist' obligates following unjust laws (such as voter disenfranchisement) but not just laws (such as the *Brown v. Board of Education* decision). King, *Testament of Hope*, 164.
18 King describes unjust and just laws in other ways: 'An unjust law is a code that a numerical or power majority group compels a minority group to obey but does not make binding on itself. This is *difference* made legal. By the same token, a just law is a code that a majority compels a minority to follow and that it is willing to follow itself. This is *sameness* made legal' (WW 71). Or: a 'law is unjust if it is inflicted on a minority that, as a result of being denied the right to vote, had no part in enacting or devising the law' (WW 71).

highest respect for law' (WW 72). It is no surprise that King here refers to Augustine's distinction between laws in the City of God and laws in the earthly city, and to Martin Buber's 'I-Thou' and 'I-It' relationships, since those two philosophers also display tendencies of sacramental work and desire.

The possibility for changing the changeable into the Unchangeable, the inessential into the essential, renders work the means for unhappy consciousness to overcome its separation from the Unchangeable. Using Paul Tillich's claim that 'sin is separation', King casts segregation as just this type of separation from the Unchangeable (WW 71). 'Is not segregation', asks King, 'an existential expression of man's tragic separation, his awful estrangement, his terrible sinfulness?' (WW 71). Racial segregation is the legalisation of the separateness that sacramental work desires to overcome.

King does this work through nonviolent direct action; the goal is not to destroy or nullify America, but to work to bring out its higher self, to end segregation and separation and unify the nation. Since, Hegel writes, the world of 'actuality is for consciousness the form of the Unchangeable, it [consciousness] is unable to nullify it [the world of actuality]' (PS 220). In Christian language, God made the world for humans to work on and enjoy. We cannot simply reject the world outright because it is God's gift to us, and we are the stewards of this gift. As Hegel puts it, 'this comes about through the Unchangeable's itself having *surrendered* its embodied form, and having *relinquished* it for the enjoyment of consciousness' (PS 220; emphases added).

King's work toward a good – however shaky this good might be – speaks to what Hegel called 'a relation of two extremes': a passive and an active side (PS 221). On the one side unhappy consciousness 'stands as actively present'; on the other side what it is present to is itself as 'a passive actuality' (PS 221). Both sides, however, belong to the Unchangeable. When the individual acts on the world, doing God's work, they are not just acting on a purely passive world, for the supposedly passive world is only there, to be worked on, because the Unchangeable made it so. While the action of the changeable, Hegel writes, 'appears as the *power* in which actuality is dissolved ... this power which it [the world] displays in its activity [is really] the beyond of itself' (PS 221; emphasis added).

In Hegel's unhappy consciousness, the individual might initially assume it is the active force of change, but it is really passive, a pawn in God's plan. The actions of the changeable thus really belong to the Unchangeable, as the actions of the slave really belong to the master or the work of missionaries really belongs to their God. Unhappy consciousness thus renounces itself as passive and dependent in its labour. It is not *my* work, but *God's* work. Hyppolite considers this 'the humiliation of man'.[19]

At the same time, this is precisely what the entire structure of unhappy consciousness seeks to do: self-renunciation. The changeable individual 'assigns the essence of its action not to itself but to the beyond', the Unchangeable (PS 222). Sacramental work and desire are meant to consist of 'two moments of *reciprocal self-surrender*' (PS 222). As the Unchangeable surrenders and renounces itself to the world, the changeable individual also surrenders and renounces itself to the Unchangeable.

Turning to King, then, and riffing off the biblical text, we could say that he was called *and* he was chosen. His fitness for the call reinforced the work he did; in turn, King understood his work to be the work of God. His platform, his preaching, and his implementation of nonviolent direct action as a strategy for change were the Unchangeable acting through his work; and yet, he recognised that the good of social transformation would not be possible without the work of individuals. King's work may have been his God's work. But it was also work that *he* had to do.

Beloved Community

King's goal was 'redemption and reconciliation ... [through] the creation of the beloved community'.[20] King calls this form of community *beloved* because the relations composing it are

---

19 Hyppolite, *Structure and Genesis*, 212.
20 King, *Testament of Hope*, 8.

relations of love. This love is not 'some sentimental emotion' but what is signalled by the Greek term *agape*.[21] To clarify, King cites the three Greek terms for 'love' used in the New Testament: *eros*, *philia*, and *agape*. *Agape* means 'understanding, redeeming good will for all men, an overflowing love which seeks nothing in return ... the love of God working in the lives of men'.[22] *Agape* is a love between people rooted simply in God's love of them, which allows one to love 'the person who does the evil deed while hating the deed he does'.[23] In Hegel's terms, King's *agape* is the proper relation of the changeable to the Unchangeable within oneself and to another; it is a way of one person reconciling with the Unchangeable within themselves by reconciling themselves with the Unchangeable in others.

Creating a beloved community will 'require a qualitative change in our souls as well as a quantitative change in our lives'.[24] The kind of change King envisions requires a certain means of achieving that change. This means, of course, is nonviolence. Speaking of one of 'the most persistent philosophical debates ... the question of ends and means', King sees nonviolence as the 'only way to reestablish the broken community', to build the beloved community out of the shards of the ideals that were cracked on racist realities.[25] 'The aftermath of nonviolence is the creation of the beloved community, while the aftermath of violence is tragic bitterness.'[26] To be more precise, nonviolence is the method, while the means is desegregation. '[D]esegregation is only a first step on the road to the good society', while '[i]ntegration is the ultimate goal'.[27] Without integration, desegregation merely shifts

---

21 Ibid. King's thinking about agape is rooted in the work of the Swedish Lutheran theologian Anders Nygren's *Agape and Eros* (1953) and King's own vast study of the German-American Christian existentialist philosopher and Lutheran theologian Paul Tillich.
22 King, *Testament of Hope*, 8.
23 Ibid.
24 Ibid., 58.
25 Ibid., 102, 103.
26 Ibid., 87.
27 Ibid., 118.

the symptoms while leaving the underlying problem intact. King describes a desegregated but unintegrated community as one 'where men are physically proximate without spiritual affinity ... a stagnant equality of sameness rather than a constructive equality of oneness'.[28] The beloved community is one that, through a nonviolent process of desegregation, achieved an integration of body and soul, hands and heart: 'Only integration ... unchains the spirit and the mind and provides the highest degree of life-quality freedom.'[29]

We might characterise the beloved community as a 'community of conscience'. Conscience is that which is most universal, most essential, most Unchangeable, yet it is located in the deepest depths of a particular, inessential, changeable individual. This is precisely why Black bodies play the central role.[30] Black Americans 'are the conscience of America – we are its troubled soul – we will continue to insist that right be done because both God's will and the heritage of our nation speak though our echoing demands'.[31] Black folk are closer to America's higher self than white people. 'Eventually the civil-rights movement will have contributed infinitely more to the nation than the eradication of racial injustice' because it will have uplifted the nation out of its racist, segregated, and changeable state into a higher, integrated, and Unchangeable one (WW 142). In other words, America will have been 'true to what [it] put on paper' – namely, a community of equals endowed with the right to lead fulfilling lives. 'Self cannot be self without other selves. I cannot reach fulfillment without thou ... All men are caught in an inescapable network of mutuality.'[32] Beloved community was King's vision. And he saw nonviolent direct action as a means to achieving that vision.

---

28 Ibid.
29 Ibid., 121.
30 Ibid., 69.
31 Ibid., 105.
32 Ibid., 122.

Summer, 1963

King enacts a form of sacramental work in telling the story of why the 'Negro Revolution' happened in the summer of 1963. After all, Black folk had 'for decades endured evil' (WW 3). Despite the best efforts of the South's Lost Cause narrative to recast the Civil War so that slavery was a less significant part of the story, no one could completely forget the centuries of bondage and racist violence. 'Any time', King concludes, 'would seem to have been the right time. Why 1963?' (WW 3). King performs sacramental work and desire here because he is making his actions into part of a divine plan. We see this clearly in a famous line, a paraphrase of the abolitionist Theodore Parker, which King repeated on various occasions: 'amid all of this we have kept going with the faith that as we struggle, God struggles with us, and that the arc of the moral universe, although long, is bending toward justice'.[33] Part of King's conceptualisation of nonviolence is rooted in the belief that the 'universe is on the side of justice ... [that] in his struggle for justice he has cosmic companionship'.[34] Even in his last sermon, given in the Mason Temple in Memphis on the eve of his assassination, King proclaimed from the 'mountaintop' the sacramentality of his labour as he glimpsed the 'promised land' and the 'glory of the coming of the Lord'.[35]

Perhaps most of all, the reason for the emergence of the Negro Revolution in 1963 was that it had been exactly a century since Lincoln issued the Emancipation Proclamation. Precisely one hundred years had passed yet Black folk were still not free. As Saidiya Hartman points out, post-emancipation Black people

---

33 Dr. Martin Luther King, Jr., 'Statement on Ending the Bus Boycott', from The Martin Luther King, Jr. Research and Education Institute, Stanford University. King repeated similar paraphrasing in two famous speeches and in one of his final sermons: 'How Long, Not Long', delivered in March 1965 on the steps of the Alabama State Capitol; 'Where Do We Go From Here?', delivered in August 1967 at the Southern Christian Leadership Conference; and 'Remaining Awake Through a Great Revolution', sermon delivered in March 1968 at the National Cathedral.
34 King, *Testament of Hope*, 9.
35 Ibid., 286.

lived, and still live, the 'afterlives of slavery' – they were and are simply enslaved by a new form of shackles. After the advances of Reconstruction were erased by the resurgence of white supremacy, the *Plessy v. Ferguson* decision in 1896, writes King, 'ended up plunging the Negro into the abyss of exploitation where he experienced the bleakness of nagging injustice'.[36] A Black man in 1963 'lived in a form of slavery disguised by certain niceties of complexity ... [which] had left him behind in the shadow of political, psychological, social, economic, and intellectual bondage' (WW 9). It was a century of 'psychological and social conditions' that produced the Negro Revolution (WW 13). Thus the 'centennial of emancipation gave the Negro a reason to act – a reason so simple and obvious that he almost had to step back to see it' (WW 11).

King begins *Why We Can't Wait* with the question of time: Why 1963? The question was asked in response to the repeated criticism of civil rights work: that it is untimely. From the *Washington Post* to Attorney General Robert F. Kennedy, to white moderates, white churches, and more, the constant critique of King's work was that it was poorly timed and impatient (WW 53, 73, 78). King's response was simply to point to the long period of Black suffering. The year 1963 was the centennial of emancipation, yet equality was still a dream. King writes that Black folk had 'waited more than 340 years for our constitutional and God-given rights ... yet we still creep at horse-and-buggy pace toward gaining a cup of coffee at a lunch counter' (WW 69). Criticisms about timing only came from those who did not suffer. Those who said 'Wait!' never saw 'vicious mobs lynch your mothers and fathers at will and drown your sisters and brothers at whim', as well as countless other atrocities experienced only by Black folk in America (WW 69). The cry of '"Wait!" has almost always meant "Never"' (WW 69). Why 1963? Because '[o]ppressed people cannot remain oppressed forever'. Because the 'yearning for freedom eventuality manifests itself' (WW 76). Because 'freedom is never voluntarily given by the oppressor; it

---

36 Ibid., 6.

must be demanded by the oppressed'. Because 'privileged groups seldom give up their privileges voluntarily' (WW 68).

The Negro Revolution occurred in 1963 because it was time to come to terms with a great arc of American, and global, history. Like all true revolutions it was a self-correcting of that history. King recognised that America was divided, and the Negro Revolution was meant to bring out the true sense of the nation. It was 'the resumption of that noble journey toward the goals reflected in the Preamble to the Constitution, the Constitution itself, the Bill of Rights, and the Thirteenth, Fourteenth and Fifteenth Amendments' (WW 11). Rather than rejecting, as Garvey did, the American sense of self in the divided African American self-consciousness, King's strategy for unifying African with American was to return to the foundations and ideals of America itself. America is not an Unchangeable beyond, but right here right now, on the soil of its continent. As King says, the 'Negro wants absolute and immediate freedom and equality, not in Africa or in some imaginary state, but right here in this land today' (WW 121). While, from one perspective, the Nation had nullified its meaning through racist policies, practices of discrimination, and antiblack violence, King discerned that, from another perspective, the soul of America, the Unchangeable, lives on. This is why King did not 'despair about the future' or 'fear the outcome of our struggle in Birmingham' (WW 81). He did not despair because the future of America and the promise of justice would, in the end, win out. 'We will reach the goal of freedom all over the nation', writes King, 'because the goal of America is Freedom' (WW 81).

The way to realign the Nation with its true, Unchangeable form, with true Freedom and Equality, was to bring all people back into a proper relationship with America's higher self, the true America, and the summer of 1963 was the time for this work. But this required sacramental work and desire. King considered nonviolent direct action as the form of such work. And the importance of that action was not merely what it could do to white folk but what it could do for Black folk.

Nonviolence as Passive Activity

Some have spoken of Hegel's *Phenomenology* as an ontology, others as an epistemology. Either way, Hegel's text, particularly because of its peculiar level of abstraction — and therefore its preoccupation with the purity of ideas — can often lead one to wonder about its moral, political, and ethical im/possibilities. Perhaps King wondered about this, too; he may have found a lot of utility in Hegel's ideas, but he also found a way to show how those ideas are embodied, how the dialectic can and will gain flesh in the space of concrete social activity. We see nonviolent direct action operating in this way; it provides moral and political flesh to the epistemological skeleton of Hegel's sacramental work and desire. As that work and desire follow devotion, King's nonviolent action begins with 'a process of self-purification' (WW 67). This process included many intensive workshops in which the commitment to a higher cause was stated publicly and repeatedly among other individuals, as well as exercises similar to the very stoic nonviolent resistance training developed by the Student Nonviolent Coordinating Committee (SNCC). The goal was to prepare the soul so that it would remain devoted to the higher cause as it endured the brutality and violence nonviolent direct action often entails. The principle was to realise that 'unearned suffering is redemptive ... [and] tremendous educational and transformational possibilities' can be found therein.[37] It was a question of 'learning to transform this degradation into resistance'.[38] Nonviolent training converted adversity into virtue.[39]

Bayard Rustin and Reverend Glenn E. Smiley showed King that his work as president of the Montgomery Improvement

---

37 Ibid., 18.
38 Ibid., 22.
39 Or so the logic goes. Nonviolent strategies require violence for their success, and therefore run the risk of valorising suffering in ways that encourage its perpetuation rather than its alleviation. In this way, and as the quotation shows, the suffering that results from nonviolent direct action is redemptive, and as we showed in the last chapter, redemptive suffering can be and often is deeply problematic.

Association was part of a grand global history of nonviolent direct action.[40] Though it 'did not originate in America, it found its natural home there' (WW 12). While Garvey connected his movement with the Hebrew slaves' escape from Egypt, King connected the Negro Revolution with a long tradition of fighting injustice, beginning with the 'nonviolent resistance of the early Christians' (WW 23). Their peaceful resistance had 'such an overriding power that it shook the Roman Empire', and something similar occurred later, when 'boycotts and protests ... confounded the British monarchy and laid the basis for freeing the colonies from unjust domination' while also laying the ground for the 'nonviolent ethic of Mahatma Gandhi' (WW 23). Black American nonviolence, then, was only the latest in a long history of sacramental nonviolent resistance against injustice, including anti-imperialism, decolonialisation, abolitionism, and more. Yet for King, nonviolence is sacramental because it is 'Christianity in action'; it is rooted in the 'principle of love'.[41]

Nonviolent direct action also heralds a new logic of action. While devotion is a form of pure passivity, nonviolent action is a form of activity that originates from a centuries-old subordinate social position. This is not Nietzsche's transvaluation of values. A 'posture of silent waiting', King writes, 'was forced upon [the slave] psychologically because he was shackled physically', a passive position that continued until 1963 (WW 13). Hundreds of years of enslaved passivity, followed by 'new devices [that] were found to "keep the Negro in his place"' – such as the threat of lynching and other antiblack violence, and then the Jim Crow and segregation laws and policies – were all intended to keep Black folk quiet, silent, and passive (WW 14). When white Southerners tricked themselves into believing that Black folk enjoyed serving them as second-class citizens, Black folk were forced to play along simply to survive.[42] Jailing was another form of 'passifying', as the

---

40 King, *Testament of Hope*, 82.
41 Ibid., 86, 87.
42 Recalling a Black female cook working for a white family, King describes how, though she denied having anything to do with the Montgomery bus

jailhouse meant confinement and severe beatings, and the courts mocked any claim of injustice. And yet, from this very position of passivity, King witnessed the stirrings of a 'sort of genius': the genius of nonviolent direct action, or sacramental work and desire (WW 22).

The genius was not to turn passivity into activity, a feat certain to fail, but to find a form of activity within passivity. For the Black person, the 'peaceable weapon of nonviolent action', King writes, was a 'way to divest himself of passivity without arraying himself in vindictive force' (WW 22, 23). We can call it 'passive activity', then, as it functioned by leaning into the passive position in which Black folk were kept rather than trying to escape it. It is, in King's terms, 'nonaggressive physically but dynamically aggressive spiritually', or, as Judith Butler puts it: 'cultivating aggression into forms of conduct that can be effective without being destructive'.[43]

Rather than avoiding the sites of what we might call forced 'passification', such as imprisonment, Black protestors voluntarily got themselves jailed by blatantly disobeying unjust laws. The idea was that by filling up the jails with so many Black bodies, there would soon be nowhere left to put them. King recalls a powerful moment in Birmingham 'when Negro youngsters ran after white policemen, asking to be locked up' (WW 16). By tapping into 'some mysterious source [they] ... found [the] courage and the conviction to meet physical force with soul force' (WW 16). Soul force is, we would argue, another name for what Hegel calls the 'Unchangeable'. By sacrificing the body, usually to the police, nonviolent action evokes the Unchangeable contained within a white changeable individual by externalising the Unchangeable within the Black changeable individual. King describes it this

---

boycott, when 'she walked home from her job, on feet already weary from a full day's work, she walked proudly, knowing that she was marching with a movement' that would change America (WW 15).

43 King, *Testament of Hope*, 7. Martha Gessen, 'Judith Butler Wants Us to Reshape Our Rage', *The New Yorker*, interview, 9 February 2020. We should also note here that this modality of nonviolent protest requires violence; the "passive activity" is meant to expose the violence already at the heart of American antiblack white supremacy.

way: 'we present our very bodies as a means of laying our case before the conscience of the local and the national community' (WW 66). Call it conscience, call it soul force, call it the Unchangeable – whatever we want to call it, it is the enactment of sacramental work and desire.

Thus, nonviolent action is not pure passivity, as was devotion, but passive action; it is the active form of passivity. King's strategy was to practise non-active action.[44] Located somewhere between action and passivity, it is neither active nor passive, either inactive or impassive. It is not purely passive because it's not a blindly idealistic faith in submission; and it is not purely active because it does not violently react to the acts of violence done to it. When they were confronted by such passive action, segregationist and racist white people were flabbergasted. They became 'paralyzed and confused' when the racist violence they were accustomed to enacting was wilfully submitted to by Black bodies (WW 25). White policemen had no idea how to act towards people who neither submitted nor reacted. Neither standing down by retreating nor going forward in an attack, the passive activity of nonviolence is the precise embodiment of resistance. To re-sist means to stand up, to be unmoved, to be erect, to stand firm. Etymologically, 'resistance' comes from *re* ('back, against') + *sto* ('to stand'), not unlike the German *Gegenstand*. 'We did not fight back', writes King, 'but we did not turn back' (WW 89). Nonviolent direct action was passive insofar as it received the blows of the billy clubs or the force of the fire hoses, yet it was active insofar as it walked, head held high, straight into those blows. Nonviolent resistance, in short, endures without retaliating. Hence the 'nonviolent creed': 'to resist without bitterness, to be cursed and not reply, to be beaten and not hit back' (WW 50).

It is not surprising that nonviolent action, as a form of passive activity or active passivity, stunned white America, since it is, on

---

44 Strictly speaking, as King clarifies, 'nonviolence in the truest sense is not a strategy that one uses simply because it is expedient at the moment ... [but] a way of life that men live by because of the sheer morality of its claim'. King, *Testament of Hope*, 17.

the face of it, utterly paradoxical. Nor is it surprising that King called his strategy a 'sword that heals', or a weapon that 'cuts without wounding and ennobles the man who wields it' (WW 12). It cuts yet heals because it is a just, 'practical and moral answer to the Negro's cry for justice', a cry that comes from a passive place (WW 12). At the time, nonviolent direct action was the latest, most sophisticated, form of resistance in the development of the continuous fight for freedom and equality, and in it we see a direct lineage from Douglass's physical fight with Covey to the nonviolence of the 'Negro Revolution' of 1963. The moral force of sacramental work and desire in nonviolent civil rights action replaced the physical force of the slave revolt.

This moral force was akin to an unmoved mover, a sort of Aristotelian Unchangeable, insofar as it could 'move and stir the social conscience of [the] community' without acting first and without reacting violently to violence (WW 23).[45] It was more akin to holding up a mirror or turning on the light of the divine so that the world could witness the barbarity with which white people oppressed Black folk in America. When a white policeman raised his club, King would neither flinch nor raise his own fist, but instead would slowly walk right at it, willingly accepting whatever viciousness might follow. In doing so, King would catch the violent act 'in gigantic circling spotlights', creating 'a luminous glare revealing the naked truth to the whole world' (WW 25). Here it is important that 'nonviolent resistance does not seek to defeat or humiliate the opponent, but to win his friendship and understanding'.[46] Referring to Ephesians 6:12, a significant source for King's philosophical anthropology, the fight is 'directed against forces of evil rather than against persons who are caught by those forces'.[47] Nonviolence aims at awakening white bodies from their racist slumber.

---

45 King views the logic of violence as entailing its 'futility' because violence only perpetuates violence. 'Violence solves no social problems', he writes, 'it merely creates new and more complicated ones'. King, *Testament of Hope*, 7.
46 Ibid.
47 Ibid., 8.

To use Hegelian terms, we might think of nonviolent action as a clear example of double negation or sublation [*aufheben*]. Passive action negates the action done to it not with a direct reaction but by accepting the violence and raising it up for the world to see in a luminous glare. In short, nonviolent direct action both negates and preserves at the same time. Communion with the Unchangeable and the overcoming of racial tension only occur if the divisions cutting through the world are revealed and overcome. Hence, King writes:

> we who engage in nonviolent direct action are not the creators of tension. We merely bring to the surface the hidden tension that is already alive ... [because] injustice must be exposed, with all the tension its exposure creates, to the light of human conscience and the air of national opinion before it can be cured. (WW 73)

This luminous glare is the light cast by the Unchangeable that reveals what Hegel calls a 'sanctified world' (PS 219) or what King calls the beloved community centred on an 'ethics of love'.[48]

King offers an example of a sanctified world: a Sunday afternoon during the events in Birmingham, when hundreds of demonstrators marched from the New Pilgrim Baptist Church to the city jail in order to hold a prayer meeting (WW 90). Determined to shut it down, Bull Connor, the Commissioner of Public Safety, brought out the policeman and the fire hoses. When the marchers politely refused Connor's orders to stand down, he shouted to his men: 'Dammit. Turn on the hoses' (WW 90). At the very moment when Connor ordered the release of the dogs and the opening of the hoses, the nonviolent activists did not raise their fists but rather burnished 'their greatest weapon – their heart, their conscience, their courage, and their sense of justice' (WW 25). Racism and bigotry, they believed, are not changed by guns and knives but by the invisible force of soul that calls us to our better selves, the Unchangeable part of us. Why this change occurs is mysterious, which might be why King calls it the 'miracle of nonviolence' (WW 31). What followed was not a wretched scene in which

---

48 Ibid.

Black people succumbed to the pressure of a water hose, but a miracle: 'Bull Connor's men, their deadly hoses poised for action, stood facing the marchers ... as though hypnotized' (WW 90). They did not turn on the hoses and they did not raise their batons. They just stood there, stunned into inaction. When the marchers realised they were without obstruction, hundreds of them simply walked right through the crowd of policemen. At just the right moment, the Unchangeable shining out from the Black faces of those brave souls evoked the Unchangeable held within the white faces holding their sagging fire hoses.

Though nonviolent action might bring broken bones, burns, scars, and sometimes death itself, King and other civil rights fighters laboured in the name of a higher good, an Unchangeable essence that might one day make America into the promised land depicted in the souls and documents of the nation's founding fathers. For King, nonviolent direct action is a form of sacred service; that is, it is work that we do but that is not ours. We labour not for our personal gain but so that we might uplift the better part of everyone and negate our lower, debased selves. Those who laboured for civil rights were, King writes, 'more concerned about realizing [their] righteous aims than about saving [their] skins' (WW 49). King resisted not out of selfish aims but for the betterment of his children, for all of America's youth, for Black people, for all oppressed people, for America. Nonviolence, he said, was 'the instruction of our national salvation'.[49] The goal was simple: to wake up on the day when people 'will no longer be judged by the color of their skin but by the content of their character' (WW 'Dedication').

The March on Washington

With the increasing signs of success of the Civil Rights Movement, Black folk had 'rediscovered the fighting spirit' which, we might say, connects King directly to Douglass, Nat Turner, and others

---

49 Ibid., 64.

who fought against slavery with soul and body (WW 101).[50] 'In the summer of 1963 ... Helplessness was replaced by confidence' (WW 100–1). Simply adding up the numbers of integrated places or providing jobs for Black people, however, does not capture the success of the Revolution, nor does pointing to the passing of the Civil Rights Act in 1964 (WW 101). The 'full dimensions of victory can be found only by comprehending the change within the minds of millions of Negroes' (WW 101). One hundred years after Lincoln signed the Emancipation Proclamation on behalf of Black slaves, in the 'summer of 1963, the Negroes of America wrote an emancipation proclamation to themselves'. Through committed nonviolent direct action, Black folk worked to 'bury the psychology of servitude'. As a psychological victory, it was 'invisible but vast' (WW 101). Black suffering that had been, until that summer, merely a quiet 'lament became a shout and then a roar'. 'White America was forced to face the ugly facts of life as the Negro thrust himself into the consciousness of the country' (WW 102).

On 28 August 1963, what King calls the 'summer of our discontent' ended with a grand climax: the March on Washington. The marchers came from nearly every state in the Union, including 'adherents of every faith, members of every class, every profession, every political party, united by a single ideal': America (WW 113). For the first time, white churches openly supported and participated in – and the media conveyed the importance and value of – a Black organised national event. 'Millions of Americans, for the first time, had a clear, long look at Negroes engaged in a serious occupation' (WW 114). White folks were forced, many from the bright TV screens shining in their homes, to view Black folks as equally American. White eyes had witnessed the violence suffered by the Black bodies of the marchers and protesters, and then they witnessed the peaceful and dignified march through Washington D.C. The stereotypes distorting the fight for equality

---

50 King gestures toward this: 'The heroic but spasmodic and isolated slave revolts of the antebellum South had fused, more than a century later, into a simultaneous, massive assault against segregation' (WW 106).

dissolved as the dignity of fellow citizens shone on those dark faces pictured on screen and in the papers.

Then King took the stage. With encouragement from Mahalia Jackson, he proclaimed to the world the highest maxim of his sacramental work and desire – 'I have a dream...'. Dr Martin Luther King's face became synonymous with America: '*I have a dream*' became '*America has a dream*'. Speaking to the higher sense of America, to the Unchangeable values that form the essence of the nation, King's words bounced off the white marble facades of the surrounding monuments to democratic values. King performed there the highest form of sacramental work and desire. His desire was his dream and his work was his speech. On the National Mall, at the heart of the nation, King incarnated the essence America. As Hegel might put it: King became the Unchangeable in changeable form.

While, in many ways, the summer of 1963 was a great success, centuries of oppression and suffering were not erased so quickly.[51] Despite uplifting white people by calling upon their Unchangeable conscience within, the ugliness of racism returned in the Fall of 1963. There was, King discovered, 'a poverty of conscience of the white majority' (WW 103). Since the 'basic recalcitrance of the South [had] not yet been broken', it was unclear whether the 'Negro Revolution' was victorious (WW 131). This is not surprising, as King well knew, because every successful revolution does two opposing things at once: 'It attracts to itself fresh forces and strength, and at the same time crystallizes the opposition' (WW 108). In short, every new success brings an emboldened enemy.

Racism simply reached too far into the depths and the heights of America.[52] As King notes, the 'strands of prejudice toward Negroes are tightly wound around the American character' (WW

---

51 We see countless examples of this still. From the murder of unarmed Black men, to racialised poverty, to the re-emergence of white supremacy, to mass incarceration and more, King's dream remains, in undeniable ways, merely a dream.
52 Fanon once called racism a 'dialectical gangrene'. Fanon, 'Racism and Culture', 36.

110). From its very beginning, America has been racist. If we simply 'X-ray our history', we find that its racism is rooted in the nearly genocidal racism against Indigenous Americans, and before that in the anti-Semitism of the European inspiration of the founding fathers.[53] Since the nation's foundation, this 'long-standing racist ideology has corrupted and diminished our democratic ideals' (WW 110). It seemed, in many ways, that the 'hope [of the Revolution] was destined to die a cold death' (WW 103). Against such deep-seated and expansive structural racism, the sacramental work and desire of the Civil Rights Movement could never have succeeded completely. Another type of relation to the Unchangeable, another moment of unhappy consciousness, would be necessary.

The Individual's Work

Part of the reason for the necessity of an-other mode of unhappy consciousness is that sacramental work and desire ultimately returns to the individual as the site of transformation. The reciprocal self-surrender – for Hegel, of the Unchangeable to the changeable and the changeable to the Unchangeable, and for King, of Black and white souls to conscience and American ideals – does not necessarily entail the true communion of the Unchangeable and the changeable because it is still 'affected with division' (PS 222). This division keeps the universal and the individual, the Unchangeable and the changeable, apart. The reason: while the individual consciousness works diligently to overcome its individuality, it ends up finding itself everywhere. Individual labour was supposed to be given over to the Unchangeable; it was supposed to be God's work, not ours. But this is only a farce. Martin Luther King, Jr did, after all, win the Nobel Peace Prize. Even as he accepted it in

---

53 For the story of the deep roots of anti-Indigenous and antiblack racism, see Ronald Sanders' *Lost Tribes and Promised Lands: The Origins of American Racism* (Boston: Little Brown and Company, 1978). Sanders tells the history of how racial prejudice was grounded in political, religious, and economic forces originating in fourteenth-century Spanish anti-Semitism.

the name of the work he'd done, and even as he gave the proceeds to the movement, it was nevertheless *his* prize, *his legacy*.

Here is where the trouble lies: sacramental work is, undeniably, the individual's work, in this case King's work. Put differently, although this working is supposed to deny the self and attribute everything to God, it actually reaffirms the essentiality of the finite self, while God is reduced to a superficial element. At best, sacramental work and desire is done *in the name of God*. The same failure to renounce and surrender oneself also applies to labour as a form of gratitude. The 'entire movement', writes Hegel, 'is reflected not only in the actual desiring, working, and enjoyment, but even in the very giving thanks where the reverse seems to take place, in the *extreme of individuality*' (PS 222). The reason: *we* are the ones working on and changing things, while God is just a fictional idea, a fancy name, that contributes nothing to our work. *We* are the ones working, day in and day out; *we* finite persons change the world; no one and nothing else but *us*. The individual self tried to overcome itself through work, to act merely as an instrument in God's handmade plan, but it inevitably ends up emboldening itself.

At the end of a day's work, the changeable individual is forced to admit the hypocrisy of its renunciation. 'Consciousness feels itself therein', writes Hegel, 'as this particular individual, and does not let itself be deceived by its own seeming renunciation, for the truth of the matter is that it has *not* renounced itself' (PS 222). The goal of sacramental work and desire was to bring the changeable into communion with the Unchangeable by eliminating the division between them. Despite all its hard work, however, the 'result is the renewed division into the opposed consciousness of the *Unchangeable*, and the consciousness of willing, performing, and enjoying ... in order words, the consciousness of *independent individuality* in general' (PS 222). Thus, unhappy consciousness sees itself as divided: one half is working, seen as a way of giving thanks, yet another finds that even in giving thanks it asserts itself.

Through its irreducible will and deed, the changeable individual's sacramental work and desire does the opposite of what it set out to do. It tried to deflate its independence as an individual in order to submit to the will of God, yet it ended up inflating its very independence. It discovers this through the experience of doing sacramental labour. 'In positing himself as the lowest', writes Hyppolite, 'he is the highest'.[54]

King knew this. He was aware of the danger. He knew that it was 'possible for one to be self-centered in his self-denial and self-righteous in his self-sacrifice', cultivating a martyr complex that will, in the end, return all the focus *back on the individual*.[55] King could not alleviate the dynamic; though he was aware of the pitfalls of sacramental work and desire, he nevertheless kept pushing. He kept doing the work – which is to say, *he* kept doing the work; though Bayard Rustin introduced him to non-violent resistance; though Howard Thurman had taught him the concept of beloved community; and though A. Philip Randolph had already laid the groundwork for massive organising, King became – perhaps in spite of himself – the face of the movement; for better or worse, he became its indisputable leader, garnering the accolades and receiving the criticism. He might have been able to call President Lyndon B. Johnson on the phone, but he would also succumb to his notoriety. At a moral level, this showed up in his infidelity, manifesting itself through his sexual escapades beyond his marriage. And at an existential level, this dynamic led to his assassination: having become the *leader*, he was also the primary *target*. If he could be eliminated, so the logic went, the movement would die with him.

And in a way, it did.

But in another way – and from another place – the sacramental work wouldn't be extinguished simply because one individual was murdered. There was another leader who, like Zora Neale Hurston, knew that each individual could be powerful; she sought not to become the singular leader, but instead to cultivate a sense of leadership in others. Her name was Ella Baker, and we now turn to her.

---

54 Hyppolite, *Structure and Genesis*, 212.
55 King, *Testament of Hope*, 41.

Ella Baker

> The Negro must quit looking for a savior,
> and work to save himself.
> – Ella Baker[56]

Ella Baker also engaged in sacramental work. But her work and her sacrament were different. Her work involved empowering others, bringing others to an awareness of their own capacities, cultivating the knowledge and wisdom in others. It was still sacramental work, the kind of work that sought to bring out the ideals of the world through those oppressed by the world. At a rally in 1964, Baker proclaimed her commitment to – and her responsibility for – doing the work of realising freedom, a freedom that the United States professed to uphold.

> And so all of us stand guilty at this moment for having waited so long to lend ourselves to a fight for the freedom ... of the American spirit, for the freedom of the human spirit for freedom, and this is the reason I am here tonight, and this is the reason, I think, that these young men who have worked and given their bodies in the movement for freedom. They are here not because they want to see something take place just for the fun of it, they are here because they should know, and I think they do know, that the freedom which they seek is a larger freedom that encompasses all mankind [sic]. And until that day, we will never turn back.[57]

Baker and King knew that societal transformation was a laborious task, that desire takes work. Both upheld visions of equality, democracy, and justice – visions that, for both of them, were central to the fulfilment of the American democratic experiment. But while King struggled with the power of his personality, while he struggled with being a hero (and eventually becoming a

---

56 Baker quoted in Barbara Ransby, *Ella Baker and the Black Freedom Movement: A Radical Democratic Vision* (Chapel Hill: University of North Carolina Press, 2003), 171.
57 Ella Baker, 'Address at the Hattiesburg Freedom Rally', 21 January 1964, at: <https://voicesofdemocracy.umd.edu/ella-baker-freedom-day-rally-speech-text>

martyr), Baker sought to encourage – to empower – her comrades to do the work themselves. Ella Baker was an organiser. If King was a minister, Baker was a missionary for Black freedom. And while she engaged with a host of different institutions and organisations – from the NAACP to the Southern Christian Leadership Conference (SCLC) and the SNCC – she nevertheless grounded herself in the political praxis of organising and leadership development. She wanted everyone to know that they could be, that they already were, leaders; she desired for everyone to participate in the transformation of US society, and did the work to cultivate indigenous leadership in the marginalised and oppressed corners of the country.

Sometimes, this work required dealing with national institutions, in order to be carried out on a larger stage. But even as she did that large-scale work, Baker was committed to local autonomy: the people on the streets already had the knowledge, the will power, and the desire to transform themselves and their circumstances. They did not need a charismatic leader. They only needed a push, some encouragement, someone to believe in them, and Baker was one of the people to do it. If King was the prince of the Civil Rights Movement, Baker was its mother. 'Baker's message', Barbara Ransby writes, 'was that oppressed people, whatever their level of formal education, had the ability to understand and interpret the world around them, to see that world for what it was and to move to transform it.'[58] Ransby is correct: King was a preacher, but Baker was an *organiser*.

This difference is not merely one of a title. King's vocation led him to be and remain at the forefront of the Civil Rights Movement, and he did so because he heard the call to lead. He was the movement's primary spokesperson, its most notable and famous proponent. But unlike King, Baker did not make herself a model to emulate; in Hegelese, she did not make her changeable individuality into the Unchangeable Universal. This is where Baker pushes this moment in the unhappy consciousness into its next moment: King uncritically took on the call to lead, along

---

58 Ransby, *Ella Baker*, 7.

with all the baggage, while Baker was aware of her individuality and was thereby able to self-determine, which is to say to self-negate, in ways that King never could. Responding to a question about her strained relationship with King, she replied, 'After all, who was I? I was female, I was old. I didn't have any Ph.D.'[59] There was, for Baker, no privilege in seeing from the mountain-top, since there was plenty of wisdom in the fields and the valleys, and that is where she did her sacred labour.

Overall, Baker valued deliberation over oration, collectivity over leadership, collaboration over inspiration. Rather than a cult of personality, she sought to co-cultivate personal relationship through communal action. Rather than give soaring speeches, her work was the day-to-day organisational and logistical work required to bring thousands of people together. Rather than lead them to the mountain top, she met people where they were, on their own terms. Her labour concerned the tedious and mundane minutiae – ordering a stage or finding rides, working the mimeograph machine, distributing fliers, making phone calls, knocking on doors. She did not meet with esteemed political leaders like Lyndon Johnson or receive international recognition or a Nobel Prize, because she was too busy sitting for hours on the porches of unemployed Mississippi farmers, celebrating their own sacred work and desires. Rather than impose her grand dream of reaching the end of an historic arc of justice, she listened to the dreams of the most oppressed and marginalised Black Americans.

Historians of the Civil Rights Movement have contrasted King and Baker in terms of a difference in approach between charismatic leaders and grassroots activists, between mobilising for big events like the March on Washington and organising communities to feel empowered enough to assess their own needs and begin fighting their own battles. Local autonomy is essential, especially when it is at odds with the visions of leaders. Baker thus moved from group to group – from the YWCA to the NAACP, SCLC, SNCC and dozens more – because she was committed to building a mass movement rather than to the success of any one organisation.

---

59 Quoted in Ransby, *Ella Baker*, 172.

This difference in approach made *all* the difference. Organising a mass movement and speaking for a movement are two different things. One focuses on the leader, around whom a cult of personality could (and in King's case would) develop; the other focuses on people, empowering them to take responsibility for their futures and make a difference. As Ransby puts it:

> Baker understood that laws, structures, and institutions had to change in order to correct injustice and oppression, but part of the process had to involve oppressed people, ordinary people, infusing new meanings into the concept of democracy and finding their own individual and collective power to determine their lives and shape the direction of history.[60]

This kind of work was ongoing. It didn't stop, and it was sacred. 'We are not in the final stages of the freedom struggle', Baker once proclaimed:

> We are really just beginning ... because even tomorrow, if every vestige of racial discrimination were wiped out, if all of us became free enough to go down and to associate with the people we wanted to associate, we still are not free. We aren't free until within us we have that deep sense of freedom from a lot of things.[61]

Baker's 'goal' was not a single 'end' but rather an ongoing 'means', a 'process', and that process requires that one give one's life – yes, as a gift – to the ideals to which one is committed, doing the daily, mundane work of actualising those ideals in the furthest corners of life. It was not that Baker did not participate in the work of transformation; it was that the *content* of this work required a different kind of self-realisation, one steeped not simply in bettering others, but in encouraging them to help them better themselves. Liberation is an everyday, endless struggle.

This kind of work, to which Baker was committed, did not carry with it the burden of self-inflation. Or, more precisely, it did not carry with it the *same kind* of self-inflation as King's work did.

---

60 Ransby, *Ella Baker*, 1.
61 Baker, 'Address at Hattiesburg Freedom Rally'.

Baker did not struggle with the fact that she was the one doing the work and that she enjoyed it and found meaning in it – not in the same way as King, anyway. Instead, she embraced this fact, she asserted herself, recognising the work as *her* work rather than pretending she was doing the work of the Unchangeable. She spoke her mind; she did not defer. 'I did not just subscribe to a theory', she said, 'just because it came out of the mouth of the leader'.[62] While she was often relegated to the role of a glorified secretary, she knew such work was sacred, and thus never hesitated to provide her insight, her wisdom, her perspective.

She shunned the spotlight. While King wrote books and gave speeches that were transcribed and recorded, while he left a record (sometimes against his own wishes) of his intimate life, Baker

> tried not to leave [a trail]. There is no memoir or diary, nor are there boxes of intimate personal correspondence. What remains is, for the most part, her public voice and presence as documented in over thirty archival and manuscript collections of organizations and individuals across the country.[63]

All that we get from Baker is *the work*. 'Her ideas were written in her work', Ransby notes; and that work was 'a coherent body of lived text spanning nearly sixty years'.[64] Rather than a political theory, she offered only political praxis. When we see Baker, we see the sacramental work and desire of social transformation in concrete action; we see a self that is always in flux, always in movement, always on the move. More than this, we see a self who is *developed* in and through community. While Baker saw King as someone who 'did not situate himself among [the people] but remained above them', she saw fit to remain *with* the people, to stay where they were, all in the name of helping them change their circumstances through their own sacramental work and desire.[65]

---

62 Quoted in Ransby, *Ella Baker*, 174.
63 Ibid., 7. While working for the SCLC when King was injured, she even had the thankless task of promoting King's new book *Striving for Freedom*. Ibid., 193.
64 Ibid., 1.
65 Ibid., 191.

Perhaps this is why some scholars think of Baker's organising strategy as primarily 'receptive' – a term that, as we know, has gendered implications. According to Mie Inouye, Baker's approach to organising – which required listening to those on the streets and in the farms – has been deemed 'nonideological' because it appeared that she didn't 'force' her ideas on others.[66] That part is true. Baker 'was neither dogmatic nor rigid in her thinking'; she 'never articulated a blueprint for social change ... her political beliefs changed in response to new experiences'.[67] Baker was uninterested in imposing her own ideological frame on the work of social transformation, and for this reason, she is often understood as nonideological. Because she did not give people her own idea(ls), because she listened more than she lectured, and because she changed her views based on what she heard, she is often seen as someone whose personal idea(l)s were rarely, if ever, expressed in her organising work. We read Baker as 'meeting people where they are', and, in that regard, we assume she did not seek to push people in a particular direction.

But this isn't quite true. As Mie Inouye points out, Baker *did* have a theory of social change; she did have a political vision, and a robust, dynamic one at that. While that vision met people where they were, it didn't *stay* there. 'Baker saw her role as an organizer ... as *starting* with them there and trying to move them, gradually, somewhere else.'[68] So, yes: Baker sat on porches and listened. But she also had an ideology of 'radical democracy', wherein the goal of the Civil Rights Movement was 'the realization of "full freedom" and "full dignity as a human being"'.[69]

This is why Ransby associates Baker with Paolo Freire's radically democratic teaching.[70] As a radically democratic teacher, Baker did not orate from a self-assigned privileged position of access to the

---

66 Mie Inouye, 'Starting with People Where They Are: Ella Baker's Theory of Political Organizing', *American Political Science Review*, 24 September 2021, 1–14.
67 Ibid., 4.
68 Ibid., 1.
69 Ibid., 4–5.
70 See Ransby, *Ella Baker*, 361–3.

truth, but taught and mentored by listening and learning, for truth was shared by a collective. Like Hurston, she listened to the lives and stories of Black people in their everyday existences, but was far more explicitly focused on distinctly racial and political ends. Baker celebrated the 'collective wisdom of sharecroppers, maids, and manual laborers'.[71] Rather than Du Bois' 'Talented Tenth', she valued the 'bottom tenth', those oppressed and marginalised by social hierarchies, as part of a radical class analysis. Of her many job titles in the many organisations at which she worked, perhaps 'field organiser' best describes her blend of theory and praxis.

Baker *knew* that she was as much a part of the transformation as others. She knew that she carried a sense of the Unchangeable – which she might have called 'full freedom' and 'full dignity' – within her. But rather than hindering her, it empowered her. More than this, it empowered her to empower others. *Strong people don't need strong leaders* was her motto, and she lived this out in all that she did.[72]

Such a disposition would inevitably set her in opposition to others, those who had a different sense of leadership and organising in mind. While she was willing to work with anyone who was engaged in the Black freedom struggle, she never hesitated to point out when someone's ego was going unchecked. 'Instead of the leader as a person who was supposed to be a magic man', she once said, 'you could develop individuals who were bound together by a concept that benefited the larger number of individuals and provided an opportunity for them to grow into being responsible for carrying out a program'.[73] This was why Baker saw the single charismatic leader as a detriment to the movement, and she never hesitated to speak her mind about this – even when that person was King himself: 'In December 1958, at the third annual Montgomery Improvement Association Institute on Nonviolence, the program theme was "A Testimonial to Dr. King's Leadership" ... [Baker] asked King directly why he allowed such hero worship,

---

71 Ibid., 365.
72 Ibid., 188.
73 Quoted in ibid.

and he responded simply that it was what the people wanted.'[74] While King hid behind 'what the people wanted', Baker directly called into question the very structure of leadership that encouraged him to become a hero.

She did not do this because she hated King – in fact, quite the opposite: 'some of the King family have said that I hated him, but I didn't'.[75] Her initial impressions of King were quite positive; she knew that a spokesperson had a place in the movement. But she also knew that dangers arose when that spokesperson's ego was left unchecked. She witnessed other leaders become disaffected about the movement, and she saw other leaders trying to emulate King. She also saw how the press sought to divinise King, to make him a 'magic man', to turn him into what she called a 'miracle performer'.[76] In other words, Baker recognised the dangers of self-inflation that come with sacramental work and desire. She saw them play out in King's life: 'King drained the masses of the confidence in themselves.'[77] King's mesmerising speeches passified, rather than actuated, the masses. This is where Baker's sacramental work and desire go beyond King and move into the kind self-mortification we will see exemplified by Malcolm X in the next chapter.

Ultimately, King's failures were not his own; they were baked into the American ideals with which he sought to bring the country back in line. In other words, his failure was to think that sacramental work would successfully raise the changeable individual into the Unchangeable universal. But Baker's sacramental work demanded an awareness and transformation of the structure of leadership itself: it did not require self-inflation, but instead a self-*situatedness*, a lodging of oneself within the community, a making sense of one's circumstances and of the meaning of one's work and desires within the communities to which one is committed. Ella Baker was neither self-aggrandising nor self-negating based on external

---

74 Ibid., 187–8.
75 Quoted in ibid., 191.
76 Ibid.
77 Ibid., 187.

determinations; she was, instead, a self-in-community. Her work was the community's work because it was self-consciously her work. Her life was always refracted through those she engaged with and those she trained because she used her own self-conscious power of self-determination to cultivate that same power of self-determination in others. And remember: if (as Hegel's Spinoza says) all determination is negation, then self-determination is self-negation, but where the determination comes from within, not from without. Like Hurston, Baker understood that we already have all we need. While Hurston sought to record Black life as lived, Baker sought to engage with Black self-determining life as a profoundly sacramental site of social transformation.

The (Gendered) Loss of Self

Baker was there, right along with King. In fact, she was doing this work long before King, and continued doing it long after him. Like King, she was formally educated (though not to the same degree); like King, she was a powerful orator (though not with the same reception); and like King, she was effective (though that effectiveness is too often overshadowed). Despite these differences, both were rooted in the Black Southern Baptist Church.

The parenthetical statements in the last paragraph speak to a dynamic that we have been tracing throughout this text – namely, that Black women are often overlooked in spite of their dynamism, their brilliance, and their capacity to express, diagnose, and transform Black life. Baker was no different. She may have been overshadowed by King, but she knew, perhaps better than he did, that the development of Black spirit is rife with dangers and contradictions. Thus, while King preferred soaring orations in front of large demonstrations, she preferred the boring, tedious process of organising every detail. While King looked to the spotlight, Baker looked to the streets. She was a seemingly unstoppable engine of transformation, a radical teacher-activist and a democrat in the most powerful sense of the word. She was central to the SCLC's success. She was a primary mentor to SNCC activists. She was the creative fire of the NAACP. She trained organisers, empowered everyday people, and cultivated community spirit. She was an individual embodiment of collective power, offering the clearest articulation of the end of this moment of unhappy consciousness and the beginning of the next. And yet, she was dismissed.

Maybe we should put that last sentence differently: and yet, *she* was dismissed. She was not overshadowed by King simply because he was charismatic; she was not relegated to secretarial work because she could not speak well. She was charismatic in her own right. Any examination of her public comments will demonstrate her oratorical capacities. Baker was an indomitable force in the world, especially one so steeped in patriarchal organisations like the Black Southern church. And yet, *she* was dismissed. Which is to say, she was dismissed because she was a woman – *I was female. I was old. I didn't have any PhD.*

Ransby illuminates the gendered dynamics between Baker and King: at the end of the day, King 'kept Baker at arm's length and never treated her as a political or intellectual peer'.[78] She initially worked for the SCLC with no office and with borrowed equipment; she and other women were regularly sidelined in favour of their ministerial and male counterparts. They were placed backstage, relegated to the margins of the work. This was a problem, and it demonstrates the profoundly sexist dynamics of the Civil Rights Movement.

But these sexist dynamics also reveal a different modality of self-development, a different modality of sacramental work and desire in the development of Black spirit. Even though she 'had the oratorical chords, [Baker] resented oratory'.[79] She was content to be what Ransby calls a Gramscian 'organic intellectual', one whose 'teaching method resembled a conversation more than a tutorial'.[80] As an organic intellectual, Baker did not seek to lead the masses but to assist them in birthing their own answers based on their already existing knowledges and experiences. She sought to teach, not to preach; she sought to speak *with* people, not *at* them.

---

78 Ibid., 173.
79 Ibid., 361.
80 Ibid.

Perhaps it was this organic intellectual development that separated Baker from King. She resented the teaching profession because it relegated women to subservient spheres, but she still taught. And that teaching occurred within the context of community – which meant that Baker's self-identity, her self-fashioning, came from within the relationships she cultivated. As we stated earlier, Baker never shied away from the fact that she, too, was doing the work; she had a self, and she self-consciously embraced it rather than pretended her work was in the name of the Unchangeable.

Yet because of the way gender operates even now, because Black women are often still dismissed or tokenised or rendered invisible, Baker's selfhood appears to be submerged under the movements she helped cultivate. In other words, while Baker cultivated a self, the self she cultivated does not appear as *dominant*. She was assertive, but she listened; she spoke, but she also changed her mind when presented with ideas from others. She knew she was doing the work, but she also knew she was not – and could not be – the only one doing it. There was a balance. There had to be. The key point is that she struck this balance through her own will and work.

Unfortunately, the balanced selfhood she cultivated – one that listened as much as it spoke, one that taught as much as it learned – was overshadowed by people like King. Which is to say, Baker does not appear in the same way King does. Her influence is *felt*, not always spoken; it resonates in the lives she touched, not through the words she left on the page. In this regard, if it were not for historians of the Civil Rights Movement and people seeking to extend her legacy, we might not know who Baker was or how important she was. Her selfhood was muted in the face of King's (self-)aggrandisement. Her changeable individuality was self-determining, a negation that self-consciously came from within. A different word for this is autonomy; another is self-mortification.

But this is not merely a victimhood narrative. Baker was *content* to lead from within. She left no personal trail because that was not what mattered to her. She determined herself. From a certain vantage point, it might appear that her selfhood was lost to King and others. But the truth is, Baker was there. Always there. She was there as a woman, engaging in what we might call a Black feminist politics. Channelling Diane Nash, Ransby writes, 'Ella Baker was a feminist more in what she did than what she said.'[81] King spoke; Baker organised. There is room for both. While King dismissed her, Baker knew there was room for both. This is why her sacramental work and desire sublate King's, in accordance with Hegel's logic: 'Because the result, the negation, is a *determinate* negation, it has a *content*. It is a new concept but one higher and richer than the preceding – richer because it negates or opposes the preceding and therefore contains it, and it contains even more than that, for it is the unity of itself and its opposite.'[82] Baker's selfhood may not have shown itself in loud and performative ways, but she, too, did the work of self-fashioning. She just did it in a way that was self-determining, self-negating, autonomous – on the way to self-mortifying.

Conclusion

If we pay close attention to the messy dialectics underlying Hegel's *Phenomenology*, we see that every moment hearkens back to others in complex and nonlinear ways. The slave's work returns as the stoic's commitment and, in different ways, through the first two moments of the unhappy consciousness; the sceptic's struggle is foreshadowed in the doubleness of the slave and the master, and it prefigures the unease present in devotion and sacramental work and desire. We celebrate the ways that Hegel's *Phenomenology* does not run in a straight line or even in circles; it runs backward and forward again and again, leaving traces we can never fully track.

But we still try, and from a perspective that lurks within but is suppressed by Hegelianism in general: the perspective of Blackness. In this phenomenology of Black spirit, we have been tracing a different kind of movement. We can see how, in King, we also

---

81 Ibid., 366.
82 Hegel, *Science of Logic*, 21.38.

glimpse Marcus Garvey, W.E.B. Du Bois, Booker T. Washington, and Frederick Douglass. More than this, we find in Ella Baker hints of Zora Neale Hurston's devotion, glimpses of Anna Julia Cooper's critical scepticism, shades of Ida B. Wells' stoic commitment, and traces of Harriet Jacobs' patient and evasive escape from slavery. Neither King nor Baker subsume these prior men and women into their own selves, but instead announce their continued resonance, their power, their capacity to speak to Black life and to criticise the violence of antiblackness and misogynoir. Selfhood rarely appears so solid or so bold, and it always shows itself in community. In the case of Martin Luther King, Jr and Ella Baker, this is precisely what happened. The difference is that, while King did not realise the work was his own, Baker was self-conscious of the fact and thus was able to determine her selfhood in ways that exceeded King's grasp. This is why her work was the community's work, while King's was only his own. This is why Baker's labour continued through the community, while King's work died along with him. Baker's commitment, in short, was the community's commitment because she determined the role of her individuality. In that regard, her selfhood appeared muted, clothed in her grey suits and ladies' hats, in short, a decorous Southern Black Baptist woman. But key here is that this muting, these hats and her decorum, were her choice and determination. Baker had a degree of autonomy that King never had. Thus, rather than lead others, or force her determination on them, she sought to cultivate their own local autonomy. Autonomy, we all know, means self-determination. And as Hegelian logic shows, all determination is negation. In this sense, autonomy is self-negation, a determination from within. The next moment of unhappy consciousness pushes this self-negating process to the extreme: it becomes *self-mortification*. Malcolm X and Angela Davis represent this final moment in this phenomenology of Black spirit.

6

Self-mortification

Malcolm X and Angela Davis

Ella Baker threw herself into the community. She never wrote much. All we have are the traces of her found in what she said and who she taught. Perhaps this is why her memory – *if* she is remembered – is subsumed under King's monolithic legacy. After all, there is no Ella Baker bust at the Capitol, no holiday in her name. Baker worked in the shadows of mythologised men, in the wings, quietly directing backstage for the star of the political show.

As the last chapter demonstrated, however, Baker maintained a strong sense of self. She knew who she was and what she could do. She understood her value, her effectiveness, her power. And yet, she also knew that her power was nothing without others. Her power was to *empower*. Her selfhood was characterised by her capacity to help others fashion themselves. She may have been a charismatic, powerful speaker, and she certainly had the strategic and intellectual gifts to lead a movement. She just chose to lead from within, from the *middle* (*Mitte*), which is to say, her selfhood, her self-identity, was situated within, in relation to those she sought to empower.

Such a self can be easily read as self-negation, as it appears – but *only* appears – that Baker lost herself in the movement. While it would not be accurate, it is possible to interpret her life and legacy as a perpetual work of self-abnegation in the service of a larger ideal. There may be no widespread recognition of her, but that was not her aim. Freedom was. *Black* freedom. To the extent that she contributed to that, it would seem that Baker was satisfied. Like Hurston, Baker might have died without the recognition and resources that she deserved, but the truth remains that her work was a work of self-negation – by which we mean that she *actively* limited herself in favour of the community.

219

Limiting oneself (*sich einschranken*), however, is different to *mortifying* (*sich kasteien*) oneself. We might not remember Baker the way we should, but that is not because of her. It is because of us. It is because her work of self-negation succeeded, because she was the agent in the work of limiting herself in the name of something greater. Self-negation, unhappy consciousness learns, is still an act of the subject. In Hegel's Spinozist terms, all negation, including of itself, is still a determination. Negation, then, should not be read as a mere loss of self. When read through Baker, it should be seen as the active determination of giving oneself over to the ideals to which one is committed – Black freedom, true equality, the people. Sacramental work and desire takes hold when – and perhaps only when – the one who engages in it realises that *they* are doing the work and are inescapably present therein. Once that realisation takes hold, the one who engages in sacramental work can, like Baker, engage in the work of negation *as a constructive act*. Baker lived. She knew who she was. In so doing, she gave (of) herself to various communities; she gave (of) herself to a movement.

This is not the case for everyone, though. Sometimes, the realisation of oneself in sacramental work can produce other possibilities. King was an example. King became synonymous with the movement, through which his personality, his ego, expanded. He won the prizes and the recognition. His bust is at the Capitol.

But there is another possibility: self-mortification. In Hegel's *Phenomenology*, this third moment of unhappy consciousness is another attempt to overcome the changeable individual in order to reach the Unchangeable essence. This time, though, the changeable individual is more completely and radically determined, that is, negated. In its relation to the Unchangeable, writes Hegel, 'consciousness takes its own *reality* to be *immediately a nothingness* [*Nichtige*]' (PS 225). This negation is so extreme that Hyppolite calls the third moment of unhappy consciousness the 'stage of renunciation and alienation' insofar as it gives up on reaching the Unchangeable through itself and instead reduces itself to a mere thing, or, even worse: to nothing.[1]

---

1 Hyppolite, *Structure and Genesis*, 212.

The goal is the same as the previous two moments of unhappy consciousness – to raise itself up and attain a higher truth by eradicating its changeable individuality – but its method is more severe, more complete. Devotion was the moment of immediate relation to the Unchangeable, but it struggled to feel the divine deeply and purely. Devotion failed because it missed the feeling of God and disgusted itself by realising that what it thought was a sense of the divine was really just self-feeling. Sacramental work and desire, then, became the mediated relation to the Unchangeable. The world in which it lived was not utterly wretched but could, through labour, become a sanctified world, God's kingdom on earth. In the end, both devotion and sacramental work and desire exacerbate the issue. Since it failed to overcome its will and embodiment through work, rather than enjoying its activity in the service of God, the changeable individual mourns and agonises over each and every element. It cannot escape itself, and so is left reeling with greater and greater self-disgust, leading to a renewed attempt and a higher aim: to reduce itself to nothing, to achieve the nothingness of its inessentiality, to completely self-annihilate.

Faced with the reality that one is, unavoidably, the one doing the work, one can act to mortify oneself, to try to mitigate one's presence, to such a degree that one loses oneself – not simply in the work, but in the ideals to which one aspires. To be annihilated means to be rendered nothing (in Latin, *nihil*), akin to the German *vernichten* (often associated with the Holocaust), a combination of the prefix *ver-* (which can mean taking something to the extreme such that it becomes its opposite) and *Nichts* ('nothing'). Annihilation and *vernichten* mean complete negation without remainder. But as Hegel, of all people, shows us, there is always a remainder, there are always remains. Yet one can still aspire to become *nothing*.

There was a man whose life speaks to this desire for and enactment of self-annihilation. He went by many names, but here we call him Malcolm X.[2] We do this for two reasons. First,

---

2 As with all of the figures discussed, there is here too an untold story of Malcolm X's link to Hegel. For example, Khalil Islam – who was only recently (November 2021) exonerated for assassinating X – says he 'often

because this is the name he was most widely known by. Second, because, in a way, the Nation of Islam was right. The Nation of Islam handed out Xs to denote that Black people did not know their 'real' last names, that the surnames they had were given to them by white masters who sought to become their total source of determination. Thus, the Xs were nominal negations of white determination. We take up this insight, but, following Hegel, with a phenomenological twist. We use the name 'Malcolm X' here to denote that Malcolm *himself* lived as someone who, beyond simply not knowing his name, *lost himself* in others through his own determination. This is a life of self-mortification. Malcolm X lived and died as one wholly subsumed by what he deemed to be the Unchangeable at the various junctures of his life. He lived as nothing – nothing other than what others had determined about him. He surrendered his will to the will of others. Referring to the period before he entered the Nation of Islam, we call him Malcolm. After that, we often call him just X.

This chapter speaks to Malcolm X as an exemplar of the annihilating performances of self-mortification. While we focus on the various ways in which X was reduced to nothing – the ways in which he lived as nothing, losing himself in others – our very focus on him signals the sheer generativity of his nothingness, the possibilities that were opened in his life and in his wake. He may have been nothing, but *he* was nothing – which is to say, he left us with a life and legacy that still resonates.

While X's legacy survives the tragedy, he did not. But there are others who have taken up the work of self-mortification and not lost themselves, or who have survived different forms of self-mortification and thereby gained themselves. One such person is Angela Y. Davis. If we can be cheeky, here we move from X to Y. Davis devoted – and still devotes – her life to a greater cause, just as she did and does sacramental work and desire. We see her as a higher form of self-mortification because she determined herself

---

saw Malcolm in the 125th Street shop, reading Hegel. "Hegel was his man"'. Mark Jacobson, 'The Man Who Didn't Shoot Malcolm X', *New York Magazine*, 30 September 2007.

to and through the point that led her to the brink of annihilation. Devoted to her work, Davis was abused by the US government – reviled, imprisoned, and despised as one of America's Most Wanted criminals. Yet she never relented. She gave of herself, lost herself in and through the movements of which she was a part. But in doing so, she also gained herself. Dr Angela Y. Davis became a beacon of resistance, an embodiment of selfhood-in-community, with a raised fist and a full afro that became an emblem of Black Power. What Malcolm X only achieved in death, she experiences in life. We conclude this chapter with a meditation on Davis and her engagements, showing that self-mortification is not the last word in the phenomenology of Black spirit but a transition to the next moment. For Hegel, this next moment is Reason; for Black Thought, it is Black Power. Before that, however, we need to talk about nothing, the nothingness of Blackness – a nothingness into which X lived.

To Be Nothing

It can be terrible to be nothing. To capture it grammatically, we take up Calvin Warren's Heideggerian appropriation of Black being under erasure: ~~being~~. 'Black ~~being~~ incarnates metaphysical nothing', Warren writes, and such a reality is terrible, terrifying, and terror-inducing. Warren continues:

> Blacks, then, have function but not Being – the function of Black(ness) is to give form to a terrifying formlessness (nothing) … The puzzle of Blackness, then, is that it functions in an antiblack world without being – much like 'nothing' functions philosophically without our metaphysical understanding of being … blackness and nothing … become synonyms for that which ruptures metaphysical organization and form. The Negro is Black because the Negro must assume the function of nothing in a metaphysical world.[3]

For Warren, Blackness incarnates nothingness because 'the world needs this labor', because, in Hegelian terms, even if the slave gains

---

3   Warren, *Ontological Terror*, 5–6.

awareness of the value of their own work, they are nevertheless compelled to do it by one who wills their annihilation.[4] In this sense, our *Phenomenology of Black Spirit* has been an exploration of those who have been rendered nothing, those whose erased existence merely functions to support the coherence of the white world.

In this regard, Malcolm X is an exemplar of the nothingness that Blackness incarnates. X lived this dynamic so thoroughly that we do not know what to call him. We settle on Malcolm X, we said, knowing it is a misnomer. Because the different names matter: call him 'Malcolm Little', and you're referring to a child who was scorned by his teacher and abused by his parents; call him 'Detroit Red', and you're speaking of a young man who ran the streets, conked his hair, hustled (sometimes through sex work) to make money, and ended up in jail; call him 'Malcolm X', and yes, you are merely speaking of the public figure who came to prominence during the 1950s and '60s, but you're also referring to the national minister for the Nation of Islam, the mouthpiece of the honourable Elijah Muhammad – which is to say, you're speaking of a man whose self-identity was overdetermined by another's political and religious agenda. Perhaps, then, in an attempt to dignify him, you call him 'El-Hajj Malik El-Shabazz', the last name he took. Yet in doing so, you negate much of his earlier life, preferring the man who was assassinated for his outspokenness. Little, Red, X, Shabazz – he went by all of them. These names – save perhaps the last one – were *given* to him; most of them were not his own, and by the time he chose a name for himself (though even it was another's name), he would be killed.

Malcolm X existed for others. His existence was demarcated and determined by the desires of those who needed his labour for their worlds to cohere. In insisting on his role as a figure of self-mortification, we resist the tendency to suggest *why* this was the case. To be sure, we could explore psychoanalytically his relationship to his murdered father and institutionalised mother, or emphasise his relationship to his dismissive teachers, but such

---

4 Ibid., 81.

analyses would only provide more evidence for the fact that this man lived – willingly or unwillingly – as nothing, as the very force against which the world militated. He was brilliant, but he was shunned by his teacher; he was a gifted orator, but he was reviled by the public; he was committed to the ideals of the Nation of Islam, but he was eventually dismissed, cast out, and abandoned. Through it all, he struggled financially, personally, and spiritually. Then he was assassinated. On a certain reading, the man known by many names, the man we call Malcolm X to signal his uncertain and annihilated existence, lived and died as nothing.

To be nothing, Warren says, can be terrible. But it also can be powerful. It can be a space of life. X might have lived as nothing, but this nothingness inspired. It spoke – it still speaks – to a kind of nothingness as generative as it is terrifying, as care-filled as it is denigrated.

> Having been said to be nothing ... we putatively speak nothing. Such speaking echoes, such speaking reverberates, but such speaking is considered – in normative theological-philosophical thought – nothing. Nothing of consequence. Nothing of weight. Nothing of materiality.[5]

Ashon Crawley demonstrates that nothingness is more than loss, that Blackness – as nothingness – is 'a tradition of the ever overflowing, excessive nothingness that protects itself, that – with the breaking of families, of flesh – makes known and felt, the refusal of being destroyed'.[6] Malcolm X lived and died as nothing. But it would be wrong to assume that this nothingness was sheer and total annihilation, without remainder. Though X was killed, he lived on in and through the Black Power movement that erupted in the late 1960s and early '70s and still rumbles today. James Cone, the most prominent Black liberation theologian of the twentieth century, for example, found X's work indispensable for developing his own political and theological claims. X may have lived a life of

---

5   Ashon Crawley, *Blackpentecostal Breath: The Aesthetics of Possibility* (New York: Fordham University Press, 2016), 197.
6   Ibid.

tragic self-mortification, but his legacy survives the tragedy. X was nothing, but that nothingness carried – and carries – multitudes.

Self-mortification, in this sense, is a moment of active nihilism and pessimism. Predetermined as nothingness, self-mortification utterly rejects the problems with sacramental work and desire: 'its actual work thus becomes a doing of nothing, its enjoyment a feeling of wretchedness' (PS 225). While the previous moment in unhappy consciousness strove to reach the Unchangeable by throwing itself completely into doing God's work and desiring only to serve him, in this moment '[w]ork and enjoyment … lose all *universal content* and *significance*' (PS 225). 'His actual action becomes the action of nothing', writes Hyppolite, 'his enjoyment becomes the feeling of his misfortune'.[7] The reason is that if work and desire had any meaning, 'they would have an absolute being on their own', which would thus lead away from, rather than toward, the Unchangeable (PS 225). This is why unhappy consciousness previously failed to reach communion with the divine; the harder it worked, the more it dedicated itself to serving God, the more it asserted itself and diminished God. Thus, in self-mortification, sacramental work and desire 'withdraw into their particularity' (PS 225). As mere particulars, they can be completely annihilated.

Once works and desires, as well as feelings, are reduced to nothingness, there is little left for unhappy consciousness. If the individual's will, body, and world are truly worth nothing, are utterly meaningless, then the individual becomes nothing too. In the face of the Infinite, the particular is infinitesimal. Unhappy consciousness thus turns from unhappiness to wretchedness.

Through the different phases of his life X struggled with this wretchedness. Though a powerful speaker, and an undeniably brilliant and gifted individual, X nevertheless actively risked and thereby lost himself in and through those he adored and with whom he found meaning. As we will see, X's self-mortification often shows itself through the many names he was given by others. As such, this chapter turns on the names X was given – and therefore adopted – in order to underscore self-mortification's

---

7 Hyppolite, *Structure and Genesis*, 213.

near-total annihilating effects. From 'Detroit Red' to 'Malcolm X' to 'El-Hajj Malik El-Shabazz', the man born 'Malcolm Little' seems never to have found a stable and generative sense of self. In fact, early on, he thought of himself as an animal.

From 'Detroit Red' to 'Satan': X's Early Years

> I lived and thought like a predatory animal.
> – Malcolm X

Hollowed out to the point of emptiness (*Nichtigkeit*), unhappy consciousness relates to itself merely 'as *this actual individual* in the animal functions [*tierischen Funktionen*]' (PS 225). Before, unhappy consciousness paid no attention to those seemingly natural but often embarrassing necessities of individual biological life – the need to eat, sleep, expel waste, etc. Even traditional Christians did not repudiate food and sex, as the Eucharist and procreation are central to Christianity. Now that unhappy consciousness is adamant about reducing all parts of its individuality to nothingness, however, these too must be annihilated. Our whole inhabitation of the world, every little detail, must be reduced to nothing. 'These are no longer performed naturally and without embarrassment', writes Hegel, as mere trifling and meaningless matters with which one need not be concerned, but become ways in which 'the enemy reveals himself in characteristic shape' (PS 225). Sexual temptation, culinary delights, defecation, and so on are now 'object[s] of serious endeavor, and precisely matters of the utmost importance' because they are elements of individuality that must be obliterated (PS 226). Self-mortification means, in one sense, mourning and agonising over every particular element of self. Hence unhappy consciousness must be intensely, perhaps obsessively, focused on its animal functions. This is precisely what we see in X's early life.

They called him 'Sandwich Red', 'Harlem Red', even 'Detroit Red', so that people could distinguish him from the other 'Reds' at the clubs – 'St. Louis Red' and 'Chicago Red'. When he worked on the railroads, he drank and smoked nonstop (MX 77, 78). When he returned to his old neighbourhood in Lansing, Michigan, he wore loud zoot suits and spoke differently than he had before (MX 79). In Harlem, he sold and used drugs, fled from the police, and slept with all sorts of women (MX 84). Living like this, he writes, 'you become an animal, a vulture, in the ghetto' (MX 102). For Malcolm, this kind of activity was tantamount to being nothing, to losing oneself, to becoming what Hortense Spillers might call a 'thing ... being *for* the captor'.[8]

One of the clearest steps toward the reduction of himself to a thing was 'conking' his hair. 'Conk', which comes from the word 'congolene', was a caustic hair straightening gel made from lye, which Black men used in the early to mid-twentieth century in order to chemically straighten or relax their naturally 'kinky' hair. Famous musicians – Chuck Berry, Little Richard, James Brown, The Temptations, and so on – sported conks. Conks were used to make a Black man's hair appear like a white man's, which is why Malcolm considered it his 'first really big step toward self-degradation ... literally burning my flesh to have it look like a white man's hair' (MX 54). The brainwashing of Black folk was so extreme that 'they would even violate and mutilate their God-created bodies to try to look "pretty" by white standards' (MX 54). The conk was one of many steps on the path toward total the self-mutilation of Malcolm's Blackness.[9]

Years of street hustling and burglary, increasing the risk with every new crime, pushed Malcolm closer and closer to death. While he would feel the threat of death throughout his life, it was at that time truly constant. 'I expected then, as I still expect today, to die at any time. But then, I think I deliberately invited death in many, sometimes insane ways' (MX 138). There was, for example, the episode before his first burglary, when Malcolm played Russian Roulette in front of his accomplices (MX 143).[10]

---

8   Spillers, 'Mama's Baby', 67.
9   Strangely, the homophone 'conching' is the process of making chocolate. See Elena Blanco et al., 'Conching Chocolate is a Prototypical Transition from Frictionally Jammed Solid to Flowable Suspension with Maximal Solid Content', *Proceedings of the National Academy of Sciences* 116: 21 (2019): 10303–8.
10 Malcolm later admitted to Alex Haley that he had 'palmed the bullet', and so was not really in danger of shooting himself (MX 416).

Or the day he was arrested, when he 'narrowly escaped death twice' in one day – once by the angry husband of Sophia, the white woman with whom he was sleeping, and whose home he was burglarising, and once by the detectives who caught him at the pawn shop (MX 149). It is no surprise that he described his life during this period as 'walking on my own coffin' (MX 146). Out on the streets, hustling to survive in a white world, Malcolm unwittingly became what he understood to be a mere animal, which is what the *white devil* had told him he was. 'I had sunk to the very bottom of the American white man's society' (MX 15).

And yet, there was a bottom beneath the bottom. Before Malcolm's transformation occurred, he would be reduced even further – from an animal to Satan. In the *Phenomenology*, Hegel writes that 'the enemy reveals himself in his characteristic shape', referring to Martin Luther's association of the devil with faeces or a 'giant anus' (PS 225).[11] The father of the Protestant Reformation thought that his personal struggle with constipation was literally a struggle with the devil, who was trying to reduce him to his mere animal functions. His physical ailments became his model for spiritual struggle. To defeat the devil, Luther focused intensely on his and the world's filth: 'as I have often said: I'm like a ripe shit [*Dreck*] and the world's like a gigantic asshole [*Arschloch*]'.[12] Unable to distinguish where the spiritual world ended and the physical world began, the possibility of revealing the sanctity of the world was extinguished. The entire world is an anus and we are the faeces stuck in it, he might say. There is no escape. 'The enemy', Hegel's term for the devil, 'renews himself in his defeat, and consciousness, in fixing its attention on him, far from freeing itself from him, really remains forever in contact with him, and for ever sees itself as defiled' (PS 136). A changeable

---

11 See John Farrell, *Paranoia and Modernity: Cervantes to Rousseau* (Ithaca: Cornell University Press, 2006, 74; Rictor Norton, *A History of Homophobia*, '4 Gay Heretics and Witches', 15 April 2002, updated 18 February 2011, at <http://rictornorton.co.uk/homopho4.htm>; originally featured in *Gay News* 87 (1976): 15–16.
12 Martin Luther, *Luther's Works, Vol. 54: Table Talk*, ed. and trans. Theodore G. Tappert (Philadelphia: Fortress Press, 1967), 448.

individual, confined to its base self and its petty actions, is left 'brooding over itself, as wretched as it is impoverished [*ebenso unglückliche als ärmliche*]' (PS 225). In Hegel and in Luther, the animal functions and the metaphysical enemy converge. Satan shows itself as animality.

Malcolm X embodies this dynamic too well during his early life. During his first year in prison, his sense of self was annihilated in several ways. As with every prisoner, he was reduced to a prison number.[13] He explains: 'your prison number became a part of you. You never heard your name, only your number. On all of your clothing, every item, was your number, stenciled. It grew stenciled on your brain' (MX 152). Malcolm Little had to be reduced to a prison number (which he would later forget) before he could become Malcolm X. The state of his cell also brought him closer to his animal functions, as his toilet was a bucket and the smell of faeces was constant. 'I don't care how strong you are', he writes, 'you can't stand having to smell a whole cell row of defecation' (MX 152). Describing how he spent that first year, he wrote: 'I would pace for hours like a caged leopard, viciously cursing aloud to myself' (MX 153). These curses were often aimed at God, Hegel's Unchangeable; so often that Malcolm soon earned another name: 'Satan' (MX 153).

From Red to X: Prison Education, Letter-Writing, and White Devils

And yet, names change. Lives shift. Transformations occur. Perhaps one of the generative dimensions of Malcolm X's version of self-mortification is the way it shows that one can always change. His life reveals selfhood as a dynamic process of self-de/re/transformation.[14] He might have been an animal-turned-devil in his early years, but this would not remain the case.

---

13 Malcolm's mother too was reduced, as he puts it, to 'a case, a number' when she was at the State Mental Hospital at Kalamazoo (MX 21).
14 Hence the subtitle of Marable's biography: 'Life of Reinvention'. Manning Marable, *Malcolm X: A Life of Reinvention* (New York: Viking, 2011).

While in prison, Malcolm met a man called Bimbi, and he was awestruck. Bimbi, whose real name was John E. Bembry, was Black and an intellectual, a combination Malcolm had not imagined possible.[15] Malcolm called him the 'first man I had ever seen command total respect … with his words' (MX 154). As books were his secret, Bimbi was the prison 'library's best customer' (MX 154). Such was the respect he commanded, other prisoners, of whatever race, listened to Bimbi speak about the 'science of human behavior … about historical events and figures' (MX 154). Without cursing or intimidation, Bimbi offered ways of thinking without the confusion, frustration, and anger that had previously blinded Malcolm. Bimbi advised Malcolm to 'take advantage of the prison correspondence courses and the library' (MX 154). Malcolm took that advice, and his life began to transform. Two things guided this transformation: Elijah Muhammad and books.

Malcolm learned of Elijah Muhammad through his brother Philbert, who introduced Malcolm to 'the "natural religion for the Black man" … something called "the Nation of Islam"' (MX 155). Eventually, all of his siblings converted to the Nation of Islam, including his brothers Reginald and Wilfried, and others in the Little family. One day, while visiting Malcolm, Reginald spoke of Allah, the one true God who posed '360 degrees of knowledge, "the sum total of knowledge"' (MX 158). This 'God had come to America', Reginald explained, and 'let Elijah know … that the devil's "time was up"' (MX 159).

Reginald helped Malcolm see that the Satan moniker he had acquired was actually brainwashing that the white man had deluded him into believing was his true essence. Malcolm was not Satan, the white man was – all of them without exception.[16] Upon hearing this, Malcolm's mind, already reeling from the impression had Bimbi left on him, began 'involuntarily flashing across the entire spectrum of white people' (MX 159). After Reginald left, Malcolm's world and sense of self were annihilated. All the faces of

---

15 Les Payne and Tamara Payne, *The Dead Are Arising: The Life of Malcolm X* (New York: Liveright, 2020).
16 Ibid., 268.

the white people he had known ran on a loop through his mind. When Reginald returned a few days later, they talked for several hours about how the white devil had 'brainwashed the Black man' (MX 161). Reginald explained:

> 'You don't even know who you are ... You don't even know, the white devil has hidden it from you, that you are of a race of people of ancient civilizations, and riches in gold and kings. You don't even know your true family name, you wouldn't recognize your true language if you heard it. You have been cut off by the devil white man from all true knowledge of your own kind. You have been a victim of the evil of the devil white man ever since he murdered and raped and stole from your native land.' (MX 161)

An essential part of this brainwashing was the *whitening of history*. As white authors wrote the books, they played what Malcolm called a 'skin game', lying about human history (MX 179). In this history, the great achievements, advancements, and civilisations of people of colour were erased and replaced with stories of white glory, even while they 'pillaged, murdered, raped, and exploited every race of many not white' (MX 162).[17] This history of lies traces back to the very beginning, to the first humans who came, Malcolm emphasises, from Africa. Citing Mendel's genetics, he argues that 'starting with a Black man, a white man could be produced; but starting with a white man, you never could produce a Black man – because the white chromosome is recessive' (MX 175). At their origins, humans were Black. White people painted our true dark skin pale, and have been painting ever since. Yet 'history's greatest crime was' the kidnapping, enslaving, and torturing of Africans, because this truly severed Black folk from the 'glorious history of the Black man' (MX 182).

---

17 Malcolm describes how little he learned about Black history in school: 'I remember, we came to the textbook section on Negro history. Mr. Williams [his teacher] laughed through it practically in a single breath, reading aloud how the Negroes had been slaves and then were freed, and how they were usually lazy and dumb and shiftless ... telling us between laughs how Negro's feet were "so big that when they walk, they don't leave tracks, they leave a hole in the ground"' (MX 29).

Once they had been enslaved, the white devil began a process of multigenerational brainwashing. It taught Black folk that 'Black was a curse', that God was white and loved only white people, that 'his native Africa ... was peopled by heathen, Black savages, swinging like monkeys from trees' (MX 162). Once this self-hatred and auto-disgust was sufficiently cultivated and passed down through generations, a whitened history made Black folk 'obey and worship the white man' *because* he is white (MX 162). Black folk, by comparison, were reduced to savage animals, if not mere things.[18]

Upon hearing this, Malcolm felt annihilated. For weeks, he barely ate, surviving almost solely on water, and nearly starving. He just sat in his room and stared at nothing. The doctor visited him but gave no diagnosis. Malcolm was experiencing 'the hardest thing, also the greatest thing, for any human being to do; to accept that which is already within you, and around you' (MX 164). The white doctor could not help him because the malignancy of Blackness is whiteness itself. The 'white man's society was responsible for the Black man's condition in this wilderness of North America' (MX 171). *To be nothing is terrible.*

Malcolm learned that the white devil's brainwashing led to the 'deafness, dumbness, and blindness ... afflicting the Black race in America' (MX 179). White people had constructed society so that Black folk were reduced to mere animal functions: sex, labour, bare life. Malcolm began to see his 'earlier self as another person', a 'personification of evil' (MX 170). Reginald and his other siblings explained to Malcolm that they learned their true history, the one concealed by white paint, from 'The Honorable Elijah Muhammad', 'The Messenger of Allah' (MX 161). He taught that the 'key to a Muslim is submission' (MX 162). To become a Muslim, Malcolm learned, meant submitting yourself completely to Allah, reducing your changeable individuality to nothing, negating your entire person. Malcolm's mind and body

---

18 Malcolm describes how, when he was a child, his family were viewed by the Welfare people who tore them apart: 'In their eyesight we were just *things*, that is all' (MX 12).

had been annihilated, but this set him on the path toward transforming Malcolm Little/Detroit Red into Malcolm X. Out of his annihilation, he began educating himself.

Malcolm X's education began with what he called 'a homemade education' or 'my prison studies' (MX 171). Though he had only finished the eighth grade, and had thought little of study since, something always stirred in Malcolm pre-X. When he first went to prison, his sister Hilda had suggested he 'study English and penmanship' so that they could correspond (MX 154). Yet it took Malcolm a year to be able to write a decent letter. He later became interested in Latin, inspired by Bimbi's talk of etymology. He soon became frustrated in his studies, however, because every book he picked up contained words he could not understand. So he decided to not only read the dictionary but to copy it out on a legal pad, all of it, 'down to the punctuation marks' (MX 172). Once he'd copied out a page, he would read his handwriting over and over, reviewing the words he did not remember. Copying the dictionary cultivated in Malcolm an ability 'to read and *understand*' the deep significance of books, which opened a universe of infinite possibilities (MX 173). The 'ability to read', Malcolm echoes Douglass, 'awoke inside me some long dormant craving to be *mentally alive*' (MX 179; emphasis added).[19] Later, when asked 'What's your alma mater?', he always answered: 'Books' (MX 179). Black literacy was always a source of power and a weapon against whiteness.

When he transferred to the Norfolk Prison Colony, he found an impressive collection of books donated by a 'millionaire named Parkhurst', which focused especially on religion and history (MX 157). The library was stuffed with shelves and boxes of books, even rare volumes. He consumed Du Bois, Socrates, H.G. Wells, Abolitionists' pamphlets, Herodotus, Plato, Schopenhauer,

---

19 We see here the shared intention with Elijah Muhammad's teachings. As Malcolm said at the opening of Temple Fifteen in Atlanta: 'That may shock you, but, oh, yes, you just don't realize how our whole Black race in America is mentally dead'; Elijah Muhammad's teachings are meant to 'resurrect the Black man from the dead' (MX 223).

Nietzsche, Spinoza.[20] He read about history, science, philosophy, religion – everything he could get his hands on. Most of all, Malcolm read about the history of white violence and the theft of people of colour from Africa, in America, in India, in China. He learned of resistance to and rebellion against the white devil, such as Nat Turner's rebellion and the 'Boxer Rebellion' in China (MX 176, 178). His reading provided 'indisputable proof that the collective white man had acted like a devil in virtually every contact he had with the world's collective non-white man' (MX 177).

Malcolm *lost* himself in his studies. He read all day and most of the night. When the lights went out, he pushed up against the front of his cell so he could read from the hall light. Studying was the most liberating experience of his life, Malcolm reported: he 'had never been so truly free' as he was when reading book after book sitting in his cell, partially because 'prison enabled me to study far more intensively than I would have if my life had gone differently and I had attended some college', given the distractions that come with college campuses (MX 173). He so enjoyed reading that once, when out of prison, he said that he would have preferred a purely scholastic life, if he 'weren't out here every day battling the white man' (MX 180).

While he learned of the white devil through Elijah Muhammad's teachings, Malcolm developed the concept further. In Hegelese, the white devil is the return of the slave master. No longer an external self-consciousness, forcing another into slavery, the white devil is now an internal master, subjugating Black consciousness from within. While the stoic discovered that it had an internal mastery with which it identified itself, the self-mortifier discovers a mastery opposed to itself within. This is the internalisation of

---

20 Once Malcolm discovered that Spinoza was a 'Black Spanish Jew', he really started digging him. The rest of it, however, was mixed. 'The Oriental philosophers were the ones I preferred', writes Malcolm, because he believed that 'Occidental philosophy had largely borrowed from the Oriental thinkers … Obviously Socrates got some of his wisdom among the East's wise men' (MX 179). For Malcolm, the 'whole stream of Western philosophy has now wound up in a cul-de-sac', as a result of white philosophers' 'neurotic necessity to hide the Black man's true role in history' (MX 180).

the white master. The white devil, Malcolm explains, is not 'any *individual* white man' but 'the *collective* white man's *historical record*' (MX 266). Malcolm uses the term 'devil' in order to point out the 'collective white man's cruelties, and evils, and greed, that have seen him *act* like a devil toward the non-white man' (MX 266).

While the white devil is international, appearing throughout history whenever racism is present, there is a special kind of devilishness in the American white man: deceitful hypocrisy. Malcolm compares the US to South Africa: 'America is worse than South Africa, because not only is America racist, but she also is deceitful and hypocritical. South Africa preaches separation and practices separation ... America preaches integration and practices segregation.'[21] At an Oxford Union Debate, Malcolm continued this thought: 'I have more respect for a man who lets me know where he stands, even if he is wrong, than for the one who comes up like an angel but is nothing but a devil.'[22]

The Mediator's Syllogism

> This was my first step toward self-degradation: when I endured all of that pain, literally burning my flesh to have it look like a white man's hair ... look around today ... It makes you wonder if the Negro has completely lost his sense of identity, lost touch with himself.
> – Malcolm X

Yet amidst all of the misery – having become Satan, having lost himself in his studies, having struggled and suffered – an undeniable connection with the divine emerges. Linked to the 'feeling of its wretchedness and the poverty [*Unglücks und die Ärmlichkeit*] of its actions', writes Hegel, there is 'the consciousness of its unity with the Unchangeable' (PS 226). The very attempt to annihilate ourselves and our world only occurs by means of a relation with

---

21 Malcolm X, *Malcolm X Speaks: Selected Speeches and Statements*, ed. George Breitman (New York: Grove Press, 1965), 75.
22 Malcolm X, 'Oxford Union Debate, Dec. 3, 1964', <https://www.youtube.com/watch?v=auWA7hMh5hc>

the Unchangeable, because the 'essence of the negative movement in which consciousness turns against its particular individuality' is mediated by a relation with the Unchangeable (PS 226). Put differently, since the reduction to nothingness is constituted by the idea of the Unchangeable, the negative relation of the changeable to itself contains a positive significance. Making the world meaning*less* is actually meaning*ful*. As Hegel puts it, auto-annihilation, '*qua relation*, is *in itself positive*, and will bring consciousness itself to an awareness of its *unity* with the Unchangeable' (PS 226). Or in Hyppolite's words, 'Unhappy consciousness must develop to the point of complete self-negation in order that through that negation it may discover its universality.'[23]

Self-mortification produces a mediated relation, which introduces a kind of mediation not yet seen in the *Phenomenology*. From the first moment of sense-certainty, it was assumed that mediation was the problem. The way to attain certainty – of sense, of self, of essence – was through immediate contact with the object. Mediation was the enemy. Yet in the moment of self-mortification, unhappy consciousness learns that mediation is the solution. This mediated relation forms a 'syllogism' (PS 227). The changeable individual is the first term insofar as it is opposed to the second term: the Unchangeable. These two extremes of the syllogism are 'united ... only through a third [or middle] term': a mediator (PS 227). 'Through this middle term [*Mitte*] the one extreme', Hegel continues, 'the Unchangeable, is brought into relation with the unessential consciousness, which equally is brought into relation with the Unchangeable only through this middle term' (PS 227):

Changeable individual to Mediator
<u>Mediator to Unchangeable</u>
Changeable to Unchangeable

There is a double relation, flowing from extreme to extreme, and the third term 'ministers to each in its dealing with the other' (PS 227). The prior failure of unhappy consciousness to overcome

---

23 Hyppolite, *Genesis and Structure*, 214.

the divide and bring the changeable into communion with the Unchangeable was due to the lack of a mediator. What is this mediator, this third or middle term? Another individual. 'This middle term is itself a conscious being' (PS 227). The appearance of the mediator through the mortification of the self and the annihilation of the world makes explicit what had been implicit all along. It is just that the individual could not see it until it was externalised in the form of another individual. The historical example of this mediator is the priest. For Malcolm X, it is Elijah Muhammad. Hence the X syllogism:

Malcolm Little to Elijah Muhammad
Elijah Muhammad to Allah
Malcolm X to Allah

In X's case, Muhammad was the priest. As mediator, the priest allows the unhappy consciousness to self-alienate, as it has been trying to do all along. Elijah Muhammad's determination was what gave X a sense of self amidst his nothingness. The messenger of Allah empowered X to speak boldly – not as himself, but as a mouthpiece for the minister and the Nation – and therefore for God. 'In the mediator', writes Hegel, 'consciousness frees itself from action and enjoyment so far as they are regarded as its own' (PS 228). No longer do the feelings, actions, or desires of an individual belong to that individual. Work and desire are no longer *mine* but those of another. Unhappy consciousness had previously failed partially because it is impossible for the Unchangeable to take on the work and desires of the changeable; but with another person, such as a priest, this is possible. 'The action, since it follows upon the decision of someone else, ceases, as regards the doing or the *willing* of it, to be its own' (PS 228). We act not because we will it but because it is willed by another.

The changeable individual, Hegel writes, 'rejects [*stöß ab*] the essence of its will, and casts [*wirft auf*] upon the mediator or minister its own freedom of decision, and herewith the responsibility for its own action' (PS 228). Since the priest has 'a direct relationship with the Unchangeable being', the changeable individual no longer precludes itself from reaching the communion that it needs (PS 228).

The problem with devotion and sacramental work and desire was that the individual could not completely renounce itself, and so was prevented from true union with its essence. With self-mortification, however, complete self-renunciation of individuality is possible because another individual accepts it. We can relate to the priest, as another person, in a way that we can never relate to God, since God is superhuman. The unhappy consciousness renounces (*abstößen, verzichten*) its will in order to substitute another's will in its place. Hegel calls it 'the surrender [*Aufgeben*] of one's own will' (PS 230). It thus grounds its individuality not in its own will, but in the will of another. We act not because we feel it is right, not because we desire it, and not even because we will it, but because the priest asks it of us. What the unhappy consciousness 'does is foreign to it' (PS 228). In this way, its actions are grounded in a way that conceals the reflexive origins of this self-punishment. In the master-slave dialectic, the slave substituted the master's desires for its own; now, the unhappy consciousness substitutes the will of the priest for its will. Whatever it may earn through work or enjoy from satisfying desires is completely denied.

Unhappy consciousness thereby 'truly and completely deprives itself of the consciousness of inner and outer freedom, of the actuality in which consciousness exists *for itself*' (PS 229). It eliminates any trace of individuality. Nothing is left but a mere thing, 'something that's nothing', X writes.[24] Or as Hegel puts it: 'It has the certainty of having truly divested itself of its "*I*", and of having turned its immediate self-consciousness into a *Thing*, into an *objective* existence' (PS 229). To successfully renounce itself, unhappy consciousness had to sacrifice itself *in toto* (*wirkliche Aufopferung*). Only once the *I* is annihilated (*vernichtet*) is the changeable individual no longer able to deceive itself into thinking it is feeling God directly or working only for the sake of a divine plan.

Notice what is happening. When the changeable individual surrenders its will to that of the priest, this is 'at the same time

---

24 Malcolm X, *By Any Means Necessary* (New York: Pathfinder, 1992), 56.

not a one-sided action' (PS 230). When the unessential extreme surrenders its will, so does the essential extreme. When the individual substitutes the will of the mediator for its will, it implicitly internalises the Unchangeable essence within its changeable self. It thus makes the Unchangeable will into *its* will; its particular will becomes the 'universal will' (PS 230). Here is the trick: the gap between infinite and finite, essential and unessential, Unchangeable and changeable, that which unhappy consciousness has been trying to overcome all along, is here overcome. Since the Unchangeable is already changeable, and now the changeable is already Unchangeable, the misery that plagues the unhappy consciousness has been relieved, at least in principle.

Hegel writes, 'in the sacrifice [of one's will for another's], consciousness, having nullified [*aufgehoben*] the *action* as its doing, has also *in principle* obtained relief [*abgelassen*] from its *misery* [Unglück]' (PS 230).[25] This is merely 'in principle' because the unhappy consciousness does not realise what it has accomplished; it is not aware that it has already crossed over the divide separating the changeable from the Unchangeable. The inessential will of the individual has already become the essential will of the divine, but it does not yet take itself to be that. Hegel says this explicitly: 'Hence, for consciousness, its will does indeed become universal and essential will, but consciousness itself does not take itself to be this essential will' (PS 230). Instead, the unhappy consciousness 'lets the mediating minister express this certainty' (PS 230).

Since the changeable individual does not recognise that its will, formerly particular and unessential, has become universal and essential, the truth of this moment remains implicit, merely 'in principle [*an sich*]' (PS 230). Put differently, God's will enters the world through the surrender (*Aufgeben*) of the individual will. In a way, once one stops trying and completely gives up, God's will becomes actualised in and through particulars.

---

25 Terry Pinkard translates *abgelassen* as 'purging'.

The Break with Elijah Muhammad

Yet the point of a mediator is that he is just another individual. The priest is no closer to God than anyone else is. Elijah Muhammad was merely human, another finite being, just like Malcolm. He is thus unnecessary. Each individual is her own mediator in relationship with the Unchangeable. Malcolm X eventually recognised this, and in so doing, began the work of breaking with Muhammad and the Nation of Islam.[26]

For twelve years, Malcolm devotedly served Elijah Muhammad. Whatever Elijah willed became Malcolm's will. Whatever Elijah ordered, Malcolm performed flawlessly. What Elijah advised, Malcolm followed without question. Thus anything Malcolm said or did was attributed to Elijah Muhammad. Malcolm always made it 'crystal clear that I was Mr. Muhammad's *representative*' (MX 29). Even when the media took photographs of Malcolm, he would hand them one of the many photos of Muhammad that he always kept, 'asking them, "Please use Mr. Muhammad's picture instead of mine"' (MX 291). He had so completely substituted his will for Elijah Muhammad's will that there was nothing left of him. Malcolm puts it well: 'I don't think I could say anything which better testifies to my depth of faith in Mr. Muhammad than that I totally and absolutely rejected my own intelligence' (MX 295). Malcolm 'believed in him as a *divine* leader ... believed that he had no human weaknesses or faults, and that, therefore, he could make no mistakes and that he could do no wrong' (MX 365).

Malcolm describes his adoration for Elijah Muhammad by pointing to the 'Latin root word *adorare*', which 'means much more than "adoration" or "adore." It means my worship of him was so awesome that he was the first man I feared', the fear of 'one who has the power of the sun' (MX 212). Given Muhammad's

---

26 In his *Philosophy of History*, Hegel also speaks of Martin Luther's overcoming of the priest: 'there is no longer a distinction between priests and layman; we no longer find one class in possession of the substance of the Truth, as of all spiritual and temporal treasures ... and this subjectivity is the common property of *all mankind*'. G.W.F. Hegel, *The Philosophy of History*, trans. J. Sibree (Mineola, NY: Dover, 2004), 416.

divinely appointed status, Malcolm said he would 'devote the rest of my life to telling the white man about himself – or die' (MX 185).

Since, however, Malcolm X 'believe[d] in Elijah Muhammad more firmly than he believed in himself', since he was such a devoted and sacramental worker, desiring precisely what the Supreme Minister told him to desire, he eventually 'face[d] a psychological and spiritual crisis' that completely transformed him (MX 210). For Elijah Muhammad was, of course, only another person, just like Malcolm X. Before he was christened the 'honourable prophet', he was simply Elijah Poole, from Sanderson, Georgia.[27] Prophet Elijah Muhammad was, in the end, just another man subject to human desires.

In Hegel's account of the minister, there is little explanation as to how the changeable self-mortifying unhappy consciousness realises that he is in communion with the Unchangeable. In the final paragraphs of the chapter, before transitioning into Reason, the changeable consciousness' communion with the Unchangeable remains 'in principle', merely implicit. This is where Hegel leaves the story, and the next chapter begins with this 'in principle' communion having become explicit for consciousness, but without explaining how this occurred.

Malcolm X's break with Elijah Muhammad fills in Hegel's silence here. Despite considering him the 'Servant and Apostle' of Allah, Malcolm writes, and believing 'he had been divinely sent to our people by Allah himself', Elijah Muhammad was simply a changeable individual, just like Malcolm (MX 214). In 1963, X finally admitted this.[28] It was one of the hardest things he had to confront, since Elijah Muhammad had brought him out of the depths of his nothingness by acting as the mediator between him and the Unchangeable. Malcolm X had held a blind faith in the

---

27 Payne, *The Dead Are Arising*, 251.
28 Les Payne sees Muhammad's willingness to work with the Klu Klux Klan and the American Nazi party, rather than King and the civil rights advocates and committees, as sowing the first seed in what became Malcolm's loss of faith and trust in Elijah Muhammad. See Payne, *The Dead Are Arising*, chapter 14.

Messenger insofar as Elijah was the means to connect with his higher identity, to connect to a Black God: Elijah's Allah.

When X finally admitted to himself that Muhammad was no closer to the Unchangeable than he was himself, he was wrecked, even though he had heard rumours of the so-called Prophet's licentious behaviour since the Fall of 1955.[29] Given X's adoration, Elijah Muhammad had left him looking like a 'total fool', a 'dupe', and 'deeply hurt' (MX 296, 297). Unable to say it himself, X cites the news report of the offending acts: 'Elijah Muhammad, 67-year-old leader of the Black Muslim movement, today faced paternity suits from two former secretaries who charged he fathered their four children' (MX 295). At the same time as he was ostracising members of the Nation of Islam, including X's brother Reginald, for adultery and other immoral acts, Elijah Muhammad was guilty of the same things. Such hypocrisy was intolerable to X, but when he confronted Elijah, the Supreme Minister's response was to silence him.

Elijah Muhammad's immorality was a betrayal 'worse than death' (MX 305). The clearest form of this betrayal, and the final blow that forced X to turn away from the Nation, was Elijah's 'willing[ness] to hide, to cover up what he had done' (MX 306). After twelve years of never thinking of himself, after more than a decade of substituting Elijah Muhammad's will for his own, X self-reflected, and when he did so he discovered that he contained within himself the will of God.

Malcolm X was already his own mediator in his relationship with Allah, the Unchangeable. Thus, out of his own personal struggles with the changeable in himself and in every individual, Malcolm X broke with the Nation of Islam because *each person is their own mediator to Allah.*

Mecca

Following the break with Muhammad, X began to establish his own organisation. He called it Muslim Mosque, Inc., and located

---

29 Ibid., 278.

it in Harlem. The goal, he writes, was to offer a 'religious base, and the spiritual force necessary to rid our people of the vices that destroy the moral fiber of our community', and to be the 'working base for an action program designed to eliminate the political oppression, the economic exploitation, and the social degradation suffered daily by twenty-two million Afro-Americans' (MX 316). To prepare to serve Allah in this new role, X had to make a pilgrimage to Mecca, known as the Hajj, one of the five pillars of Islam. The Hajj is a mandatory religious duty, which every orthodox Muslim must do. 'The literal meaning of Hajj in Arabic', X writes, 'is to set out toward a definite objective' (MX 322). On 13 April 1964, X boarded a plane at JFK Airport, and did just that. He would return transformed once again.

After some delays, Malcolm X finally reached Mecca. No longer relying on Elijah Muhammad for communion with the Unchangeable, X entered communion with the Kaaba, the 'House of God'. He performed the rites of the Hajj, the first of which was to enter a state of holiness, *Ihram*, which required removing one's clothes and putting on 'two white towels. One, the *Izar*, was folded around the loins. The other, the *Rida*, was thrown around the neck and shoulders, leaving the right shoulder and arm bare' (MX 323). The purpose of *Ihram* is to show the equality of all pilgrims in front of Allah, regardless of race, sex, class, etc. After different types of ritual prayers, X was led by a *Mutawaf* ('the one who guides') to the Kaaba, a 'huge Black stone house in the middle of the Great Mosque', around which 'thousands upon thousands of praying pilgrims, both sexes, and every size, shape, color, and race in the world' were turning (MX 336). This is called the *Tawaf*, literally 'going about'. Malcolm entered the mass, stretching himself toward the Kaaba. He repeated the circumambulations of Kaaba three times, and performed sacred prayers, walks, and other rites at the appropriate times. When *Ihram* ended, he 'cast the traditional seven stones at the devil', and others (though not X) had their hair and beards cut (MX 337).

When asked by his fellow pilgrims what impressed him most, X said: 'The *brotherhood*! The people of all races, colors, from all over the world coming together as *one*! It has proved to me the power of the One God' (MX 338). He put down his thoughts in several letters sent to his family and his assistants at Muslim Mosque, Inc. At the heart of these letters was 'a *new insight* into the true religion of Islam, and a *better understanding* of America's racial dilemma' (MX 339; emphases added). The insight was that Islam is the 'one religion that erases from its society the race problem' because, through it, 'the "white" attitude was removed from their minds'. 'I have never seen before', writes X, '*sincere* and *true* brotherhood practiced by all colors together, irrespective of their color' (MX 340; emphases added). It produced an epiphany: 'if white Americans could accept the Oneness of God, then perhaps, too, they could accept *in reality* the Oneness of Man – and cease to measure, and hinder, and harm others in terms of their "differences" in color' (MX 341). In short, Islam cultivated brotherhood, unity, oneness unlike anything Malcolm had ever before imagined.

His epiphany: the race problem in the US was not white people but *whiteness*. Before, X admits, he 'made sweeping indictments of *all* white people' (MX 362). To be a white person was to be a devil, and there was no escaping it. But after meeting blue-eyed, blonde-haired, pale Muslims on the Hajj, who treated him as a true brother and equal, X realised that '*some* American whites do want to help cure the rampant racism which is on the path to *destroying* this country!' (MX 362). Again, the problem is not white individuals but whiteness. In the US, the 'seeds of racism are so deeply rooted in the white people collectively, their belief that they are "superior" in some way is so deeply rooted, that these things are in the national white subconsciousness' (MX 363). It is difficult for a white person to recognise how his own whiteness is the subordination or degradation of non-white people. 'The white man', writes X, 'can't separate himself from the stigma that he automatically feels about anyone, no matter who, who is not his color' (MX 363). Or again: 'it isn't the American white *man* who is a racist, but it's the American political, economic, and social *atmosphere* that automatically nourishes a racist psychology in the white man ... which brings out the lowest, most base part of human beings'. Put differently, 'the white man is *not* inherently evil, but America's racist society influences him to act evilly' (MX 371).

For Malcolm X, the 'Holy City of Mecca had been the first time I had ever stood before the Creator of All [the Unchangeable] and felt like a complete human being' (MX 365). By mortifying himself again, X overcame the division of the unhappy consciousness and raised up his changeableness into the Unchangeable. Through the Hajj, X reached a new stage of his continuous development.

He was born Malcolm Little, who became Detroit Red on the streets and Satan in prison. His life in this first stage was a life of changeableness, in which there was no hope for communion with an Unchangeable beyond. 'In the ghettoes the white man has built for us, he has forced us not to aspire toward great things [e.g. the Unchangeable], but to view everyday living as *survival*' (MX 90). Through a process of self-mortification, through books and the Prophet and his Nation of Islam, Satan became Malcolm X. At this stage, the changeable self, the 'negro' denigrated and subordinated as it was by the white devil, surrendered to the newly accessible Unchangeable, which appeared as the God of the Nation of Islam, Allah, the truly Black God. After Elijah Muhammad betrayed him, and his subsequent pilgrimage to Mecca, there was a further process of self-mortification: Malcolm X became El-Hajj Malik El-Shabazz.[30]

The self that had been surrendered to Allah, through the mediation of Elijah Muhammad, reached true communion with a new sort of Unchangeable: Allah, the One and only God. No longer simply a Black God, as Allah was for the Nation of Islam, the Sunni God was the Unchangeable for all peoples, regardless of race. As El-Shabazz writes, the Sunni 'belief in one God had removed the "white" from their *minds*, the "white" from their *behavior*, and the "white" from their *attitude*' (MX 347). The

---

30 'El-Hajj' designates one who has completed the pilgrimage to Mecca. 'Malik' means 'king'. 'El-Shabazz' refers to the 'especially strong Black tribe of Shabazz' in Yakub's History, a key lesson from the teachings of the Nation of Islam.

Unchangeable was not exclusive to any one race, Black or white, but was instead the erasure of racial divisions. What maintained the separation from the Unchangeable, for El-Shabazz, was whiteness itself.

X had come into a sense of himself. He had submitted to Allah. He had even given himself a new name. El-Hajj Malik El-Shabazz was no longer Malcolm X. He was something else, some*one* else. The process of self-mortification had come to an apex. X became his own mediator, living his life in relation to Allah, to he who would empower him to continue the work of deconstructing whiteness. He was still submitting – Islam, after all, means 'submission' – but this submission was different. It *gave* him a sense of self, one that would open him to engaging with other people from different vantage points, from different perspectives – even different religions. The hard boundary Elijah Muhammad's Nation of Islam drew between races and other orientations no longer had weight. It was time to work together, to self-determine anew. With El-Shabazz's openness, we can transition to Angela Davis. But before we do, we leave you with words from his most famous speech, 'The Ballot or the Bullet', delivered less than a year before his assassination:

> I'm still a Muslim; my religion is still Islam ... Just as Adam Clayton Powell is a Christian minister who ... takes part in the political struggles to try and bring about rights to the Black people in this country; and Dr. Martin Luther King is a Christian minister ... who heads another organization fighting for their civil rights in this country ... I myself am a minister, not a Christian minister, but a Muslim minister; and I believe in action on all fronts by whatever means necessary.
>
> ... it's time for us to submerge our differences and realize that it is best for us to see that we have the same problem, a common problem, a problem that will make you catch hell whether you're a Baptist, or a Methodist, or a Muslim, or a nationalist. Whether you're educated or illiterate, whether your live on the boulevard or in the alley, you're going to catch hell just like I am ... All of us have suffered here, in this country, political oppression at the hands of the white man, exploitation at the hands of the white man, and social degradation at the hands of the white man.

Now in speaking like this, it doesn't mean that we're anti-white, but it does mean we're anti-exploitation, we're anti-degradation, we're anti-oppression. And if the white man doesn't want us to be anti-him, let him stop oppressing and exploiting and degrading us.[31]

As Malcolm X became El-Hajj Malik El-Shabazz, he unearthed the potential for Black liberation and Black Power.[32]

Sadly, we can only speculate about who El-Shabazz would have been. Because, sometimes, demons return. On 21 February 1965, after he went public with the inconsistencies within the Nation of Islam — and particularly the hypocrisy of Elijah Muhammad — El-Shabazz was assassinated. Because Malcolm X was the man everyone knew, because he was the one at the forefront of public consciousness — which is to say, because the world still castigated, denigrated, and militated against him — the 'authorities' never determined with certainty who killed him. Even in death, he would be dismissed.

And yet, he lives on. We still write about him. In his conjunction, Malcolm Little/Malcolm X/El-Hajj Malik El-Shabazz remains a fixture in our collective consciousness. Whether he is remembered as a controversial rabble-rouser or a sensitive man who, in struggling to find himself, was nevertheless committed to the lives of Black people, he remains, his remains are a remainder and reminder. Malcolm X showed that to be nothing can be so much more than wallowing in nothingness. He may not have lived to see his influence. But it remains.

And it will remain.

---

31 Malcolm X, 'The Ballot or the Bullet', speech delivered in Cleveland, Ohio, 3 April 1964, at <http://www.edchange.org/multicultural/speeches/malcolm_x_ballot.html>

32 For a more fully developed articulation of his thought considered as a whole, see Michael E. Sawyer, *Black Minded: The Political Philosophy of Malcolm X* (London: Pluto Press, 2020).

Angela Davis

If X-turned-Shabazz went fully toward self-mortification, Angela Davis offered, and still offers, a more radical approach. Davis shows that selfless commitment and erasure of oneself need not necessarily result in the return of the individual, but can instead result in *service to the collective*. As Davis embodies, in losing oneself, one is reborn, but now as more than a changeable individual.

Davis's life is not simply one of ascetic dedication but of collective commitment. She moved in step with the various groups of which she was a part, such that her fate was linked to the fate of the group. Evoking Ella Baker's insistence on the centrality of the movement, rather than the man, Davis pushed X's process of self-mortification to its logical conclusion: while X became a vessel for the power of (a) personality, Davis traffics in the power of the collective. While X lived a life of isolated (near-)asceticism; Davis lives a life of collective commitment. Davis intimates this in the preface to her autobiography:

> I was reluctant to write this book because concentration on my personal history might detract from the movement which brought my case to the people in the first place. I was also unwilling to render my life as a personal 'adventure' – as though there were a 'real' person separate and apart from the political person. My life would not lend itself to this anyway, but even if it did, such a book would be counterfeit, for it could not convey my overwhelming sense of belong to a community of humans – a community of struggle against poverty and racism.[33]

Even in her autobiography, Davis tried not to make it about her; she tried to situate herself as merely an ordinary woman who had been subjected to 'the very same forces that have shaped and misshaped the lives of millions of people'.[34] In this sense, Davis also led a life of asceticism, of nothingness. She moved through the world as a member of a collective, found herself in the worst

---

33 Angela Davis, *Angela Davis: An Autobiography* (New York: Random House, 1974), viii.
34 Ibid.

of conditions, and experienced the revilement and denigration that, as we noted earlier, might be understood as a staple of Black existence. She was wrongly accused and hunted, then imprisoned and isolated, regularly starved and mistreated, and deemed one of the greatest threats in America.

None of this was new. When she was a girl, she witnessed the bombing of a Black neighbour's home; while in prison, she made her bed with the mice. Seeing these things – *experiencing* these things – shifted her perspective and sharpened her resolve. If she was to be nothing, she would be so boldly, and with an eye toward her community.

In 1970, she was on the lam from the federal authorities. She was on the FBI's ten most wanted list, and she was wanted in California for possessing a firearm that had been used in a courtroom uprising and killing of a judge. The police eventually arrested her in New York, where she was put in jail for almost two years before being moved to California. During this time, Davis was isolated in the psych ward of the jail, where she witnessed prison doctors sedating many of the women inmates, reducing them to shells of themselves. She experienced institutional annihilation.

The isolation soon got to her. But there were people on the outside – literally right outside the jail, and throughout the world – who gave her resolve, who chanted her name. 'I discovered that if I concentrated hard enough', she writes, 'I could hear echoes of slogans being chanted on the other side of the walls. "Free Angela Davis." "Free All Political Prisoners."'[35] The Rolling Stones and Bob Dylan would write songs about her. Thousands of people wrote letters of support. Such echoes stabilised her, buoyed her as she endured the destabilising and disorienting reality of incarceration.

And yet, she seems to not have desired a self – or, put differently, she was content to lose herself in the movement. Newspapers carried her name in their headlines; she'd become known to millions. But this did not inflate her ego. It only served to sharpen her acknowledgement that she was a stand-in for the

---

35 Ibid., 31.

violence of the state. 'Knowing my name was now familiar to millions of people', she writes, 'I felt overwhelmed. *Yet I knew that all this publicity was not really aimed at me as an individual.* Using me as an example, they wanted to discredit the Black Liberation Movement, the Left in general and obviously also the Communist Party. I was only the occasion for their manipulations.'[36] This was not about her. Or, put differently, it was about her *only to the extent that she stood in for something else*. 'Angela Davis' was not an individual agent. She was, instead, a stand-in for a larger cause – one that was as controversial as it was generative. There was no separation of the individual from the work, she knew. Davis the political actor and Davis the woman from Alabama were one and the same.

Davis knew this, though. And – perhaps unlike X – it neither fuelled a further desire for admiration nor did it foster excessive adoration for others. Instead, Davis, ever the dialectician, recognised that her existence was nothing without others – others who lived, and others who suffered and died. She was reminded of this regularly, and when things would get really, *really* rough in that New York jail, Davis would remember: *others had been through this, too*.

> I fought the tendency to individualize my predicament. Pacing from one end of this cell to the other, from a bench along one wall to a bench along the other, I kept telling myself that I didn't have the right to get upset about a few hours of being alone in a holding cell. What about the brother – Charles Jordon was his name – who had spent, not hours, but days and weeks in a pitch-dark strip cell in Soledad Prison, hardly large enough for him to stretch out on the cold cement, reeking of urine and human excrement because the only available toilet was a hole in the floor which could hardly be seen in the dark.[37]

She would ask herself: What about 'the brother who had painted a night sky on the ceiling of his cell' because he needed to see the night sky?[38] What about so many other political prisoners, Black

---

36 Ibid., 32.
37 Ibid., 36.
38 Ibid.

and white, throughout the world? For Davis, 'all the countless others whose identities were hidden behind so much concrete and steel, so many locks and chains', demanded that she not 'indulge even the faintest inclination toward self-pity'.[39] Davis refused to succumb to self-pity. Instead, she would do what she had done before. She would educate and organise. She would inform and support.

After long legal battles, Davis eventually left the psych floor in the jail and – though not without struggle – found herself with other inmates. It was here that she would continue her work of pouring herself into others. At night, she and the other inmates discussed communism and resistance; they would go on hunger strikes; they would find ways to support one another in resistance.[40] Jail was not pleasant, but she had found comrades, she made friends, she formed coalitions. When it came time to be transferred to California, Davis was not only thinking of herself, she was thinking of those she had to leave behind.

> My anger gave way to pangs of regret at having to leave behind all my friends locked up in that filth. Vernell ... Would they drop that phony murder charge? Helen ... would she go home? Amy ... so old, so warm ... what would happen to her? Pat ... Would she write her book exposing the [House of Detention]? And the organizing for the bail fund ... Would it continue? Harriet ... So committed to the struggle – would they continue to try to break her will?[41]

If, as Hegel claims, self-mortification is a movement in which consciousness takes itself to be 'nothingness', and if such nothingness – especially when refracted through Black life – translates into an ontological and existential wretchedness, then Davis' incarceration announces that such nothingness, such wretchedness, can be as generative as it is vile, as filled with possibility as it is marked by utter doubt. During that time in the New York House

---

39 Ibid.
40 Ibid., 50–3.
41 Ibid., 77.

of Detention, Davis knew that the state's goal was to *force* her into a psychological state of self-mortification; they sought to kill her spirit, to make an example out of her robust engagement. They desired for her to lose her mind within those cells, to lose *herself* while incarcerated.

The truth is, she *did* lose herself, just not the way the state intended. This is why her self-mortification is different from X's. Davis became an informal educator, defining the term 'imperialism' and encouraging her fellow inmates to develop their critical sensibilities.[42] She worked with the other women to develop chants for the protesters demonstrating on her behalf – ensuring that she was mentioning them as much as others mentioned her.[43] She even became a maternal figure for a young woman who did not have money for food.[44] This was not the first time Davis helped others out this way. When she was younger, she would steal coins from her father's stash to help other kids buy food for lunch.[45]

When she was in college at Brandeis, she was involved in protests about the Cuban Missile Crisis. James Baldwin had come to speak, but on hearing that the 'Crisis had erupted', stopped his lectures midway.[46] A rally was organised, and it was here that she met Herbert Marcuse – her eventual mentor and the source of her Hegelianism – for the first time.

What is important in all of this is that Davis never stopped committing herself to larger causes, even as it meant the erasure of her individuality and her rebirth as an icon for international revolution. While an undergraduate, she travelled to Helsinki to engage with the Communist Youth Festival, and organised with and for her international peers and friends. She witnessed the French antagonism toward Black Algerians, and recognised the sheer injustice of the US's foreign policy position toward Cuba.

---

42 Ibid., 70.
43 Ibid., 73.
44 Ibid., 62.
45 Recall that the US government's 'free and reduced-price lunch' program hadn't started yet; they'd need to discover – and then steal the idea from – the Black Panther Party before they would introduce it.
46 Ibid., 102.

Throughout her life, she was committed to the cause of *collective* liberation, and this meant – more than anything else – that her life was not her own. Though she struggled with what this meant, she willed it. Much like Malcolm X, Davis devoted her life to others, and yet, in this midst of this intense, self-sacrificial, devotion, she found a way to *life*, by willing herself through the totalising nothingness that seems to have engulfed X.

In fact, Malcolm X had something to do with Davis' ability to practise the work of *generative* self-mortification. The irony, perhaps, is that her formal studies *included* an engagement with X, who spoke at Brandeis during her time there as a student. According to Davis, X helped her 'to construct a psychological space with which I could "feel good about myself"'.[47] As she elaborates in her *Autobiography*:

> Malcolm X began his speech with a subdued eloquence … I was fascinated by his description of the way Black people had internalized the racial inferiority thrust upon us by a white supremacist society. Mesmerized by his words, I was shocked to hear him say, speaking directly to the audience, 'I'm talking about you! You!! You and your ancestors, for centuries, have raped and murdered my people!' … Malcolm was addressing himself to white people, chastising them, informing them of their sins, warning them of the Armageddon to come, in which they would all be destroyed.[48]

While Davis found 'a kind of morbid satisfaction listening to Malcolm reduce white people to virtually nothing', she could not fully resonate with his message. At the time, it was because of religious differences. 'Not being a Muslim', she writes, 'it was impossible for me to identify with his religious perspective'.[49] But eventually, the critique went deeper. Davis struggled with the nationalistic nature of X's ideas, especially given her Marxism and feminism.[50] Part of her critique of nationalism is that it does

---

47 *Angela Y. Davis Reader*, 290.
48 Davis, *Autobiography*, 130–1.
49 Ibid., 109.
50 *Angela Y. Davis Reader*, 290, 291.

not sufficiently attend to the heterogeneous composition of all communities. '[W]e need to be more reflective, more critical, and more explicit about our concepts of community. There is often more heterogeneity within a Black community ... than in cross-racial communities.' 'What is problematic is the degree to which nationalism has become a paradigm for our community-building processes.'[51]

Perhaps the main problem with nationalism as a model for organising is that it is rooted in ideological similarity (evoking the problems we saw with Garveyism). The very *form* of nationalism, Davis contends, is not necessary, and can be detrimental, to coalition work. To demand ideological affinity before collectivities can be formed is to replicate and perpetuate forms of exclusion and repression, such as calculations about who is 'Black enough' or who is 'more feminist'. Different definitions of Blackness or feminism, Davis writes, 'should not prevent us from creating movements that will put us in motion together, across all our various differences'.[52] Difference, conjunction, and contradiction generate, rather than impede, political momentum.

Out of Mortification, Coalitions

Davis practises a mode of self-mortification steeped in the dynamic process of coalition-building. She moves with the collective, not merely decentring or abnegating herself in the process but constantly drawing upon herself as an expression, example, or embodiment of larger problems – as well as of the movements developed to combat them.

Unlike King, Davis does not build coalitions around universalist ideals like personhood or humanism but on the material conditions and historical forces that compose contemporary social formations. Unlike X, Davis's life is not organised around an actual divine being – whether that divine being be physical or not. Such ideals require mediation; they involve priests or idols

---

51 Ibid., 299.
52 Ibid., 304.

who, in the end, turn out to be merely human. Davis distrusts ideals and idols because they so easily entail and/or obscure forms of exclusion, neglect, or marginalisation. Instead of nationalism and ideology, Davis builds coalitions across differences and around concrete *issues* – prison abolition, secure health care, reproductive justice, housing – or 'points of junction constructed by the political projects we choose to embrace'.[53]

This kind of project-building allows Davis to move differently regarding race and antiblackness. While thinkers like X underscored the metaphysical and political dimensions of antiblackness, recognising the demonic and oppressive nature of white supremacy, Davis shows that while Black, brown, Native American, Asian, and Chicano people are forever the first victims of racism, white people too are affected. She thus asks: who does racism aid? Racism does not benefit the masses of white people, especially not working-class people, but capitalist corporations, which are very few in number. One of the most effective strategies in the maintenance of power is to divide and conquer, for the few to divide the masses, and race in America has been the most effective means for separating people with political, economic, and social affinities that cross racial differences.

Davis saw this intentional social fragmentation in the racist strategies through which Hitler and the Nazis gained power, and this led her to diagnose the advanced racism emerging in late-twentieth-century America as a crossbreed of fascism and corporate capitalism. By insisting on racial divisions which were both inspirations to and reflections of Nazi anti-Semitism, capitalists aimed to stave off the formation of a movement that Davis calls *revolutionary*. Beyond Garvey's return to Africa, beyond King's dream of a new world, beyond X's diasporic unity, Davis practises a mode of political action for revolutionising *this* world.

Davis thus turns away from the religiosity of King and X to an outright political project. And more to the point, this political project shifts the *terms* by which one engages in the work of selfmortification. Davis loses herself in collective political struggles;

---

53 Ibid.

she is steeped in the coalitions – as temporary or as longstanding as they may be – that are built in service of changing the material conditions of those struggling the most. But that's the thing about coalitions: they're fragile, and necessarily so. Davis understands failure to be a necessary part of the work of coalition-building. Hence she writes:

> we often assume that the disbanding of a coalition or alliance marks a moment of failure, which we would rather forget. As a consequence, we often fail to incorporate a sense of the accomplishments as well of the weaknesses. Without this memory, we are often condemned to start from scratch each time we set out to build new coalition forms.[54]

Similar to Hegel, Davis sees the failure of a movement as productive, rather than destructive.

In place of movements that rise and fall with a dynamic leader like King or X, Davis emphasises the decentred structure of coalitions. Although white violence might destroy a dynamic leader and thereby the movement based on them, the coalitions that Davis envisions and builds transform and grow. To evoke Deleuze and Guattari's critique of arboreal logics in favour of rhizomes: rather than basing a coalition on a single identity, embodied by a charismatic leader and imposed by an oppressive history, the power of coalitions resides in their capacity to generate new political identities that are composed of, but not reducible to, the various members of a coalition.[55] Beyond the most obvious coalitions, Davis advocates for the 'creation of *unpredictable* or *unlikely coalitions* ... Not only prisoners, immigrant workers, and labor unions, but also prisoners *and* students.'[56]

---

54 Ibid., 298.
55 Gilles Deleuze and Félix Guattari, *A Thousand Plateaus*, trans. Brian Massumi (Minneapolis: University of Minnesota Press, 1987), 'Introduction'.
56 *Angela Y. Davis Reader*, 324; emphasis added.

Conclusion

We will not continue chronicling Davis's life – not because she doesn't deserve it, but because to do so would be to risk hagiography, which would run counter to what appear to be Davis's own interests. It would also reproduce what Victor Anderson calls the cult of 'heroic genius', wherein we celebrate exemplary figures for being just that – exemplary.[57]

And yet, in a way, we are already guilty of this. Throughout this text, we have traced the lives and thoughts of 'extraordinary' people – those who, for better or worse, in both explicit and implicit ways, have shaped the collective memory and social imagination of Blackness in the United States and the world. Read in this way, Davis is the culmination of a line of figures who have shaped our sense of what Blackness was and is. Angela Y. Davis stands as the final moment of *this particular phase* of the phenomenology of Black spirit.

But we do not want to end this text that way. To do so would be counterintuitive to what Davis and X were about, as it would situate both of them in the realm of the heroic. It would render them exemplars in ways that neither strove – or strives – to be. They were (are), like so many other figures we have engaged in this text – especially Black women – simply committed to doing the work of demonstrating, and cultivating respect for, the profound generativity and possibility present within Black life. And yes, we mean Black *life* – not simply Black 'thoughts' or Black 'ideas'.

So much of Hegel's work is situated within the realm of epistemology. To sit and think with him is to underscore how knowledge is produced, how knowledge moves and develops over time, how history moves in and through ideas. Throughout this text, however, we have traced the movement of *Black* spirit – a movement that is (we ardently argue) as existential as it is epistemological, as ethical as it is ontological, as concrete as it is idealistic. It is fitting, then, that we end with figures – with lives – whose very

---

57 Victor Anderson, *Beyond Ontological Blackness: An Essay on African American Religious and Cultural Criticism* (London: Bloomsbury Academic, 2016), 80.

existence exposes the unsettled and inextricable relation between life and knowledge, between ethics and epistemology, between bodies and ideas.

It is also fitting that we end this text with two thinkers who embodied and still embody the both generative and devastating capacities of living as nothing, of existing as nothingness. As we noted in the introduction to this chapter, recent discussions in Black studies have focused on nothingness as a central analytic for understanding Blackness. Some, like Warren, emphasise the ontological and metaphysical terror of such an existence; others, like Crawley, emphasise the generativity present within communities who have been said to have and to be nothing.

Here, we try to emphasise *both*. X's life was tragic. There is no doubting that. He lived a life of deep struggle and extreme re-invention. His existence was constantly overdetermined by others. But he also lived a life of *meaningfulness*. Like so many of the lives we have engaged with in this volume, X's life may have meant little-or-nothing for many, but for others it means and meant so much. He spoke boldly. He cared deeply. He was affected by new possibilities. He welcomed transformation. Though his life ended tragically, the man who we know and name as Malcolm X strove for greater life, for fuller meaning, throughout his forty years on this planet. And though it can be argued that he only experienced that sense of greater life and fuller meaning in his final years, he nevertheless left a lived legacy of that struggle and striving. In many ways, Malcolm X is the exemplary figure of and for Warren's Black nihilism. But in other ways, he announces that there is everything in the nothingness.

Perhaps this is what Davis knew and still knows. Perhaps her recognition that coalitions fail, that she is nothing outside of the political life she leads, and that a movement can only be as strong as the masses who comprise it – perhaps these recognitions announce another perspective on nothingness. Maybe Davis's writings – on the tripartite dimensions of race, class, and gender oppression, or on the possibility and necessity of prison and police abolition – maybe these writings, like Crawley's, are *also* love letters to those who have been said to be and to have nothing. And maybe she wrote, and continues to write, because she knows that she, too, is nothing outside of those with whom she organises and for whom she cares.

In this regard, perhaps Angela Davis – like Harriet Jacobs and Ida B. Wells and Anna Julia Cooper and Zora Neale Hurston and Ella Baker – demonstrates that nothingness might mean *no-thingness*, by which we mean, no sense of oneself as an atomised, isolated, and impassible individual. Beyond the philosophical rhetoric, beyond the propaganda, beyond the sophisticated reflections on race, gender, class, slavery, fascism, and the prison-industrial complex, perhaps the most profound critique and augmentation of Hegel's *Phenomenology* that these figures – especially these Black women – embody, express, and articulate, is that Black spirit is as *lived* as much as it is thought.

In this sense, the phenomenology of Black spirit names something that many of us recognise but too often forget: the thinking is in the living, and the living is what matters.

Conclusion

Idealism and Black Power

> Like an owl exploding in fire …
> – Amiri Baraka, 'Somebody Blew up America'

Afterword, or the Phenomenology of Afterlives

As always, the dialectical movement relinquishes (*entäußert*) yet bears forth and recollects all that has come before. Everyone from Douglass and Jacobs to X and Davis, to the many, many others who we have not named, compose Black spirit's coming-to-be and relinquishing into time. This 'relinquishing, however, is likewise the relinquishing of itself' (PS 807). 'In its own self', Hegel continues, 'this self-relinquishing relinquishes itself [*diese Entäußerung sich an ihr selbst entäußert*] and, in that way, is in its extension as well as in its depth, in the self' (PS 808). This is especially true of Black history, marked as it is by irremediable loss, violent erasure, and a wake of dispossession.

Black spirit, we think, resonates strongly with how Hegel speaks of the path taken through his *Phenomenology* – 'a path of despair' (PS 78). For the protagonist moving along it, Hegel writes, 'this path has negative meaning …, and what is the retaliation of the concept will count, instead, to it, as the loss of itself, for on this path, it loses its truth' (PS 77). In Black history, there is an even deeper kind of loss, one that is more Hegelian than Hegel could have realised: a loss that loses itself. Given this loss of loss, Black spirit cannot simply turn inward and recollect all that has gone before, but must instead formulate what Hartman calls wayward lives in spaces, often in 'urban commons where the poor assemble, improvise the forms of life, experiment with freedom, and refuse the menial existence scripted for them'.[1] Perhaps the best way to think of this improvisational recollective insistence of previous moments in later moments, of all that was lost and forgotten in the fire and sea, is to evoke Hartman's notion of afterlives. In this book, we have recomposed Hegel's *Phenomenology* so that it becomes a book about the intersecting afterlives of slavery and loss, as well as the joy and vitality bound up with them; or perhaps it is a book of afterlives of afterlives, weaving and unfolding until the movement of these entangled afterlives unfolds itself through a gallery of shadows, the dispossessed absolute living in its own wake.[2]

But there is plenty left of the *Phenomenology*. This book only follows Chapter IV, 'The Truth of Self-Consciousness'. We skipped the preceding three chapters on 'Consciousness', and stopped before the subsequent hundreds of pages on 'Reason', 'Spirit', 'Religion', and 'Absolute Knowing'. But this is where we must stop. No one or two people should tell this whole story, and we are not even sure that this dialectical parallelism should continue. If, however, others want to continue where we ended, we invite them to extend the dialectical parallelism beyond Chapter IV. To assist with this, we gesture to what might come next in this phenomenology of Black spirit. At the end of unhappy consciousness, after self-mortification, Hegel transitions to Reason. For us, the rise of Reason is a parallel to the rise of Black Power.

The Rise of Reason

Put simply, Reason is the dialectical synthesis of consciousness and self-consciousness. It can only happen at the end of unhappy consciousness because, through its necessarily self-defeating attempts to reconcile the changeable with the Unchangeable,

---

1 Hartman, *Wayward Lives*, 2.
2 Thinking of Hegel's subsequent claims that art (religion too) is similar to philosophy in its ability to regard the absolute (albeit not conceptually), we can gesture to Kara Walker's Black cut-paper silhouettes that evoke the kind of 'gallery of pictures' that Hegel describes in the final paragraph of his *Phenomenology*.

the protagonist finds that it universalises itself *through* its failed attempts to overcome or eliminate individuality. By inadvertently universalising itself, self-consciousness provokes the first full integration of otherness, though an otherness that first appears as a full articulation of individuality – the mediator. In this sense, Reason is the overcoming of the inchoate individuality marking self-consciousness and the emergence of the seeds of sociality that will only be actualised in the chapters on Spirit.

As we saw in Chapter 6, the final act of self-mortification has 'driven its being-for-itself outside of itself and made it into an existent' (PS 231). The changeable individual finally unified itself with the Unchangeable universal – true reconciliation of its unhappiness came about through the 'actual, completed sacrifice [*wirklich vollbrachten Aufopferung*]', the purging of changeableness and individuality (PS 230). Individuality reaches this state of universality through its history of self-negations; Reason thus emerges when 'the singular individual is the universal' (PS 231). Put differently, the individual 'I' has become a universal 'I'. By purging itself of itself, through practices of self-mortification, self-consciousness universalised itself. In this new shape of self-consciousness, the changeable became Unchangeable and the Unchangeable changeable. This is Reason.

In historical terms, writes Hyppolite, 'Hegel envisages the transition from unhappy consciousness to reason as the transition from the medieval church to the Renaissance and modern times'.[3] Religiously, Reason is the moment of Protestantism; philosophically, it is the moment of Idealism. For Hegel, Martin Luther and Descartes are versions of the same kind of reconciliation of the changeable and the Unchangeable, as well as the rise of Reason, that mark – on standard European historiographies – the beginning of Modernity.[4] Luther's version keeps the moment of

---

3 Hyppolite, *Structure and Genesis*, 223.
4 It is perhaps underappreciated how much Hegel took from Luther. As Frank Ruda puts it, 'Hegel himself claimed that it is philosophy's task to articulate in the medium of the concept what Luther articulated in the medium of feeling.' Frank Ruda, *Abolishing Freedom: A Plea for a Contemporary Use of Fatalism* (Lincoln: University of Nebraska Press, 2016), 11.

reconciliation in the worldly beyond while locating the Unchangeable in every Christian (every man is a priest); Descartes' version, as seen in his *Le Monde*, more fully embeds the Unchangeable in an individual mind and says: let us pretend that God does not exist, and articulate what the structure of the world would be if he created the world again. Reason is the shape of spirit that places the Unchangeable in the changeable individual.

Reason, then, is the middle term between the changeable and the Unchangeable; but rather than taking the form of an external mediator, it is the mediator that is self-consciousness itself. Each individual self now mediates its *own* relation between individual and universal. The priest is unnecessary, as is the king. Reason does not so much kill God as distribute it in every subject. Modernity is marked by the emergence of a much more robust 'I' – when subject becomes substance and substance subject. As such, self-consciousness feels a new degree of certainty, a new power to know and create the world. Modern subjectivity realises that it is the *whole* of reality, the *whole* of truth; truth and reality are no longer beyond but immediately present to and dependent on the mind, the *I*. As Hegel says, self-consciousness 'discovers the world as *its* new real world, which in its permanence holds an interest for it which previously lay only in its transiency; for the existence of the world becomes for self-consciousness its own *truth* and *presence*' (PS 232). The world is no longer seen as an other, an externality that must be worked on and eliminated. For the world now is nothing but what it is in and for self-consciousness. 'It demonstrates itself to be this *along the path* in which … otherness as an *intrinsic being* vanishes' (PS 233). Self-consciousness gained the previously divine power to create and shape the world – *everything* – through itself, through thinking, through the cogito.

Hence Reason brings complete certainty. More than sense- or self-certainty, Reason is certain that *it* is *all* of reality. As Reason further develops into later idealisms, and science displaces religion as the institution controlling truth, thinking is emboldened to contend that it *is* the world completely, that there is no otherness or external world that it cannot reach. The 'I' is all of reality and all of reality is the 'I'.[5] Thinking *is* existing and what exists is what the *I* thinks. Knowledge of the world, for Reason, is self-knowledge. The rise of the power of rationality is the claim that the 'I' can know everything, that there is nothing 'I' cannot know. Hence the reputation of science as hegemonic and totalising. As Francis Bacon put it, nature must submit to the power of reason. In fact, Hyppolite notes, the term 'world [*die Welt*]' itself becomes a new term, designating not only a subjection of externality but a decentring of the world and a recentring on the subject, in what Kant called a Copernican Turn: 'Up to now it has been assumed that all our cognition must conform to objects ... Hence let us once try whether we do not get farther with the problems of metaphysics by assuming that the objects must conform to our cognition.'[6] Before, there was just otherness, externality, the beyond. Now, there is a realm of experience wherein the self is the organising and constituting force. *The* world is now *my* world.

As with all of Hegel, however, Reason will fail to deliver on what it promises. Its fatal flaw is that its certainty that it is all of reality is merely immediate, a claim rather than a demonstration. 'It merely asserts [*versichert*] that it is all reality, but does not itself comprehend this' (PS 233). To comprehend itself as all of reality requires other subjects in a more robust way. But such otherness does not truly happen until the rise of spirit, first sparked as it is for Hegel by Antigone's defiant burial and mourning.

The Rise of Black Power

The corresponding moment to Hegel's Reason in the phenomenology of Black spirit is *Black Power*. Black Power spans various histories, movements, and organisations in Black Thought, though its overarching aim seems consistent: full self-determination *of, by, and through* Black people.

---

5 Hyppolite, *Structure and Genesis*, 225.
6 Immanuel Kant, *Critique of Pure Reason*, trans. and ed. Paul Guyer and Allen W. Wood (Cambridge: Cambridge University Press, 1998), Bxvi.

Beyond respectability, separation, or integration, the key word here is *power*, *Macht*, *Kraft* – a power that is thoroughly and exhaustively Black. Black is power in the sense of the capacity to self-determine, which for Hegel means to negate all of reality. Black Power is the capacity for the total self-negation/total determination of the Black self and the Black world. In this sense, Black Power, like Hegel's Reason, is the immediate certainty of itself as being all of reality; it is making reality Black, outside and in spite of whiteness. Black Power is the complete wresting of the power to make, shape, name, form, choose, destroy, and recreate Blackness. Black Power, in short, is the certainty of the capacity for Black people to determine reality.

Black Power grew out of the criticisms of the Civil Rights Movement, especially those made by Malcolm X and Angela Davis. In this vein, in the early 1960s, Robert F. Williams, the president of the Monroe, North Carolina Chapter of the NAACP, criticised King's philosophy of nonviolence, articulating a criticism Baker and Davis both shared. Williams' 1962 book *Negroes with Guns* forcefully depicts this criticism through stories of the violation of Black people and their rights during peaceful civil rights protests and marches. Rather than nonviolence, Williams detailed a policy of self-defence and self-reliance. Insofar as self-defence involves the power to determine life or death (evoking Hegel's definition of the master), it is the clearest, earliest depiction of Black Power, and the concrete forms of Black self-reliance and self-determination are rooted therein. The transition from unhappy consciousness to Reason is a move from the forms of self-mortification in Malcolm X and Angela Davis, respectively, to the self-defence of Black Power.

Learning from Malcolm X and Williams, Huey P. Newton and Bobby Seale further developed these seeds of Black Power by forming the Black Panther Party for Self-Defense. Newton and Seale pushed Black Thought into a revolutionary and anti-imperialist programme for achieving full Black self-determination. One of the main sparks for the Panthers was the continuous destruction of Black life, as seen in the deaths of King, Malcolm X, and, especially, the police brutalisation and murder of Black people across the US. In the explosive anger and insurrection that followed such killings, Newton and Seale discerned an internal strength and immanent power in Black people to stand up to the police, one that they thought could be organised into lasting political power. They studied California gun laws and organised groups to police the police. They raised money to buy guns by selling Mao Tse-tung's *Little Red Book*. In Seale's words, they would 'sell the books, make the money, buy the guns, and go on the streets with the guns. We'll protect a mother, protect a brother, and protect the community from the racist cops.'[7] With guns and books in hand, they tracked incidents of police brutality around Oakland. When they heard of an incident they would immediately show up on the scene, openly carrying their guns in order to prove that the cops were not the only ones with such powers, often reading aloud from law books to inform the victims of their rights, to cite laws demonstrating that they were innocent, and to threaten officers who violated constitutional rights. These police patrols effectively demonstrated the power of Black people to self-determine and self-organise. When Betty Shabazz, Malcolm X's widow, came to speak at a February 1967 conference held in his honour, members of the Black Panther Party formed her armed escort.[8]

Alongside policies and practices of self-defence, the Black Panther Party developed networks to found and support Black-owned bookstores and presses, farms and grocers, media and schools, hospitals and ambulance services, and more. All of these were seen as forms of self-defence – medical self-defence, educational self-defence, economic self-defence, and so on. In total, there were more than sixty such 'Black Panther Party Survival Programs', the most famous of which was the 'Free Breakfast for School Children Program'. Inspired by social research on the value of breakfast for effective education, and the belief that alleviating

---

[7] Bobby Seale, *Seize the Time: The Story of The Black Panther Party and Huey P. Newton* (Baltimore: Black Classic Press, 1991), 79–83.

[8] Josh Bloom and Waldo E. Martin Jr., *Black Against Empire: The History and Politics of the Black Panther Party* (Berkeley: University of California Press, 2013), 49.

hunger and poverty was essential for Black liberation, the Black Panthers cooked and served free breakfasts to inner city children at local community centres and churches.

Since white society had failed and abandoned Black communities, the Panthers organised ways to cultivate Black self-determination and self-reliance. This is perhaps most clearly articulated in their 'Ten-Point Program'. A sort of combined Black Bill of Rights and Black Declaration of Independence, the Program had two sections. The first, called 'What We Want Now!', articulates what the Black Panthers demanded from American society. The second, 'What We Believe', outlines the Party's philosophical ideas and sets out the rights Black people should have but are denied. In essence, it amounted to a Constitution of Black Power. Here is the first section:

1. We want freedom. We want power to determine the destiny of our Black Community.
2. We want full employment for our people.
3. We want an end to the robbery by the Capitalists of our Black Community.
4. We want decent housing, fit for shelter of human beings.
5. We want education for our people that exposes the true nature of this decadent American society. We want education that teaches us our true history and our role in present-day society.
6. We want all Black men to be exempt from military service.
7. We want an immediate end to POLICE BRUTALITY and MURDER of Black people.
8. We want freedom for all Black men held in federal, state, county and city prisons and jails.
9. We want all Black people when brought to trial to be tried in court by a jury of their peer group or people from their Black Communities, as defined by the Constitution of the United States.
10. We want land, bread, housing, education, clothing, justice and peace.[9]

---

9   Ibid., 71.

The second section is longer, but the first point captures the parallel with Hegel's Reason: 'We believe that Black people will not be free until we are able to determine our destiny.'

In 1967, Seale and Newton 'drafted' Stokely Carmichael into the Black Panther Party, giving him the rank of Field Marshal, and later promoting him to Prime Minister.[10] Born in Trinidad and raised in Harlem, Carmichael was a philosophy major at Howard when he became active in the Civil Rights Movement. First participating in the Freedom Rides to desegregate interstate travel, organised by the Congress of Racial Equality, he later acted as a field organiser for SNCC (where he worked with Ella Baker) and co-founded the Lowndes County Freedom Organization, whose mascot was a Black panther. In 1966, Carmichael took over SNCC chairmanship from John Lewis. The following June, James Meredith began his 'March Against Fear', intending to walk from Memphis to Jackson, Mississippi. He was shot by a white sniper on the second day. While Meredith was hospitalised, Carmichael (and others) continued the march until he was arrested. Upon his release, he gave his first Black Power speech:

> We been saying 'Freedom' for six years and we ain't got nothing yet. What we are gonna start saying now is Black power ... from now on when they ask you what you want, you know to tell them: Black power, Black power, Black power![11]

The six-hundred person crowd started repeating the slogan 'Black Power', and it spread throughout the country and the world.[12]

---

10 Ibid., 92.
11 Cited in Joel D. Aberbach and Jack L. Walker, 'The Meanings of Black Power: A Comparison of White and Black Interpretations of a Political Slogan', *The American Political Science Review* 64:2 (1970): 367.
12 In an interview, Carmichael/Ture explained that the introduction of the term at the march was part of a larger SNCC strategy that came out of organised field work and preparation of the community. Interview with Stokely Carmichael, conducted by Blackside, Inc. on November 1988, for *Eyes on the Prize II: America at the Racial Crossroads 1965 to 1986*. Washington University Libraries, Film and Media Archive, Henry Hampton Collection, Question 51.

Though rumblings of Black Power echo throughout the history of Black Thought – Frederick Douglass had used the phrase (albeit in a different sense), Marcus Garvey was close to formulating it, Richard Wright used it, and Angela Davis did even more – it was Carmichael's formulation that made it a fully formed concept which changed the history of Black spirit. His subsequent book *Black Power: The Politics of Liberation* (co-written with Charles V. Hamilton) was intended 'to define and encourage a new consciousness among Black people which will make it possible for us to proceed toward those answers and those solutions'.[13] Black Power expressed a 'sense of peoplehood: pride, rather than shame, in Blackness, and an attitude of brotherly, communal responsibility among all Black people for one another'.[14] Black Power, for Carmichael, is a call for the unity and self-determination of Black people *in, through, and by* Blackness. It is no surprise that he was the first to theorise 'institutional racism'.[15]

While Black Power galvanised many young Black people, it worried others, especially the older Black generations who still believed in the Civil Rights Movement. King called it 'an unfortunate choice of words'. The NAACP's Roy Wilkins derided it as 'the raging of race against race'. The director of the National Urban League, Whitney Young Jr, said: 'Anyone can arouse the poor, the despairing, the helpless. That's no trick. Sure they'll shout "Black power", but why doesn't the mass media find out how many of those people will follow those leaders to a separate state or back to Africa?'[16] And Black Power terrified white people. It paid no attention to white fragility – by tiptoeing around sensitive topics, treading lightly, trying to see 'all sides', and so on. Integration, Carmichael and others argued, had failed as a project, while separatism was short-sighted. Instead, Black Power made Blackness the sole source of meaning. No matter what the

---

13 Kwame Ture and Charles V. Hamilton, *Black Power: The Politics of Liberation* (New York: Vintage Books, 1992), xvi.
14 Ibid., xvi.
15 Ibid., 4–5.
16 Michael T. Kaufman, 'Stokely Carmichael, Rights Leader Who Coined "Black Power", Dies at 57', *New York Times*, 16 November 1998.

response, once it was out of the bag and on the lips of almost every Black person, there was no stopping it.

Black Power urges pride in Blackness, proclaims the beauty of Black bodies, celebrates the genius of Black history – and not just for Black people but for everyone. It means that Black people have the right and power to define themselves and to make white and non-Black people accept those definitions as real, valid, and meaningful. Black beauty *is real* beauty, Black pride is about *historical acts*, and Black genius *is true* brilliance. White people feared the claims of Black Power because it forced them to confront their whiteness like never before and admit the power of Blackness.

In parallel with Hegel's Reason, Black Power, we argue, can be viewed as an emergent form of Black self-consciousness that is certain that its world is Black, that the determinations of Black people are real and have objective significance, even as the system of white supremacy tries to paint it differently. Black Power is nothing short of a complete redefinition of Blackness. Black Power is a practice rooted in the claim that Blackness is self-sufficient and has no need of whiteness.

In this sense, Black Power is radically different from white power. While Black Power is marked by self-sufficiency, white power is the parasitical need to denigrate Blackness and non-whiteness. Unlike Brooker T. Washington's hand metaphor – 'In all things that are purely social we can be as separate as the fingers, yet one as the hand in all things essential to mutual progress' (SBF 34) – Black Power raises a clenched fist, a symbol of collective self-determination, self-organisation, and solidarity. Black Power is, then, not the negation of whiteness, but the negation of the negation that is antiblackness. Black Power is the collective overcoming of the humiliation, shame, and degradation that whiteness has cast upon Black people for centuries. While Du Bois lamented the white yardstick against which he was forced to measure himself, Black Power redefines what is considered beautiful, valuable, and meaningful. Black Power is the reformation of all categories according to Black measurements. Nothing in Black Power takes up white models or ideals – not freedom, not living, not aesthetics, not politics, and so on.

Black Power represents a fundamental turning point in the Black liberation struggle and a new stage in Black self-consciousness. It signals a shift in form and content, one that grew out of all that came before it – from Douglass and Jacobs' escape from slavery, to Washington and Wells' raising of Freed peoples, to Du Bois and Cooper's theorisation of divided Black consciousness, to Garvey and Hurston's devotion to Black life and individuality, to King and Baker's sacramental labour, to Malcolm X and Davis's extreme practices of self-mortification – but which brought about a racial pride never seen before. This was the time of the rejection of the term 'Negro' as a white imposition, and the reclamation of 'Black' and 'African American' as Black acts of naming, defining, and imaging Blackness. Blackness now means self-respect, self-reliance, self-defence, self-determination, and self-organisation. It was, in short, a revolution of Black Spirit.

Black Power brought a wave of celebration and recognition of Blackness – the rise of Black studies programs, the introduction of Kwanzaa, the celebration of Black History, the spread of Pan-Africanism (alongside the fall of European colonialism), the formulation of Black feminisms, the articulation of Black Marxism and the Black Radical Tradition, and much more. One of the clearest formulations of this new shape of Black Spirit is the emergence of a Black Aesthetic and the Black Arts Movement, as theorised by the poet Amiri Baraka (formerly LeRoi Jones).[17]

According to Larry Neal, 'Black art is the aesthetic and spiritual sister of the Black Power concept.' Neal continues:

> the Black Arts Movement proposes a radical reorganization of the western cultural aesthetic. It proposes a separate symbolism, mythology, critique, and iconography. The Black Arts and the Black Power concept both relate broadly to the Afro-American's desire for self-determination and nationhood.[18]

---

17 As always, the women in the Black Arts Movement are under-recognised and appreciation, though a recent work seek to change that. See La Donna L. Forsgren, *Sistuhs in the Struggle: An Oral History of Black Arts Movement Theater and Performance* (Evanston, IL: Northwestern Press, 2020).

18 Larry Neal, 'The Black Arts Movement', *The Drama Review* 12:4 (1968): 29.

A new Black Aesthetic reflected and shaped the new emerging Black self-consciousness, the sensuous reflection of Black beauty, truth, and genius.[19]

At the start of this Conclusion, we placed a Baraka quote that played on Hegelian imagery. As we close, we end with another of his poems. Doing so again parallels Hegel's own *Phenomenology*. As he ended his book with lines from a Friedrich Schiller poem (admittedly misquoted), we end here with the last lines of Amiri Baraka's poem called, unsurprisingly, 'Hegel':

> Either I am wrong
> or he is wrong. All right
> I am wrong, but give me someone
> to talk to.[20]

---

19 See Verner D. Mitchell and Cynthia Davis (eds), *Encyclopedia of the Black Arts Movement* (Lanham, MD: Rowman & Littlefield, 2019).
20 LeRoi Jones (Amiri Baraka), 'Hegel', in *Black Magic: Collected Poetry, 1961–1967* (Indianapolis: Bobbs-Merrill, 1969), 23–4. This poem belongs to an earlier collection called *Sabotage*, covering the period 1961–63.

Bibliography

Aberbach, Joel D. and Jack L. Walker. 'The Meanings of Black Power: A Comparison of White and Black Interpretations of a Political Slogan', *The American Political Science Review* 64:2 (1970): 367–88.

Agamben, Giorgio. *Homo Sacer: Sovereign Power and Bare Life*. Translated by Daniel Heller-Roazen. Stanford: Stanford University Press, 1998.

Amato-Fox, Matthew. *Exposing Slavery: Photography, Human Bondage, and the Birth of Modern Visual Politics in America*. Oxford: Oxford University Press, 2019.

Anderson, Sybol S.C. *Hegel's Theory of Recognition: From Oppression to Ethical Liberal Modernity*. London: Continuum, 2009.

Anderson, Victor. *Beyond Ontological Blackness: An Essay on African American Religious and Cultural Criticism*. London: Bloomsbury Academic, 2016.

Baker, Ella. 'Address at the Hattiesburg Freedom Rally', 21 January 1964, <https://voicesofdemocracy.umd.edu/ella-baker-freedom-day-rally-speech-text>

Basevich, Elvira. 'Reform or Revolution? On the Political Use of Violence in the Historical Constitution of Objective Spirit in Du Bois and Hegel', special Issue of *Hegel Bulletin* (forthcoming).

Basevich, Elvira. 'W.E.B. Du Bois's Critique of Radical Reconstruction (1865–77): A Hegelian Approach to American Modernity', *Philosophy and Social Criticism* 45:2 (2019): 168–85.

Basevich, Elvira. *W.E.B. Du Bois: The Lost and the Found*. Cambridge: Polity Press, 2021.

Bernasconi, Robert. 'Hegel at the Court of the Ashanti', in *Hegel After Derrida*, edited by Stuart Barnett. London: Routledge, 1998, 41–63.

Bernasconi, Robert. 'With What Must the Philosophy of World History Begin? On the Racial Bias of Hegel's Eurocentrism', *Nineteenth-Century Contexts* 22 (2000): 171–201.

Bernasconi, Robert and Sybol Cook, eds. *Race & Racism in Continental Philosophy*. Bloomington, Indiana: Indiana University Press, 2003.

Bird-Pollan, Stefan. *Hegel, Freud and Fanon: The Dialectic of Emancipation*. London: Rowman & Littlefield, 2015.

Blanco, Elena, Daniel J. M. Hodgson, Michel Hermes, Rut Besseling, Gary L. Hunter, Paul M. Chaikin, Michael E. Cates, Isabella Van Damme, and Wilson C. K. Poon. 'Conching Chocolate is a Prototypical Transition from Frictionally Jammed Solid to Flowable Suspension with Maximal

Solid Content', *Proceedings of the National Academy of Sciences* 116:21 (2019): 10303–8.

Blight, David W. *Frederick Douglass: Prophet of Freedom*. New York: Simon & Schuster, 2018.

Bloom, Josh and Waldo E. Martin Jr. *Black Against Empire: The History and Politics of the Black Panther Party*. Berkeley: University of California Press, 2013.

Bright, Liam Kofi. 'Du Bois' Democratic Defense of the Value Free Ideal', *Synthese* 195:5 (2018): 2227–45.

Buck-Morss, Susan. *Hegel, Haiti, and Universal History*. Pittsburgh: University of Pittsburgh Press, 2009.

Burke, Victoria. 'Essence Today: Hegel and the Economics of Identity Politics', *Philosophy Today* 51:1 (2007): 79–90.

Camara, Babacar. 'The Falsity of Hegel's Theses on Africa', *Journal of Black Studies* 36:1 (2005): 82–96.

Cannon, Katie. *Black Womanist Ethics*. Eugene, OR: Wipf and Stock, 1988.

Chamayou, Grégoire. *Manhunts: A Philosophical History*. Translated by Steven Rendall. Princeton: Princeton University Press, 2012.

Chandler, Nahum Dimitri. *X: The Problem of the Negro as a Problem for Thought*. New York: Fordham University Press, 2014.

Ciccariello-Maher, George. '"So Much Worse for the White": Dialectics of the Haitian Revolution', *Journal of French and Francophone Philosophy/Revue de la philosophie française et de langue française* 22:1 (2014): 19–39.

Cole, Andrew. *Birth of Theory*. Chicago: University of Chicago Press, 2014.

Cone, James H. *The Spirituals and the Blues: An Interpretation*. Maryknoll, NY: Orbis Books, 1991.

Cooper, Anna Julia. *Voice from the South*, edited by Charles Lemert and Esme Bhan. Lanham, MD: Rowman & Littlefield, 1998.

Cooper, Brittney C. *Beyond Respectability*. Urbana: University of Illinois Press, 2017.

Crawley, Ashon. *Blackpentecostal Breath: The Aesthetics of Possibility*. New York: Fordham University Press, 2016.

Crummell, Alexander. *Africa and America: Addresses and Discourses*. New York: Negro Universities Press, 1969.

Davis, Angela. *Angela Davis: An Autobiography*. New York: Random House, 1974.

Davis, Angela. *Angela Y. Davis Reader*, edited by Joy James. Oxford: Blackwell, 1998.

Delany, Martin Robison and Robert Campbell. *Search for a Place: Black Separatism and Africa, 1860*. Ann Arbor: University of Michigan Press, 1969.

Deleuze, Gilles and Félix Guattari. *A Thousand Plateaus*. Translated by Brian Massumi. Minneapolis: University of Minnesota Press, 1987.

Descartes, René. *The Philosophical Writings of Descartes, Volume I*. Translated by John Cottingham, Robert Stoothoff, and Dugald Murdoch. Cambridge: Cambridge University Press, 1985.

Douglass, Frederick. *My Bondage and My Freedom*. New York: The Library of America, 1994.

Douglass, Frederick. *Narrative of the Life of Frederick Douglass, an American Slave*, in *Autobiographies*. New York: The Library of America, 1994.

Du Bois, W.E.B. 'Sociology Hesitant', *boundary 2* 27:3 (2000): 37–44.
Du Bois, W.E.B. *The Souls of Black Folk*. London: Penguin, 2018.
Du Bois, W.E.B. *Writings: The Suppression of the African Slave-Trade, The Souls of Black Folk, Dusk of Dawn, Essays*, edited by Nathan Huggins. New York: Library of America, 1987.
Empiricus, Sextus. *Outlines of Skepticism*, edited by Julia Annas and Jonathan Barnes. Cambridge: Cambridge University Press, 2009.
Equiano, Olaudah. *The Interesting Narrative and Other Writings*. New York: Penguin Books, 1995.
Eyes on the Prize II: America at the Racial Crossroads 1965 to 1986. Washington University Libraries, Film and Media Archive, Henry Hampton Collection.
Fanon, Frantz. *Black Skin, White Masks*. Translated by Richard Philcox. New York: Grove Press, 2008.
Fanon, Frantz. 'Racism and Culture', in *Toward the African Revolution: Political Essays*. Translated by Haakon Chevalier. New York: Grove Press, 1988.
Farrell, John. *Paranoia and Modernity: Cervantes to Rousseau*. Ithaca: Cornell University Press, 2006.
Ferguson, Stephen C. 'The Philosopher King: An Examination of the Influence of Dialectics on King's Political Thought and Practice', in *The Liberatory Thought of Martin Luther King, Jr.: Critical Essays on the Philosopher King*, edited by Robert E. Birt. Lanham, MD: Lexington Books, 2014, 87–108.
Ferris, William H. *The Philosophical Treatise of William H. Ferris: Selected Readings from* The African Abroad or, his Evolution in Western Civilization, edited by Tommy J. Curry. London: Rowman & Littlefield, 2016.
Forsgren, La Donna L. *Sistuhs in the Struggle: An Oral History of Black Arts Movement Theater and Performance*. Evanston: Northwestern Press, 2020.
Franklin, John Hope. *The Militant South 1800–1861*. Boston: Beacon Press, 1956.
Franklin, John Hope and Loren Schweninger. *Runaway Slaves: Rebels on the Plantation*. Oxford: Oxford University Press, 2000.
Gaines, Kevin K. *Uplifting the Race: Black Leadership, Politics, and Culture in the Twentieth Century*. Chapel Hill: University of North Carolina Press, 1996.
Garvey, Marcus. *Philosophy and Opinions of Marcus Garvey*, ed. Amy Jacques-Garvey, *The Journal of Pan African Studies* (ebook, 2009).
Genovese, Eugene. *Roll Jordan Roll: The World the Slaves Made*. New York: Vintage, 1976.
Gessen, Martha. 'Judith Butler Wants Us to Reshape Our Rage', *The New Yorker*, interview, 9 February 2020.
Gilroy, Paul. *The Black Atlantic: Modernity and Double Consciousness*. Cambridge, MA: Harvard University Press, 1993.
Gooding-Williams, Robert. *In the Shadow of Du Bois: Afro-Modern Political Thought in America*. Cambridge, MA: Harvard University Press, 2009.
Griffin, Emily. *A First Look at Communication Theory: Standpoint Theory*. New York: McGraw-Hill Higher Education, 2009.
Habib, M.A.R. *Hegel and Empire: From Postcolonialism to Globalism*. Basingstoke: Palgrave Macmillan, 2017.

BIBLIOGRAPHY

Hadden, Sally. *Slave Patrols: Law and Violence in Virginia and the Carolinas.* Cambridge, MA: Harvard University Press, 2001.

Harlan, Louis R. *Booker T. Washington: The Wizard of Tuskegee, 1901–1915.* Oxford: Oxford University Press, 1986.

Harris, Kimberly Ann. 'Du Bois and Hegelian Idealism', *Idealistic Studies: An Interdisciplinary Journal of Philosophy*, special issue: '"Philosophical Idealism as Anti-Racism" on the Occasion of Hegel's 250th Anniversary', 51:2 (2021): 149–71.

Harris, Kimberly Ann. 'Hegel's Dialectic and African Philosophy: Du Bois, Fanon, and James', PhD diss., Penn State University, 2018.

Harrison, Hubert. *A Hubert Harrison Reader*, edited by Jeffrey B. Perry. Middletown, CT: Wesleyan University Press, 2001.

Hartman, Saidiya. *Scenes of Subjection: Terror, Slavery, and Self-Making in Nineteenth-Century America.* New York: Oxford University Press, 1997.

Hartman, Saidiya. *Wayward Lives, Beautiful Experiments: Intimate Stories of Upheaval.* New York: W.W. Norton, 2019.

Hartman, Saidiya and Frank Wilderson. 'The Position of the Unthought', *Qui Parle* 13:2 (2003).

Hegel, G.W.F. *Elements of the Philosophy of Right.* Translated by Allen W. Wood. Cambridge: Cambridge University Press, 1991.

Hegel, G.W.F. *Science of Logic.* Translated by George D. Giovanni. Cambridge: Cambridge University Press, 2010.

Hegel, G.W.F. *The Phenomenology of Spirit*, trans. A.V. Miller (Oxford: Oxford University Press, 1977).

Hegel, G.W.F. *The Philosophy of History.* Translated by J. Sibree. Mineola, NY: Dover, 2004.

Hoffheimer, Michael. 'Hegel, Race, Genocide', *Southern Journal of Philosophy* 39 (2001): 35–62.

Hoffheimer, Michael. 'Race and Law in Hegel's Philosophy of Religion', in *Race and Racism in Modern Philosophy*, edited by Andrew Valls. Ithaca: Cornell University Press, 2005, 194–216.

Hogan, Brandon. 'Frantz Fanon's Engagement with Hegel's Master-Slave Dialectic', *Africology: The Journal of Pan African Studies* 11:8 (2018): 16–32.

Holt, Thomas C. 'The Political Uses of Alienation: W.E.B. Du Bois on Politics, Race, and Culture, 1905–1940', *American Quarterly* 42:2 (1990): 301–23.

hooks, bell. *Ain't I a Woman: Black Women and Feminism.* New York: Routledge, 2014.

Houlgate, Stephen. *Hegel on Being.* London: Bloomsbury Academic, 2021.

Hurston, Zora Neale. *Dust Tracks on a Road.* New York: Harper Perennial, 2006.

Hurston, Zora Neale. 'How It Feels to Be Colored Me', *World Tomorrow*, 1928.

Hurston, Zora Neale. 'Letter to the Orlando Sentinel', *Orlando Sentinel*, 11 August 1955, <https://teachingamericanhistory.org/library/document/letter-to-the-orlando-sentinel>

Hurston, Zora Neale. *Moses, Man of the Mountain.* New York: Harper Perennial, 2008.

Hyppolite, Jean. *Structure and Genesis.* Translated by Jean Heckman. Evanston: Northwestern University Press, 1979.

Inouye, Mie. 'Starting with People Where They Are: Ella Baker's Theory of Political Organizing', *American Political Science Review*, 24 September 2021, 1–14.

Jackson, Zakiyyah Iman. *Becoming Human: Matter and Meaning in an Antiblack World*. New York: New York University Press, 2020.

Jacobs, Harriett/Linda Brent. *Incidents in the Life of a Slave Girl*. New York: Harvest Books, 1973.

Jacobson, Mark. 'The Man Who Didn't Shoot Malcolm X', *New York Magazine*, 30 September 2007.

James, C.L.R. *Notes on Dialectics: Hegel, Marx, Lenin*. Westport, CT: Lawrence Hill & Co, 1980.

James, Joy. 'Profeminism and Gender Elites: W.E.B. Du Bois, Anna Julia Cooper, and Ida B. Wells-Barnett', in *Next to the Color Line: Gender, Sexuality, and W.E.B. Du Bois*, edited by Susan Gillman and Alys Eve Weinbaum. Minneapolis: University of Minnesota Press, 2007, 69–95.

Johnson, Thomas. *The Montgomery Advertiser*, 19 January 1956.

Johnson, Walter. 'On Agency', *Journal of Social History* 37:1 (2003): 113–24.

Jones, Alisha Lola. '"You are My Dwelling Place": Experiencing Black Male Vocalists' Worship as Aural Eroticism and Autoeroticism in Gospel', *Women and Music* 22 (2018): 3–21.

Jones, LeRoi (Amiri Baraka). 'Hegel', in *Black Magic: Collected Poetry, 1961–1967*. Indianapolis: Bobbs-Merrill, 1969.

Joseph, Celucien L. 'On Intellectual Reparations: Hegel, Franklin Tavarès, Susan Buck-Morss, Revolutionary Haiti, and Caribbean Philosophical Association', *Africology: The Journal of Pan-African Studies* 9:7 (2016).

Kant, Immanuel. *Critique of Pure Reason*. Translated and edited by Paul Guyer and Allen W. Wood. Cambridge: Cambridge University Press, 1998.

Kaufman, Michael T. 'Stokely Carmichael, Rights Leader Who Coined "Black Power", Dies at 57', *New York Times*, 16 November 1998.

Kazanjian, David. 'Hegel, Liberia', *Diacritics* 40:1 (2012): 6–39.

Kendi, Ibram X. *How to Be An Antiracist*. New York: One World, 2019.

Kendi, Ibram X. *Stamped from the Beginning*. New York: Nation Books, 2016.

King, Jr., Martin Luther. 'Statement on Ending the Bus Boycott', from The Martin Luther King, Jr. Research and Education Institute, Stanford University.

King, Jr., Martin Luther. *Stride toward Freedom*. New York: Harper & Row, 1958.

King, Jr., Martin Luther. *Why We Can't Wait*. Kolkata: Signet, 2000.

King, Jr., Martin Luther. *A Testament of Hope: The Essential Writings and Speeches*, edited by James M. Washington. San Francisco: Harper, 2003.

Kirkland, Frank. 'Enslavement, Moral Suasion, & Struggles for Recognition: Frederick Douglass' Answer to the Question – "What is Enlightenment?"', in *Frederick Douglass: A Critical Reader*, edited by B.E. Lawson and F.M. Kirkland. Oxford: Blackwell, 1999, 242–310.

Kirkland, Frank. 'Hegel and the Saint Domingue Revolution – Perfect Together?: A Review of Susan Buck-Morss' *Hegel, Haiti, and Universal History*', in *Logos: The Journal of Modern Society and Culture* 11:2–3 (2012).

Kirkland, Frank M. 'Hegel on Race and Development', in *The Routledge*

Companion to Philosophy of Race, edited by Paul C. Taylor, Linda Martín Alcoff, and Luvell Anderson. New York: Routledge, 2018, 43–60.

Kirkland, Frank M. 'How Would Hegel's *Phenomenology of Spirit* Be Relevant Today?', *Logos: The Journal of Modern Society and Culture* 7:1 (2008).

Kistner, Ulrike and Philippe Van Haute, eds. *Violence, Slavery and Freedom between Hegel and Fanon*. Johannesburg: Wits University Press, 2020.

Krell, David Farrell. 'The Bodies of Black Folk: From Kant and Hegel to Du Bois and Baldwin', *boundary 2* 27:3 (2000): 103–34.

Lacan, Jacques. 'The Mirror Stage as Formative of the *I* Function as Revealed in Psychoanalytic Experience', in *Écrits*. Translated by Bruce Fink. New York: W.W. & Norton, 2007, 58–74.

Laclau, Ernesto and Chantel Mouffe. *Hegemony and Socialist Strategy*. London: Verso, 1985.

Levinas, Emmanuel. *Totality and Infinity*. Translated by Alphonso Lingis. Pittsburgh: Duquesne University Press, 1969.

Lewis, David Levering. *King: A Critical Biography*. Urbana: University of Illinois Press, 1978.

Lewis, David Levering. *W.E.B. Du Bois: A Biography*. New York: Henry Holt and Company, 2009.

Lubet, Steven. *Fugitive Justice: Runaways, Rescuers, and Slavery on Trial*. Cambridge, MA: Harvard University Press, 2010.

Luther, Martin. *Luther's Works, Vol. 54: Table Talk*, edited and translated by Theodore G. Tappert. Philadelphia: Fortress Press, 1967.

McClendon III, John H. *C.L.R. James's* Notes on Dialectics: *Left Hegelianism or Marxism-Leninism*. Lanham, MD: Lexington Books, 2005.

Mackey, Nathanial. *Bedouin Hornbook*, Callaloo Fiction Series, vol. 2. Lexington: University Press of Kentucky, 1986.

MacLean, Nancy K. *Behind the Mask: The Making of the Second Klu Klux Klan*. Oxford: Oxford University Press, 1994.

McMurry Edwards, Linda. *To Keep the Waters Troubled: The Life of Ida B. Wells*. New York: Oxford University Press, 2000.

Malcolm X. *By Any Means Necessary*. New York: Pathfinder, 1992.

Malcolm X. *Malcolm X Speaks: Selected Speeches and Statements*, edited by George Breitman. New York: Grove Press, 1965.

Malcolm X. 'Oxford Union Debate, Dec. 3, 1964', https://www.youtube.com/watch?v=auWA7hMh5hc

Malcolm X. *The Autobiography of Malcolm X: As Told to Alex Haley*. New York: Ballantine Books, 1992.

Malcolm X. 'The Ballot or the Bullet', speech delivered in Cleveland, Ohio, on 3 April 1964, <http://www.edchange.org/multicultural/speeches/malcolm_x_ballot.html>

Malcolm X. 'The House Negro and the Field Negro', <https://www.youtube.com/watch?v=7kf7fujM4ag>

Marable, Manning. *Malcolm X: A Life of Reinvention*. New York: Viking, 2011.

Mbembe, Achille. *Critique of Black Reason*. Durham, NC: Duke University Press, 2013.

Mitchell, Michelle. *Righteous Propagation: African Americans and the Politics of*

Racial Destiny after Reconstruction. Chapel Hill: University of North Carolina Press, 2004.

Mitchell, Verner D. and Cynthia Davis, eds. *Encyclopedia of the Black Arts Movement*. Lanham, MD: Rowman & Littlefield, 2019.

Monahan, Michael, ed. *Creolizing Hegel*. London: Rowman & Littlefield, 2017.

Moody-Turner, Shirley. '"Dear Doctor Du Bois": Anna Julia Cooper, W.E.B. Du Bois, and the Gender Politics of Black Publishing', *MELUS: Multi-Ethnic Literature of the U.S.* 40:3 (2015).

Morrison, Toni. *The Source of Self Regard*. New York: Vintage Books, 2019.

Moten, Fred. *Black and Blur*. Durham, NC: Duke University Press, 2017.

Moten, Fred, *In the Break: The Aesthetics of the Black Radical Tradition*. Minneapolis: University of Minnesota Press, 2003.

Moten, Fred. *Stolen Life*. Durham, NC: Duke University Press, 2018.

Moten, Fred. 'The Case of Blackness', *Criticism* 50:2 (2008): 177–218.

Moynihan, Daniel Patrick. *The Negro Family: The Case for National Action*. Office of Policy Planning and Research United States Department of Labor, March 1965.

Nasar Meer. 'W.E.B. Du Bois, Double Consciousness and the "Spirit" of Recognition', *The Sociological Review* 67:1 (2019): 47–62.

Neal, Larry. 'The Black Arts Movement', *The Drama Review* 12:4 (1968): 29–39.

Nietzsche, Friedrich. *Genealogy of Morals* and *Ecce Homo*. Translated by Walter Kaufman. New York: Vintage, 1989.

Nisbett, Richard E. and Dov Cohen. *Culture of Honor: Violence in the South*. New York: Westview Press, 1996.

Norton, Rictor. *A History of Homophobia*. '4 Gay Heretics and Witches', 15 April 2002, updated 18 February 2011, <http://rictornorton.co.uk/homopho4.htm>; originally featured in *Gay News* 87 (1976): 15–16.

Novakovic, Andreja. *Hegel on Second Nature in Ethical Life*. Cambridge: Cambridge University Press, 2017.

Novakovic, Andreja. 'Hegel's Real Habits', *European Journal of Philosophy* 27:4 (2019): 882–97.

Nuzzo, Angelica. *Approaching Hegel Obliquely: Melville, Molière, Beckett*. Albany: SUNY Press, 2018.

Oates, Stephen B. *Let the Trumpet Sound: A Life of Martin Luther King, Jr.* New York: Harper & Row, 1982.

Painter, Nell Irvin. *History of White People*. New York: W.W. Norton, 2011.

Park, Peter K. J. *Africa, Asia, and the History of Philosophy: Racism in the Formation of the Philosophical Canon, 1780–1830*. Albany: SUNY Press, 2013.

Parks, Henry Blanton. *Africa: The Problem of the New Century; The Part the African Methodist Episcopal Church Is to Have in Its Solution*. New York: A.M.E. Church, 1899.

Patterson, Orlando. *Slavery and Social Death: A Comparative Study*. Cambridge, MA: Harvard University Press, 2018.

Payne, Les and Tamara Payne. *The Dead Are Arising: The Life of Malcolm X*. New York: Liveright, 2020.

BIBLIOGRAPHY

Pinkard, Terry. 'Introduction' to G.W.F. Hegel, *The Phenomenology of Spirit*. Translated and edited by Terry Pinkard. Cambridge: Cambridge University Press, 2018.

Pinn, Anthony, ed. *Noise and Spirit: The Religious and Spiritual Sensibilities of Rap Music*. New York: New York University Press, 2003.

Pinn, Anthony. *Terror and Triumph: The Nature of Black Religion*. Minneapolis: Fortress Press, 2003.

Purtschert, Patricia. 'On the Limit of Spirit: Hegel's Racism Revisited', *Philosophy & Social Criticism* 36:9 (2010): 1039–51.

Ransby, Barbara. *Ella Baker and the Black Freedom Movement: A Radical Democratic Vision*. Chapel Hill: University of North Carolina Press, 2003.

Robinson, Cedric J. *Black Marxism: The Making of the Black Radical Tradition*. Chapel Hill: University of North Carolina Press, 2000.

Rollin G. Osterweis. *Romanticism and Nationalism in the Old South*. New Haven: Yale University Press, 1949.

Rooney, Catherine. *African Literature, Animism, and Politics*. London: Routledge, 2000.

Ruda, Frank. *Abolishing Freedom: A Plea for a Contemporary Use of Fatalism*. Lincoln: University of Nebraska Press, 2016.

Sanders, Ronald. *Lost Tribes and Promised Lands: The Origins of American Racism*. Boston: Little Brown and Company, 1978.

Sawyer, Michael E. *Black Minded: The Political Philosophy of Malcolm X*. London: Pluto Press, 2020.

Seale, Bobby. *Seize the Time: The Story of The Black Panther Party and Huey P. Newton*. Baltimore: Black Classic Press, 1991.

Sexton, Jared. 'The Social Life of Social Death', *Intensions* 5 (2011), <http://www.yorku.ca/intent/issue5/articles/jaredsexton.php>

Sharpe, Christina. *In the Wake: On Blackness and Being*. Durham, NC: Duke University Press, 2016.

Spillers, Hortense. 'Mama's Baby, Papa's Maybe: An American Grammar Book', *Diacritics* 17:2 (1987): 64–81.

Stauffer, John, Zoe Trodd, and Celeste-Marie Bernier. *Picturing Frederick Douglass: An Illustrated Biography of the Nineteenth Century's Most Photographed American*. New York: W.W. Norton, 2015.

Stewart, Lindsay. *The Politics of Black Joy: Zora Neale Hurston and Neo-Abolitionism*. Evanston: Northwestern University Press, 2021.

Stone, Alison. 'Hegel and Colonialism', *Hegel Bulletin* 41:2 (2020): 247–70.

Taylor, Jack. 'Ralph Ellison as a Reader of Hegel: Ellison's Invisible Man as Literary Phenomenology', *Intertexts* 19:1 (2015): 135–54.

Terrell, Mary Church. *A Colored Woman in a White World*. Amherst, MA: Prometheus Books, 2005.

Thurman, Howard. *The Negro Spiritual Speaks of Life and Death*. New York: Harper & Brothers, 1947.

Tibebu, Teshale. *Hegel and the Third World: The Making of Eurocentrism in World History*. Syracuse: Syracuse University Press, 2011.

Ture, Kwame and Charles V. Hamilton. *Black Power: The Politics of Liberation*. New York: Vintage Books, 1992.

Turner, Lou. 'On the Difference between the Hegelian and Fanonian Dialectic of Lordship and Bondage', in *Fanon: A Critical Reader*, edited by Lewis R. Gordon, T. Denean Sharpley-Whiting, and Renee T. White. Oxford: Blackwell, 1996, 134–54.

Vernon, Jim. *Hegel, Hip Hop, and the Art of Emancipation*. Basingstoke: Palgrave Macmillan, 2018.

Villet, Charles. 'Hegel and Fanon on the Question of Mutual Recognition: A Comparative Analysis', *The Journal of Pan African Studies* 4:7 (2011): 39–51.

Walker, Alice. 'In Search of Zora Neale Hurston', *Ms.*, March 1975, 74–9, 84–9.

Warren, Calvin. *Ontological Terror: Blackness, Nihilism, and Emancipation*. Durham, NC: Duke University Press, 2018.

Washington, Booker T. *Up From Slavery*. Mineola, NY: Dover, 1995.

Wells, Ida B. 'Booker T. Washington and his Critics', *World Today*, April 1904.

Wells, Ida B. *Crusade for Justice: The Autobiography of Ida B. Wells*, edited by Alfreda M. Duster. Chicago: University of Chicago Press, 1992.

Wells, Ida B. *Southern Horrors: Lynch Law in All Its Phases*. Auckland: The Floating Press, 2013.

Willet, Cynthia. *Maternal Ethics and Other Slave Moralities*. New York: Routledge, 1995.

Wischmann, Anke. 'The Absence of "Race" in German Discourses on *Bildung*: Rethinking *Bildung* with Critical Race Theory', *Race, Ethnicity and Education* 21:4 (2018): 471–85.

Wood, J.T. 'Critical Feminist Theories', in *Engaging Theories in Interpersonal Communication: Multiple Perspectives*, edited by L.A. Baxter and D.O. Braithwaite, 323–34. Thousand Oaks: Sage, 2008.

Zack, Naomi, ed. *The Oxford Handbook of Philosophy and Race*. New York: Oxford University Press, 2017.

Zambrana, Rocío. 'Bad Habits: Habit, Idleness, and Race in Hegel', *Hegel Bulletin* 42:1 (2021): 1–18.

Zambrana, Rocío. 'Hegel, History, and Race', in *The Oxford Handbook of Philosophy and Race*, edited by Naomi Zack. Oxford: Oxford University Press, 2017, 251–60.

Zambrana, Rocío. 'Hegelian History Interrupted', *Crisis & Critique* 8:2 (2021): 410–31.

Zamir, Shamoon, '"Double-Consciousness": Locating the Self', in *Dark Voices: W.E.B. Du Bois and American Thought, 1888–1903*, Chicago: University of Chicago Press, 1995.

Index

abolitionists, 153
absolute nonsubjects, 44
abstract freedom, 81–87
abstract negation, 41
adjectival philosophy, 10
Africa, 147–148, 149, 159, 167–168
African American churches, 151; *see also* Black churches
African American folk culture, 122
Africanness, 144, 145, 160–162, 165, 172, 182
Afro-American Council, 95–96
afterlives, 262
afterthought, 124
Agamben, G., 39
agape, 189
Allah, 246, 247
America, 193, 203, 236, 245–246
American South, 55–56, 90–99
Anderson, V., 258
annihilation, 221
antiblackness, 3, 13, 19–20, 22, 101, 171; *see also* racism
appositional encounter, 15n24
Aquinas, T. of, 186
Arbery, A., 2
Armstrong, S.C., 77, 83
Augustine of Hippo, 187
Auld, T., 57, 61
Autobiography (Davis), 254

Bacon, F., 265

Bailey, F.A.W., 32; *see also* Douglass, F.
Baker, E., 10, 18, 206–214
  self-negation, 219–220
  v. M.L. King, Jr, 214–217, 218
Baldwin, J., 253
"Ballot or the Bullet, The" (Malcolm X), 247–248
Baraka, A., 261, 273
Barrett, W.H., 92, 93
beloved community, 188–190, 199
Bembry, J.E., 231
Bimbi, 231
Black Arts, 272
Black bodies, 93, 190; *see also* Black female bodies
Black churches, 155–156
Black colonisation, 163–165
Black death, 91; *see also* lynching
Black elites, 77
Black embodiment, 75–76
Black female bodies, 93, 127–129
Black feminist politics, 217
Black feminist scepticism *see* radical tripartite scepticism
Black feminist thinkers, 17–18
Black freedom, 219, 220
Black gaze, 123
Black God, 143, 166–168
Black history, 261
Black joy, 174–175
Black knowledge, 88
Black life, 91, 97, 101, 169, 175, 176, 258

285

INDEX

Black male bodies, 93
Black men (males), 17, 83, 129, 133, 137
Black music, 155–156
Black Panther Party for Self-Defense, 266–268
Black Power, 265–273
Black religion, 144, 146–148, 150–153; *see also* Black churches
Black self, 158
Black souls, 153, 156, 161–162
   double consciousness, 112–113, 116, 122
   equal status of, 115
   second-sight, 123
   see also white souls
Black spirit, 6, 88, 99, 114, 144, 258
Black Star Line, 149–150
Black stories, 183
Black studies, 12–13, 14
Black subjectivity, 94
Black suffering, 150–153, 162, 192, 201
Black thinkers, 16–19, 21
Black Thought, 121–122
Black women, 17, 132, 133–137, 139, 152–153, 214, 216; *see also* Black female bodies
Blackness, 22, 89
   and Africanness, 160–162, 165
   and Black Power, 272
   and gender, 20
   and nothingness, 7–9, 223–227, 259
   and *Phenomenology of Spirit* (Hegel), 3–4, 4–6, 11, 20–22
   and reason, 148–149
   versus whiteness, 123–124
   and work, 98
   see also antiblackness

brainwashing, 228, 231–232, 233
Brent, L., 17
Brightman, E.S., 178
Buber, M., 187
Buck-Morss, S., 4, 28–29, 31
Butler, J., 196

Cannon, K., 170
Carmichael, S., 269, 270
Catholic Mass, 154–155
Chamayou, G., 43, 44, 46, 63, 64
Chandler, N.D., 103
chattel slavery, 143, 152
   freedom, 83
   master-slave dialectic, 13, 31–35
   and *Phenomenology of Spirit* (Hegel), 3, 5
   stoicism, 76
   work, 54
   see also slavery
Christendom, 131
Christian ascetics, 146
Christianity, 143–144, 145, 157, 195, 227
civil rights, 121
Civil Rights Movement, 100, 190, 200, 203, 208, 211, 216, 266
cleanliness, 80, 92
coalition-building, 255–257
Cohen, D., 56
collective commitment, 249–250
collective liberation, 254; *see also* coalition-building
colour-line, 115, 126
community, 91, 180, 188–190, 199
community of conscience, 190
conceptual thinking, 84
Cone, J., 225
conks, 228
Connor, B., 199, 200

INDEX

consciousness, 42–46; *see also* double consciousness; self-consciousness; triple consciousness; unhappy consciousness
consumption, 109–110
Cooper, A.J., 17, 102, 129–140
Covey, E., 33, 50, 90
    fight with Douglass, 34, 56, 57–62, 77–79: master-slave dialectic, 62–65
Covid, 2
Crawley, A., 225
Crisis, The, 122, 131–132
Crummell, A., 166
Cuban Missile Crisis, 253
culture of honour, 55–56

Darkwater (Du Bois), 103–104
Davis, A., 18, 222–223, 249–255, 259–260
    Black Power, 270
    coalition-building, 255–257
    rape, 66
death, 91, 228–229
    fear of, 46–52, 53–54, 61
    see also lynching
Deleuze, G., 257
Descartes, R., 65, 264
desegregation, 189–190
Detroit Red, 224; *see also* Malcolm X
devil *see* Satan; white devil
devotion, 145–150, 221, 239
    and feeling, 154, 156–157
    H.M. Turner, 165–168
    M. Garvey, 156, 158–159, 162
    Zora Neal Hurston, 168–176
DeWolf, L.H., 178
dialectical parallelism, 15–19
double consciousness, 64, 110–111, 112–116, 125, 127, 129, 160

double negation, 199
Douglass, F., 33, 35–36, 50
    Black Power, 270
    bondage, 37
    fight with Covey, 34, 56, 57–62, 77–79: master-slave dialectic, 62–65
    freedom, 52, 64, 82–83
    holidays, 48–49
    humanity, 90
    music, 156
    sense of self, 71, 88
    slavery, 46
    stoicism, 75
    work, 54
drunkenness, 48–49
Du Bois, W.E.B.
    Black elites, 77
    Black music, 155–156
    and Black Power, 271
    The Crisis, 131–132
    criticism of B.T. Washington, 116–122
    double consciousness, 64, 110–111, 112–116, 125, 127, 129, 160
    Dusk of Dawn, 103–104
    Garveyism, 149, 165
    negation, 107–108, 112
    scepticism, 101–102, 129, 150
    second-sight and afterthought, 122–124
    white souls, 125–126

Earth's scepticism, 138
education
    Anna Julia Cooper, 135–136
    B. T. Washington, 77, 83, 92, 114, 118, 119, 120
    F. Douglass, 78–79
    M. Garvey, 148
    Malcolm X, 230–236, 232n17
Edwards, L.M., 92–93

INDEX

Elements of the Philosophy of Right (Hegel), 103
embodied perspective *see* standpoint theory
embodiment *see* Black embodiment
emigrationist theodicy, 167
enslaved females, 65–66
enslavement, 33; *see also* slavery
epistemology, 258
Equiano, O., 50n43
equipollency, 106
escape, 64–65
evasion, 12, 69, 70
Exodus story, 151

faith, 139
faithfulness, 147
Fanon, F., 54, 149
fear, 64–65, 159
  of death, 46–52, 53–54, 61
feeling, 154–156, 181
female bodies, 46–47, 93, 127–129
female flesh, 127–129
fight Douglass-Convey, 34, 56, 57–62, 77–79
  master-slave dialectic, 62–65
Flint, Dr., 33, 34, 68–69, 70
Flint, Mrs, 34–35
Floyd, G., 2
Franklin, J.H., 55
Free Speech, 97
freedom
  Black, 219, 220
  F. Douglass, 52, 64, 82–83
  H. Jacobs, 68, 70
  master-slave dialectic, 52
  Phenomenology of Spirit (Hegel), 42, 86
  sceptic, 106–110, 114, 128–129
  stoic, 81–87
fugitive slaves, 64

"Gain from a Belief, The" (Cooper), 138–139
Gaines, K.K., 73, 77
Garvey, M.
  Africanness, 144, 182
  Black colonisation, 163–165
  Black Star Line, 149–150
  devotion, 156, 158–159, 162
  education, 148
  faithfulness, 147
  racial purity, 159–162
  slavery, 151, 163
gender, 19–20, 96–97
  in master-slave dialectic, 33–35
  and scepticism, 102, 128–129: radical tripartite scepticism, 129–138, 139–140
gendered loss of self, 214–217
Germanic peoples, 131
Gilroy, P., 36, 61
God
  Black God, 143, 166–168
  and Black suffering, 150–153, 162
  and devotion, 145–146, 157
  M.L. King, Jr, 184
  sacramental work and desire, 204
  white God in blackface, 162–165
Guattari, F., 257

Haitian revolution, 28–29
Hajj, 244, 245
Hartman, S., 44–45, 86, 126–127, 168–169, 191–192, 261–262
Hawking, Sir J., 163
Heaven, 134
Hebrew Exodus, 151

288

INDEX

Hegel, G.W.F.
   and Dr M.L. King, Jr,
     177–180, 184
   see also *Phenomenology of Spirit*
     (Hegel)
Hegel studies, 14
Hegelian fight, 63–64
heroic genius, 258
history, whitening of, 232–233
Hitler, A., 256
Holiday, B., 99–100
holidays, 48–49
honour culture, 55–56
hooks, b., 65
house negroes, 45
hunting, 43, 46–47, 63
Hurston, Z.N., 10
   devotion, 18, 145, 168–176, 177
   Moses, 151n14
   sacramental work and desire, 181–185
   selves-in-community, 180
Hyppolite, J.
   devotion, 154, 157–158
   master-slave dialectic, 45–46, 104: negation, 38; nonabsolute subjects, 44; recognition, 39–40
   Reason, 263, 265
   sacramental work and desire, 205
   scepticism, 108–109, 110
   self-mortification, 220, 226, 237
   stoic freedom, 86
   unhappy consciousness, 183, 185, 188

"I", 83–84, 85, 105
   and Reason, 263, 264–265
   see also sense of self
"I have a dream." (King), 202

Ihram, 244
individualism/individuality
   E. Baker, 208
   feeling, 181
   M. Garvey, 161
   M.L. King, Jr, 184
   Phenomenology of Spirit (Hegel), 204
   Z.N. Hurston, 169, 171, 172–173, 174, 182
individual's work, 203–205
inner exclusion, 125
Inouye, M., 211
integration, 171
internal aliens, 125
intersectionality, 17, 130, 130n51, 131, 139
"inward" turn, 73, 74
Islam, 245, 247; see also Nation of Islam
Izar, 244

Jackson, Z., 20, 89
Jacobs, H., 17, 32, 33–34, 37, 65–71, 73, 135
jailing, 195–196
Jenkins, S., 58–59
Jesus, 143, 146, 157, 161n36
justice, 186

Kant, I., 113
King, Dr M.L., Jr
   beloved community, 188–190, 199
   Black Power, 270
   and G.W.F. Hegel, 177–180, 184
   individual's work, 203–205
   law and justice, 186–187
   March on Washington, 200–203
   "Negro Revolution", Summer 1963, 191–193

INDEX

nonviolence as passive activity, 194–200
sacramental work and desire, 183–185, 220
v. E. Baker, 206–208, 210, 213, 214–217, 218

labour, 183; *see also* work
Lacan, J., 52, 87–88
law, 186–187
law of the father, 52
leadership, 161, 213
life, 158; *see also* Black life
literacy, 78–79
Little, M., 224, 230; *see also* Malcolm X
Little, R., 231, 232, 233, 243
Lloyd, E., 52
local autonomy, 207, 208
"Lordship and Bondage", 36–39
loss, 261
love, 189
Luther, M., 229–230, 263–264
lynching, 91–92, 96, 97, 100

McDade, T., 2
Malcolm X, 18
  and Angela Davis, 254
  break with Elijah Muhammad, 241–243
  early years, 227–230
  house negroes, 45, 68
  killing, 100
  Mecca, 243–248
  mediation, 236–240
  nothingness, 224–227, 228, 259
  prison education, 230–236
  school, 232n17
  self-annihilation, 221–222
male bodies, 93
manhunts, 43, 46–47, 63
"March Against Fear", 269

March on Washington, 200–203
Marcuse, H., 253
master-slave dialectic, 4–5, 27–30, 104
  battle for recognition, 39–42
  and chattel slavery, 13, 31–35
  consciousness, 42–46
  Douglass's fight with Covey, 62–65
  fear of death, 46–52
  H. Jacobs, 65–71
  human subjectivity, 36–39
  and stoicism, 74–75
  work, 52–54
Mbembe, A., 51, 148–149, 165, 166
Mecca, 244–248
mediation, 237–238
Meredith, J., 269
merit, 79–80, 92–93
Middle Passage, 32, 41
mirror stage, 87–88
misogynoir, 17
mistresses, 34–35
modernity, 264
Montgomery Improvement Association, 194–195
Moody-Turner, S., 131–132
Morrison, T., 11–12
Moss, T., 92, 93
Moten, F., 11, 15n24, 77, 90, 125, 145
motherhood, 136–137, 137–138
Moynihan, D.P., 137
Muhammad, E., 224, 231, 238, 241–243
Muslim Mosque Inc., 243–244
Mutawaf, 244

natal alienation, 47, 48
Nation of Islam, 222, 224, 225, 231, 241

INDEX

nationalism, 254–255
Nazis, 256
Neal, L., 272
negation, 5, 8
  abstract, 41
  double, 199
  incomplete, 86
  of self, 38, 219, 220
  and stoicism, 100
  W.E.B. Du Bois, 107–110, 112
"Negro Revolution", Summer 1963, 191–193
Newton, H.P., 266–267, 269
Nietzsche, F., 152
Nisbett, R.E., 56
nonabsolute subjects, 44
nonviolence / nonviolent direct action, 180, 187, 189, 190, 191, 193
  as passive action, 194–200
normative masculinity, 32
nothingness, 5–7, 260
  and Blackness, 7–9, 223–227, 259
  and self-mortification, 237, 249, 252

objective I, 84
Ontological Terror (Warren), 7–8, 9
Orlando Sentinel, 171
Osterweis, R.G., 55n49
otherness, 46

Pan-Africanism, 165
Parker, T., 191
passification, 195–196
passive activity, nonviolence as, 194–200
Patterson, O., 42n23, 47, 55, 56, 75
People's Grocery Company, 92, 93

Phenomenology of Spirit (Hegel), 1
  and Black thinkers, 16–19, 21
  and Blackness, 3–4, 4–6, 11, 20–22
  devil, 229–230
  feeling, 181
  individuality, 204
  master-slave dialectic, 4–5, 13, 27–30: battle for recognition, 39–42; consciousness, 42, 45; fear of death, 50–51; human subjectivity, 36–39; normative masculinity, 32; work, 53
  path of despair, 261
  Reason, 265
  scepticism, 106, 107, 108, 109, 110, 111, 113
  self-consciousness, 264
  self-mortification, 263
  self-relinquishing, 261
  slavery, 12–13
  stoic freedom, 86
  stoicism, 74–75, 76, 101
  unhappy consciousness, 139: devotion, 146, 154, 157; sacramental work and desire, 185, 187, 217; self-mortification, 220, 226, 227, 236–238, 238–240
philosophy, 10, 13, 21
Philosophy of History (Hegel), 241n26
Pinn, A., 41, 146–147, 151–152, 153, 163, 166
Plessy v. Ferguson, 192
police brutality, 266–267, 268
political activism, 121–122
politics of Black joy, 174–175
prepositional philosophy, 10
prison education, 230–236
profeminist politics, 132

progress, 108
providence, universal law of, 79, 93

race, 171–172
race achievement, 182
racial purity, 159–162
racial segregation, 187; *see also* desegregation
racial uplift, 77
racism, 107, 124, 199, 203, 245–246, 256
radical democracy, 211–212
radical tripartite scepticism, 129–138, 139–140
radicalism, 161n36
Randolph, A.P., 205
Ransby, B., 207, 209, 210, 211, 217
rape, 66, 68–69, 93–94, 97, 153
reading, 78–79
Reason, 148–149, 262–265
recognition, 39–42, 44, 79; *see also* self-recognition; white misrecognition
redemption, 152–153, 164
religion *see* Black religion; Christianity; Islam
religious asceticism, 146
resistance, 197
Rida, 244
Robinson, C., 125
Rustin, B., 194, 205

sacramental work and desire, 179, 180–181, 221, 239
  E. Baker, 206–214, 220
  M.L. King, Jr, 183–185: beloved community, 188–190; divided worlds, 185–188; individual's work, 203–205; March on Washington, 200–203; "Negro Revolution", Summer 1963, 191–193; nonviolence as passive activity, 194–200
  Z.N. Hurston, 181–185
sagacity, 65
Satan, 229–230, 231
sceptic freedom, 106–110, 114, 128–129
sceptical subjectivity, 110
scepticism, 101–102
  and Black suffering, 150
  criticism of stoicism, 116–122
  double consciousness, 110–111, 112–116, 125, 127, 129
  radical tripartite scepticism, 129–138, 139–140
  second-sight and afterthought, 122–124
  versus stoicism, 104–107
  ungendered female flesh, 127–129
  white souls, 125–126
school of American slavery, 76
schools, 118, 119, 120, 232n17
Seale, B., 266–267, 269
second-sight, 122–124
second slavery, 114–115
self
  gendered loss of, 214–217
  sense of, 84, 88 (*see also* double consciousness)
self-annihilation, 221, 236–237, 239; *see also* self-mortification
self-annunciation, 182
self-certainty, 108–109
self-consciousness, 83–84, 105, 108, 110, 123, 262–263, 264
self-defence, 266, 267

INDEX

self-fashioning, 78–81, 83, 145, 174, 182, 183
self-misrecognition, 88
self-mortification, 139, 179, 220–221, 226, 227, 237–238, 239, 263
   Angela Davis, 249, 252–253, 254, 255
   Malcolm X, 221–223, 230, 246, 247
self-negation, 38, 219, 220
self-purification, 194
self-recognition, 67–69, 70; *see also* self-misrecognition
self-renunciation, 188
self-situatedness, 213
sense of self, 84, 88
sexism, 17
Sexton, J., 47
Sextus Empiricus, 105–106, 110
sexual violence *see* rape
Shabbaz, B., 267
Shabbaz, El-Hajj M. El-, 224, 246, 247, 248; *see also* Malcolm X
Sharpe, C., 170–171
Simone, N., 100
skin game, 232
slave fight *see* fight Douglass-Convey
slave trade, 11, 41
slavery, 11
   and Black God, 166–167
   misrecognition, 89–90
   Phenomenology of Spirit (Hegel), 12–13
   position of unthought, 126–127
   and redemption, 153
   school of American slavery, 76
   second slavery, 114–115
   see also chattel slavery; master-slave dialectic

slaves, 33, 75
slave's freedom, 81–83
Smiley, G.E., 194
social death, 47
song, 99–100
soul force, 196, 199
Souls of Black Folk, The (Du Bois), 103
South Africa, 236
Southern honour culture, 55–56
Southern horrors, 90–99
Spillers, H.
   captive body, 42, 46–47
   motherhood, 136–137, 137–138
   mothers, 133
   Mrs Flint, 34–35
   theft of the body, 38
   ungendered female flesh, 102, 127–129
standpoint theory, 130, 136
Stewart, L., 174–175
Stewart, M., 151, 152–153
stoic freedom, 81–87
stoic happiness, 85
stoic struggle, 77–78, 79–80
stoicism, 74–77, 99–100, 101
   versus scepticism, 104–105, 106–107
   Southern horrors, 90–93
   triple paradox of, 116–122
   white misrecognition, 87–90, 93–99
"Strange Fruit", 99–100
Student Nonviolent Coordinating Committee (SNCC), 194
subjective I, 84
subjectivity, 44, 69, 83, 94
   in "Lordship and Bondage", 36–39
   recognition of, 39–42
sublation, 199
subversion, 68

INDEX

suffering, 170; *see also* Black suffering
Summer 1963 revolution, 191–193

Tawaf, 244
Taylor, B., 2
"Ten-Point Program" (Black Panthers), 268
Their Eyes were Watching God (Hurston), 173–174
Tillich, P., 187
triple consciousness, 102, 131; *see also* radical tripartite scepticism
triple paradox of stoicism, 116–122
truth, 139
Truth, S., 135
truth telling, 97–99, 100
Tubman, H., 64, 135
Turner, H.M., 143, 162–163, 165–168

ungendered Black men, 137
ungendered Black women, 134, 135, 136–137, 139
ungendered female flesh, 20, 102, 127–129
unhappy consciousness, 143, 144; *see also* devotion; sacramental work and desire; self-mortification
Universal Negro Improvement Association (UNIA), 149, 150
universal will, 240
universities, 119, 120
unselfishness, 84–85
unthought, position of, 126–127

Veil of Race, 115, 124, 126, 129
violence, 94–95, 198n45

vocational training, 118, 119, 120
Voice from the South, A (Cooper), 130, 131, 135

Walker, A., 169–170
Walker, D., 151
Warren, C., 223, 225
Washington, B.T., 48–49, 73, 271
   Afro-American Council, 95–96
   Black embodiment, 76
   Du Bois' criticism of, 116–122
   sense of self, 88
   stoic freedom, 83–87
   stoicism, 76–77, 77–78, 79–81, 90–91, 92–93, 98, 101, 115, 116–118
wayward lives, 261–262
Wells, I.B., 17, 73–74, 135
   Black embodiment, 76
   Black life, 101
   and Du Bois' scepticism, 116–117
   gender, 96–97
   stoicism, 91–92, 97–99
   white misrecognition, 93–95
"What We Believe" (Black Panthers), 268
"What We Want Now!" (Black Panthers), 268
white devil, 235–236
white gaze, 123
white God in blackface, 162–168
white men, 131
white misrecognition, 87–90, 93–95, 98–99
white power, 271
white souls, 125–126

white supremacy, 13, 91, 163
whiteness, 62, 104, 112, 113, 114, 245
   versus Blackness, 123–124
whitening of history, 232–233
Why We Can't Wait (King), 192
Wilderson, F., 126
Wilkins, R., 270
Williams, R.F., 266
women, 19–20, 131, 152–153; *see also* Black women; enslaved females; female bodies; gender

work, 52–54, 67–68, 79, 80–81, 92, 98, 105; *see also* labour; sacramental work and desire; individual's work
work on the self *see* self-fashioning
Wright, R., 270
writing, 78–79

X *see* Malcolm X

Yancy, G., 2
Young, W., Jr, 270